Good Housekeeping

BOOK OF
BRITISH
FOOD

Happy Birthday to Barbara

Good Housekeeping

from Jen. August 2012

BOOK OF
BRITISH
FOOD

COLLINS & BROWN

First published in Great Britain in 2012
by Collins & Brown
10 Southcombe Street
London W14 0RA

An imprint of Anova Books Company Ltd

The Good Housekeeping website is
www.allaboutyou.com/goodhousekeeping

ISBN 978-1-90844-903-0

A catalogue record for this book is available from the
British Library.

Reproduction by Dot Gradations UK Ltd
Printed and bound by 1010 Printing International Ltd, China

This book can be ordered direct from the publisher. Contact
the marketing department, but try your bookshop first.

www.anovabooks.com

CONTENTS

FOREWORD

Britain's increasing interest in good food has been justly celebrated in recent years. The growing number of farmers' markets, the revival of home baking, the rise of small producers in nearly every region and every type of food – all of these show that many of us take the pleasures of the kitchen and table very seriously indeed.

At Good Housekeeping we join in welcoming those developments. But we also know that Britain had a long history of excellence in food long before chefs became celebrities and TV schedules were jam-packed with cookery programmes. Traditional British food is full of riches, made possible by both glorious regional produce and an unsung army of home cooks – people who turned those raw materials into wonderful dishes both savoury and sweet.

The Good Housekeeping Book of British Food celebrates that long history, and the cooks and producers who made it possible. This is a book about the best of British, with a survey of our regional foods followed by a generous selection of outstanding recipes. Some are ancient. Others are of recent vintage. All prove that great British food never went away. It has always been with us. And we hope that it will just go on getting better and better.

Richard Ehrlich

Richard Ehrlich
Chairman of the Guild of Food Writers

THE
REGIONS

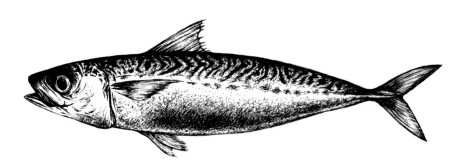

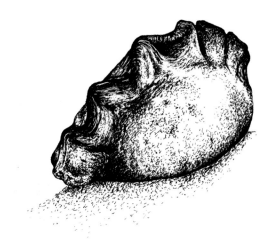

THE WEST COUNTRY

CORNWALL
DEVON
DORSET
SOMERSET
GLOUCESTERSHIRE
WILTSHIRE

The land of the West Country is so fertile that it abounds with a wealth of good produce, while the climate is the mildest in England. This generous region is defined for many people by cream teas, cooling ciders, ripe strawberries and mellow cheeses. But there is much more to offer. The West Country's riches make holidays here a delight, from the lush pastures with their gently grazing cattle to the glorious beaches of Devon and Cornwall. The seas are warmed by the Gulf Stream, another plus for holidaymakers, and the fishing industry goes back for centuries.

Spring arrives early in the West, ripening fruit and vegetables well before they are ready elsewhere. Apple orchards abound, filled with fruit to make the famous cider, and everywhere there are grassy fields supporting the dairy herds, which have made the production of cream and cheese such a popular part of the farmer's livelihood. Pig farming is also traditional, especially in Wiltshire. Crops tend to come second to livestock, although wheat, barley and oats are grown in Gloucestershire.

Moving away from the countryside, the elegant towns of Bath and Bristol have each made a contribution to West Country eating. Bath has given its name to several local goodies, mentioned later in this chapter, and Bristol, which as a port was once second only to London, used to trade in food and drink from all over the world. In recent years its waterfront has begun playing host to an increasing number of food festivals.

Famous dairying

All the breeds of cattle raised on the rich green grazing of the West Country give milk with a high butterfat content, perfect for making the cream, cheese and butter for which the region is justly renowned. No visit here would be complete without a traditional cream tea – a plate heaped high with fresh scones or splits, lavishly spread with strawberry jam and, of course, clotted cream. This type of cream is one of the best-known regional products and, as it both keeps and travels well, is often brought or posted home as a souvenir by the tourists who throng to this part of the country each summer.

Clotted cream is widely made in Cornwall and Devon, and some also comes out of Dorset. A handful of farms make it by the traditional method, but most producers use automatic separators and more up-to-date equipment. The basic idea is simple: double cream is heated, held at a high temperature for up to 40 minutes, and then cooled. The clotted cream that forms has a yellowish colour, wrinkled appearance, distinctive flavour and a very thick, grainy texture.

It is, however, cheese for which the West Country is truly celebrated. This is the ancestral home of Cheddar, probably the best-known cheese in the world. First made in Somerset, it has a history that dates back centuries – it was already highly thought of in the time of Henry II and although Cheddar is reproduced in English-speaking countries across the world, only that made in the West Country should have the right to bear the name.

Single and Double Gloucester, originally made from the milk of the handsome and recently revived Old Gloucester cow, have an equally long history, but artisan production had all but died out until the late 1980s. Along with the revival of these great British classics, the last 30 years has seen an explosion in the number of cheeses created and made by individuals to their own unique recipes – and today there are over 200 modern British cheeses made in the West Country from cow, goat, ewe and even buffalo milk. These range from Cheddar made in state-of-the-art factories to pungent washed-rind cheeses like the now famous Stinking Bishop, and Cornish Yarg, with its distinctive coat of nettles.

FOUR TOP WEST COUNTRY CHEESES

Cheddar (26kg/57lb cylinders)
Cheddar is not really Cheddar unless it comes from the green and verdant hills that are England. It was originally made in the Cheddar Gorge, Somerset, but production has spread over the centuries from Devon to Northern Scotland. Depending on its age it is referred to as mild, medium, mature or vintage.
Tasting notes: firm, dense, almost chewy texture; tangy, with a wonderful complexity of aromas and taste; nutty, rich, with a hint of fresh pastures.

Double Gloucester (4kg/9lb deep wheel)
Coloured with annatto, Double Gloucester is similar to Red Leicester but a paler orange; farmhouse examples come in elegant, cloth-covered wheels.
Tasting notes: firm body, close creamy texture, though not as firm as a Cheddar; round and mellow in flavour; delicious, zesty, with an orange tang on the finish.

Single Gloucester PDO (2.5kg/5½ lb flat wheel)
Protected under the European PDO system (see page 53) and made by only four cheesemakers, it is milder and smaller than Double Gloucester and not coloured with annatto.
Tasting notes: firm body but moist with a more open texture than Double Gloucester; delicate, buttery with a refreshing acidity.

Cornish Yarg (3kg/6lb flat wheel)
Handmade to a 17th-century recipe initially, then re-created and named after a couple called Gray (yarg spelt backwards), it is wrapped in interwoven nettle leaves, which make it one of the most distinctive cheeses on the market.
Tasting notes: crumbly like a young Caerphilly with a hint of meadow flowers and grasses while the finish is fresh and lemony.

Fish and shellfish galore

As elsewhere in Britain, the fishing industry in the West Country has been badly affected by over-fishing. But some seaside ports maintain the tradition to this day. Cornish coasts face two seas, and the fleets bring home a wide variety of fine-quality fish. Newlyn and Falmouth are the big ports in Cornwall, while in Devon trawlers operate principally out of Brixham and Plymouth. These two counties are important sources of a wide variety of both flat and round fish.

The waters of the West Country are also home to shellfish: spider crabs, crayfish, scallops and lobsters. The crabs in Cornwall are larger than those caught in East Anglia, but the two areas both claim that their crabs have the finest flavour. Besides these luxurious treats, the everyday favourites – cockles, winkles, prawns and mussels – also thrive in these seas. There are oyster beds too, in Devon and Cornwall, producing both Native and Pacific oysters.

Freshwater fish, especially salmon and trout, from rivers such as the Dart, Exe and Tamar, feature on the menus of local restaurants and are frequently served cooked with cider or cream. Fish farms have sprung up here as they have elsewhere in the country, and as well as trout and salmon, some enterprising fish farmers are producing more unusual fish, including pike, grayling and carp. Shellfish are also farmed on a small scale, with oysters, crayfish and mussels all commercially grown.

Prime meat

Pork is the prime meat of the West Country and is produced mainly in Wiltshire, which has been famous for pig farming for centuries. This is one of the best counties to visit for sausages and faggots, and the traditional hams and bacon are renowned for their high quality. The 'Wiltshire cure' – two to four days in a wet brine followed by a couple of weeks of maturation – produces sweet-flavoured, mild bacon, smoked or unsmoked. Bradenham hams, another great treat, are now relatively rare. Much more commonly found is another West Country pork speciality, Bath chaps, which are the cured cheeks of the pig.

Chickens and turkeys are bred all over the region; there are ducks too, and sometimes guinea fowl. A wide variety of wild game, including rabbit and duck, is found in Wiltshire and on the moors of Devon and Cornwall.

There is no shortage of cattle or sheep in these parts, and both Devon and Dorset produce good beef and excellent lamb. Cornwall, with its harsher landscape, has less of a tradition of livestock rearing and used, in the past, to rely mainly on the hardy goat for meat. However, the county does produce early lambs, which have a superb flavour.

OILY FISH

A lot of oily fish are caught and brought into West Country ports. These varieties tend to be excellent value for money and, as well as being full of flavour, they are exceptionally nutritious – the richest dietary source of omega-3 fatty acids. They are also, as a group, found at sustainable stock levels in the waters around the UK.

Pilchards
Rarely available fresh and usually only found locally to their fishing port. Most are exported or canned. They have a strong, oily flavour. Grill or fry whole. **Best:** between November and February.

Herring
A streamlined fish, with a steely-blue back and silvery belly. Braise, bake, fry or grill. Also available smoked or kippered, and as rollmops in vinegar. **Best:** from July to February.

Mackerel
Larger than herring, with a pattern of dark zigzags on the back and a silver belly. Firm, well-flavoured flesh. Cook as for herring, or can be soused in vinegar. Also available smoked. **Season:** all year round.

Sprats
A smaller member of the herring family (but not a young herring). Has a bluish-green back and silvery sides and belly. Bake, fry or grill. Also smoked. **Season:** October to March.

Young and tender fruit and veg

It's not hard to see why there's so much agricultural activity in the West Country. The fertile land and well-warmed climate, with its regular rainfall, make the region ideal for growing vegetables. In fact, the unusual warmth of these southerly parts means that crops are ripe well before those grown further north. In Cornwall farmers can start planting potatoes in February, a month earlier than in less sheltered places. The very first crop is ready by May and these young early potatoes and other vegetables, such as peas and broad beans, have wonderful tenderness and delicacy of flavour. Other staple main-crop vegetables, such as carrots, Brussels sprouts and onions, also grow well.

Early strawberries from the Tamar Valley are another great delicacy, and Cornwall also grows gooseberries – often, no doubt, in order to cook one of the county's best traditional dishes, Baked Mackerel with Gooseberry Sauce (see recipe, page 174). Pears are grown too, and sometimes to make perry (pear cider); they are a particularly important crop in Gloucestershire. But for the most part it is apples, apples and more apples in the West Country, reflected deliciously in regional recipes like Somerset Apple Cake (see recipe, page 227). Apple orchards flourish all over the region and usually the apples are grown for cider-making (see Cider, right).

Wonderful bakes and cakes

Probably the best-known bake of the West Country is the Cornish pasty, a portable meal originally made for farmers and miners to take to work. A good one has chunks of meat (not mince), plus potatoes and onions, inside a crisp pastry overcoat. But sometimes pasties don't live up to these high ideals – there is even a legend that the Devil refused to cross the Tamar into Cornwall because he had heard that the Cornish would put anything into their pasties!

Lots of lovely cakes come from these parts, including fruit cakes and honey cakes. Apples, of course, crop up in cakes and puddings (try Somerset Apple Cake, page 227). Lardy Cake (see page 252) also comes from the region, as do the delicious Devon Flats biscuits, made with clotted cream. There are plenty of different flours for home-bakers to choose from, as several mills in the West Country produce organic and stone-ground varieties.

The spa town of Bath is known for three baked delicacies. Bath buns are made from a rich, yeasty mixture; they are beautifully yellow inside and are topped with crushed lump sugar. Dr William Oliver, who founded the Bath Mineral Water Hospital, performed another great service when he invented the Bath Oliver biscuit as part of the simple diet prescribed for those taking the supposedly curative waters. These crisp crackers are still made today and are the ideal accompaniment to a chunk of Cheddar cheese. Look for the portrait of their originator, imprinted on one side of each biscuit. Thirdly, from Bath, comes Sally Lunn, a round, light, yeast cake. There are various legends attached to the name, but whether Sally Lunn was really an 18th-century street seller will never be known. Again, you can buy the cakes in the town, and the best way to eat them is split while still hot and filled with either whipped cream or butter.

Drinks for sipping and slurping

Cider may be better known as the classic West Country drink, but excellent beer is also brewed in the region. It was once famous for 'boy's bitters', ales of around 3 per cent alcohol that refreshed agricultural labourers after long hours in the fields. There are still refreshing and well-hopped light beers, such as St Austell's 3.4 per cent IPA, and the 50 per cent reduction in excise duty on beers of 2.8 per cent may encourage the return of beers for boys. But the emphasis today is on premium bitters and golden ales, although traditional copper-coloured beers have not been overwhelmed by the move to paler beers. Choice is strong, with close to 30 breweries in Devon and 25 in Gloucestershire and Bristol.

Wine-making is a growing venture in the West Country, even though the climate is not quite as suitable as it is in drier parts of the country. But there are commercial vineyards in Avon, Somerset, Wiltshire, Devon and Cornwall, producing a range of white, red and sparkling wines.

CIDER

West Country cider
Cider, in all styles and strengths, is the quintessential West Country drink. Traditionally, cider from this part of the country is made from cider apples, rather than the culinary and dessert varieties used in other regions. This gives farmhouse ciders their distinctive dryness. Traditional varieties have appealingly old-fashioned names such as Harry Masters Jersey, Brown Snout, Slack Ma Girdle, and Ten Commandments.

Farmhouse ciders
From bone dry to reasonably sweet, many types of cider are brewed by small producers and sold locally 'over the gate'. These farmers tend to use the cider apples known as bittersharps and bittersweets to get the flavour they want. Production is simple: the apples are pulped and allowed to ferment naturally in barrels. Different types of apple might be blended or the cider may be made from a single variety. Farmhouse ciders vary widely in quality but at their best they are excellent. If buying locally, try to taste before you buy. They are also increasingly sold via mail order or online, and are recognised as being worthy of the same kind of connoisseurship accorded to wine and beer.

Commercially produced ciders
Two of the country's largest cider producers are in the West Country and make a range of ciders of a consistent standard and flavour. Again, special cider apples are widely used. The drink is aged in vats and then carefully blended. Types available include still, dry ciders, which are fairly strong; sweet, sparkling bottled ciders; and still, mellow, dryish ciders, which are almost like wine.

A TOP WEST COUNTRY WINEMAKER

Camel Valley, Nanstallion, Bodmin, Cornwall
The top wine producer in the West Country and generally considered to be one of the finest in England. They are best known for their sparkling wines, which regularly win recognition in international wine competitions.
Top wine: Camel Valley White Pinot.

THREE TOP WEST COUNTRY BREWERIES

Blue Anchor, Helston, Cornwall
World-famous home-brew pub on the site of a monks' hospice, brewing strong Spingo ales of enormous depth and complexity.

Palmers, Bridport, Dorset
Family-owned brewery from 1794 with excellent, traditional copper-coloured beers, including 200 that celebrated the company's double century, and Tally Ho!, a strong, dark winter ale.

Uley, Gloucestershire
Craft brewery producing full-flavoured, hoppy bitters, using water from a spring that bubbles away outside. Beers include Laurie Lee's Bitter, in honour of the author of 'Cider with Rosie'.

FOOD FAIRS AND FESTIVALS

JANUARY

WASSAILING THE APPLE TREES
CARHAMPTON, SOMERSET

EASTERTIDE

EASTER TUESDAY: DISTRIBUTION OF TWOPENNY STARVERS
ST MICHAEL ON THE MOUNT WITHOUT, BRISTOL

APRIL

WIMBORNE HORTICULTURAL SOCIETY SPRING SHOW
ALLENDALE COMMUNITY CENTRE, HANHAM ROAD, WIMBORNE, DORSET

MAY/JUNE

DEVON COUNTY SHOW
WESTPOINT, CLYST ST MARY, EXETER, DEVON
ROYAL BATH AND WEST SHOW
SHOWGROUND, SHEPTON MALLET, SOMERSET

JUNE

ROYAL CORNWALL AGRICULTURAL SHOW
WADEBRIDGE

JULY

STITHIANS SHOW
PLAYING FIELDS, STITHIANS, TRURO, CORNWALL

AUGUST

HARVEST HOME
PROCESSION AT EAST BRENT, SOMERSET

OCTOBER

TAUNTON ANNUAL ILLUMINATED CARNIVAL AND CIDER-BARREL ROLLING RACE
TAUNTON, SOMERSET

THE SOUTHEAST

BEDFORDSHIRE
BUCKINGHAMSHIRE
OXFORDSHIRE
BERKSHIRE
HAMPSHIRE
ISLE OF WIGHT
WEST SUSSEX
EAST SUSSEX
KENT AND SURREY
GREATER LONDON
HERTFORDSHIRE

London produces little of its own food, but it is surrounded by areas that are rich in produce of all kinds. Rich farmlands stretch down to the coast, encompassing the Garden of England and making a cornucopia filled with soft fruits, vegetables, seafoods, meat, milk and other good things.

A kind climate, enough rain to keep the crops watered, and a fertile soil – all these bonuses are enjoyed by farmers in the Southeast. Farming of all types goes on here. Cereals such as wheat, barley and oats are grown, and root vegetables too, but the area is most famous for market gardening, with the Kent and Sussex Weald especially producing large amounts of fruit and vegetables. Relative newcomers to the scene are grapevines, rapidly becoming more widespread as the world wakes up to the excellent quality that English wine can attain.

As well as producing top-quality crops, the land is ideal for raising cattle and sheep, while the fishing industry is still important around parts of the Southeast coast.

Flourishing fruit

Its warm, moist climate and rich soil make the Kent Weald exceptionally fertile. Fruit and vegetables thrive here in the Garden of England, as they have since the 16th century. But fruit was flourishing in this area long before then. Cherries first came to England with the Romans and still turn the orchards of the Southeast into a mass of blossom every spring, even though far fewer cherry orchards exist than 30 or 40 years ago.

Several varieties of sweet cherry are grown in Kent. You'll see many different types in the shops, and it's worth buying them as they arrive. The picking period in any orchard is only about a week, so the supplies to the markets are constantly changing. If you want to cook cherries in a savoury dish, look out for red-skinned sour types. Morellos are another good choice – they have dark skin and flesh, and are also used for canning, bottling and making cherry brandy.

Apples are the other major fruit crop of Kent, the trees laden with more of that breathtaking spring blossom. Cox's Orange Pippin, one of Britain's favourite apples, was first grown in the Southeast, and many other eaters, cookers (especially Bramley's Seedlings) and cider apples are cultivated here.

Conference pears are frequently planted alongside dessert apple orchards. Also widely grown is the Comice pear, which has a melting, fragrant flesh, and the juicy and sweet Williams, often used for canning. South Buckinghamshire is known for its cherries, plums and damsons, while Victoria plums from Kent also make excellent eating.

As well as acres of fruit trees, the Southeast boasts bushels of soft fruit – much of it on offer at pick-your-own farms. Black- and red currants, gooseberries, raspberries and strawberries make a brightly coloured display throughout the summer.

A wealth of fresh vegetables

No market gardening area would be complete without plentiful vegetables, and salads galore are grown in the Southeast, as well as broccoli, beans, cauliflower and almost every other vegetable you care to name. Some counties have traditionally been associated with a particular speciality: Bedfordshire with Brussels sprouts, Sussex with mushroom farms and Hampshire with watercress. Garlic, that deliciously aromatic member of the lily family, is produced on a small scale in the UK, mostly on the Isle of Wight.

Kentish cobnuts, sometimes called Lambert's Filberts, were first grown by Mr Lambert in about 1830. They are a variety of hazelnut that has pleasant, sweet flesh. The crop is smaller now than in the past but you should still be able to find Kentish cobs in the shops during October.

DESSERT APPLES

Numerous varieties of apple are grown in the Southeast (and elsewhere in the UK). The season for apples lasts from September/November through to December/April, depending on the variety. Some of the best-known types originating here are Cox's Orange Pippin, Ida Red, Discovery, Egremont Russet, Worcester Pearmain, Spartan, and Laxton Superb. When buying, choose unblemished fruit without bruises, buy little and often, and store in a cool place, not in a bowl in a warm room. Many dessert apples can also be used successfully for cooking.

There is so much more to British apples than just the most famous names – some 1,200 varieties are grown in the UK. Commercial pressures and cheap imports have steadily narrowed the choice over recent decades, however, with the result that many fine varieties are exceedingly rare. Even some of the lesser-known varieties, such as Russets and Discovery, may be hard to find outside the area where they're grown. That's all the more reason to seek them out during their season, to support the farmers who continue to grow them.

Our apple heritage is recognised by organisations that preserve seeds from the old varieties. The most important is the National Fruit Collection at Brogdale Farm in Faversham, Kent, which has the largest seed collection in the world – and collects other fruits, as well as nuts, around 3,500 named varieties in all. The Collection is open to the public, with courses and orchard tours among other activities, and is well worth a visit. Get more information at www.brogdalecollections.co.uk.

Good grazing

Herds of dairy cattle, now mostly the ubiquitous black and white Friesian, are still a common sight in the fields of the Southeast, especially in Hampshire – although there are sizeable dairy herds, too, on the Isle of Wight and in Berkshire, Sussex and Kent.

Most farms in the Southeast are mixed, and sheep are kept on many of them, as they are happy to graze on pasture that is unsuitable for cattle. The ewes are mainly cross breeds.

Pure breeds are used only when their special characteristics make them ideal for a particular area. One famous pure breed is the Romney Marsh, which feeds on the salty pastures that border Sussex and Kent, and is robust enough to withstand the winds that sweep across the grazing grounds from the Channel.

Cattle do well in the Southeast and although many belong to dairy herds, beef production is also important. The two types of farming are closely interlinked. Some of the calves born to the dairy herd are kept to supplement the

FOOD FAIRS AND FESTIVALS

JANUARY

WASSAILING THE APPLE TREES
GILL ORCHARD, HENFIELD, WEST SUSSEX

MARCH/APRIL

CAMRA LONDON DRINKER BEER FESTIVAL
BIDBOROUGH STREET, LONDON WC2

EASTERTIDE

SHROVE TUESDAY: PANCAKE RACE
OLNEY, BUCKINGHAMSHIRE
GOOD FRIDAY: EASTER BUN CEREMONY
THE WIDOW'S SON INN, 75 DEVONS ROAD,
BROMLEY-BY-BOW, LONDON E3
GOOD FRIDAY: BUTTERWORTH CHARITY
ST BARTHOLOMEW-THE-GREAT, LONDON EC1
ROGATION DAY: BLESSING OF THE NETS AND MACKEREL
ON THE BEACH OPPOSITE THE OLD SHIP HOTEL, BRIGHTON, EAST
SUSSEX; ALSO AT HASTINGS

MAY

FESTIVAL OF ENGLISH FOOD AND WINE
LEEDS CASTLE, MAIDSTONE, KENT
HERTFORDSHIRE SHOW
SHOWGROUND, FRIARS WASH, REDBOURN,
HERTFORDSHIRE
SURREY COUNTY SHOW
STOKE PARK, GUILDFORD, SURREY

JUNE

ANNUAL SOUTH OF ENGLAND SHOW
ARDINGLY, WEST SUSSEX: LIVESTOCK

JULY

BLESSING THE SEA CEREMONY
MARGATE AND WHITSTABLE
KENT COUNTY SHOW
DETLING, MAIDSTONE, KENT
RARE BREEDS SHOW
WEALD AND DOWNLAND OPEN AIR MUSEUM, SINGLETON,
CHICHESTER, WEST SUSSEX
WHITSTABLE OYSTER FESTIVAL
HELD IN VARIOUS VENUES IN WHITSTABLE, KENT

SEPTEMBER

ENGLISH WINE FESTIVAL AND REGIONAL FOOD FAIR
BENTLEY WILDFOWL, HATLAND, NEAR LEWES, EAST SUSSEX

milk-producers, others are used for breeding, and the remainder are reared for meat.

Sussex cattle – which are large and reddish-brown – are a breed commonly found in the area. But once again, they are cross-bred in order to combine the good qualities of beef bulls and dairy cows.

Poultry and turkeys are important in the Southeast, both for egg production and for the table. The Aylesbury duck, a large, plump, white species, originated in Buckinghamshire, but the pure breed has now almost disappeared.

Pig farms are scattered throughout the Southeast, mainly in Kent and Hampshire, and there's good game to be had, with venison from the New Forest as well as excellent pheasant, partridge, quail and hare.

Cheesemaking

The Southeast was not traditionally a region known for its cheeses, but over the last 30 years things have changed. The herds of cows have given way in some places to herds of goat and sheep, and the result is over 30 cheesemakers making more than 100 different cheeses. These range from Camembert-style cheeses like Tunworth and Waterloo, to soft goats' from Rosary Goats and Golden Cross Cheese to magnificent boulders of Old Winchester, Lords of the Hundred and others too numerous to name.

CHOOSING CHEESES

- If possible, taste before you buy, and take time to decide.
- Avoid cheeses that have cracks or a dark, shiny surface around the cut edges.
- Buy small amounts. Keep in a larder or the fridge salad drawer, wrapped in foil.

Rich in shellfish

The long coastline of Sussex and Kent has made fishing an important part of life in those counties for centuries. However, the inshore fishing industry has gradually decreased over the years, especially in Kent.

Shellfish are plentiful all around the south coast. Fine lobsters are caught in pots from May to October, and shrimps, scallops, clams, whelks and superb crabs are also found in these waters.

Good-quality, well-fattened oysters are farmed in quantity in the Solent and in smaller numbers at Whitstable. Two main varieties are produced – the Flat oyster and the Pacific oyster, both of which are at their most delicious eaten raw

with a squeeze of lemon and some bread and butter. The old 'R in the month' method of telling when oysters are in season still holds good, for quality rather than health reasons, so September to April is the best time to eat them.

Oysters have had a troubled history. From being cheap and plentiful up until the start of the 19th century, they then became far scarcer and more of a luxury, because over-fishing had severely depleted the oyster beds. The industry has been revived but the stocks are always at risk from disease, bad weather and predatory sea creatures. Here as elsewhere they are an expensive treat.

From a food that used to be cheap and is now a luxury, to one that used to be pricey and is now much more affordable. Rainbow trout are farmed extensively all over the Southeast and because the methods are so efficient, trout is more widely available – and therefore cheaper – than ever before. Farms spring up wherever there is a good supply of clean cool water and many of them welcome visitors. The trout are fed on a high-protein diet and grow rapidly, producing a good weight of sweet, succulent flesh for their size.

If you're lucky, you may find 'wild' trout from Sussex, or from the River Test in Hampshire, although these tend to be consumed close to where they are caught. Other freshwater fish, such as pike and perch, are also found in local rivers but may be hard to come by outside the local area.

London is still home to Billingsgate, the famous fish market, where much of the British catch (and many imports from overseas) ends up. Although long ago moved from its former site in the City of London to the Docklands, the market continues to ply its trade as it has done for centuries. Most fish is sent directly by road from the ports and arrives in the early hours of the morning, to be rushed to fishmongers all over the country while it is still fresh.

Warm from the oven

The streets of London no longer resound to the cries of traders ringing their bells as they walk along with trays of fresh crumpets or muffins for sale on their heads. Such picturesque scenes disappeared in the 1930s, but we can still buy those wonderfully comforting foods, or even make them at home (see recipe, pages 257 and 260).

Chelsea buns are another London delicacy that fortunately have survived (see recipe, page 253). They were originally sold from the Old Chelsea Bun House in Pimlico, which was destroyed in 1839. King George III was a regular customer.

Kentish women were keen on baking and many traditional recipes exist, although few are made commercially and you probably won't see them in the shops. However, Banbury cakes can still be bought in the town of Banbury, Oxfordshire, which is also famous for the Cross mentioned in the nursery rhyme 'Ride a Cock Horse'. A Victorian replacement of the original Cross still stands.

Drinks new and old

The English wine industry has seen an extraordinary upsurge in the last 20 years. Although winemaking has gone on here since the time of the Romans, it was an activity mainly confined to the monasteries and it more or less disappeared when they were dissolved by Henry VIII. Interest in winemaking revived in the late 1940s but the real growth in both quality and quantity is a more recent development, and many of the best producers are in the Southeast.

Vines need a south-facing slope with well-drained soil to thrive, and are at the mercy of the climate. Frost kills the buds, high winds break down the vines, and if there's not enough sun, the grapes won't ripen properly. For a long time this meant that English producers focused primarily on Germanic grape varieties, which produce mostly sweet or semi-sweet wines. Then some producers realised that French grape varieties, especially those used for Champagne-style wines, could also thrive. Parts of Sussex and Hampshire are similar in soil and climate to Champagne, and sparkling wines are perhaps the finest made in England today.

Hops have been an important crop in Kent for centuries and, although less widespread now, fields of hop cones and oast houses are still a familiar part of the Kent countryside. Families from London's East End used to make an annual holiday of hop picking, but the operation is now mechanised. Hops were originally grown as a vegetable and weren't used in brewing until the 16th century. After harvesting, they are placed in the oast houses to dry out over slow-burning fires, before being sent to breweries around the country. Beers brewed in Kent tend to have a strong hoppy flavour, which can be something of an acquired taste.

The beers of Southeast England owe their character to the hops of Kent, which include such famous varieties as Fuggles and Goldings, named after the farmers who first grew them. The move away from cask beer in the 1960s led to a decline in hop growing and a switch to apple growing, but now farmers are developing hop fields again. Shepherd Neame in Faversham, England's oldest brewery, from 1698, has laid out fields where every known English hop variety is grown: visitors are welcome. Small brewers abound and the region is rich in fine country pubs.

The vast crops of fruit produced every year in Kent have other delicious alcoholic spin-offs. Cider is made from local apples, and Morello cherries are used to make delectable cherry brandy. The slight hint of almonds in the flavour comes from the crushed cherry stones that are added to the pulped fruit.

London Dry Gin is another tipple associated with the capital and the recipe, based on juniper berries and various herbs, has been the same for 200 years.

THREE TOP SOUTHEASTERN BREWERIES

Harvey's, Lewes, East Sussex
A superb family brewery, dating from 1790, on the banks of the Ouse; still producing a dark mild and arguably one of the finest of all traditional bitters, Sussex Best. Watch out for occasional sightings of the strong Imperial Extra Double Stout.

Shepherd Neame, Faversham, Kent
A large brewery; good beers, full of Kentish hop aromas and flavours, including Spitfire premium bitter, Canterbury Jack, just 3.5 per cent and bursting with citrus/hop notes, and the strong, fruity Bishop's Finger with a nickname too rude to mention.

Thame Brewery, Thame, Oxfordshire
This tiny, one-barrel brewery stands behind the delightful old Cross Keys pub and produces a succulent dark mild, Mr Splodge's, named after the pub cat, and Hoppiness, a pale bitter using American Cascade hops.

THREE TOP SOUTHEASTERN WINERIES

Chapel Down, Tenterden, Kent
Britain's largest wine producer by a good margin, Chapel Down is best known for its wide range of whites, but its sparkling wine is just as distinguished.

Ridgeview Wine Estate, Ditchling Common, East Sussex
Ridgeview makes sparkling wine only, from the classic Champagne grape varieties, and they are usually regarded as among the top producers in the country.

Denbies Wine Estate, Dorking, Surrey
A leading source of fine sparkling wines, most made from the classic Champagne grape varieties, and of Germanic-style white wines. They also produce a red of excellent quality.

WALES

CLWYD
DYFED
GWYNEDD
POWYS
GWENT
WEST GLAMORGAN
MID GLAMORGAN
SOUTH GLAMORGAN

Sweet, tender lamb from the mountains; oats, wheat and barley; soft fruits in the warmer south; fish of all types, from cockles to sea trout; creamy milk and butter; carrots, cabbage and early potatoes. These are the good things of Wales, a country where the cooking is simple and wholesome.

A land of breathtaking scenery, with its own lilting language, Wales possesses a terrain that has always presented a challenge to farmers in some mountainous areas. Those in the north, where the rugged mountains will sometimes support little other than oats and sheep, had to scrape a living from the land. In the more affluent south, where the landscape as well as the climate is kinder, the story is different. In the rolling hills dairy and beef cattle do well and it is possible to grow soft fruit, vegetables and crops of wheat and barley, the last of which is mainly used for fattening beef herds. In the warmest parts of the south, there are even vineyards.

Milk, butter, cream and cheese all feature in Welsh cooking. Lamb is popular and so are oats, which appear in many guises. Fishing from the long coastline has had its heyday and the industry, which formerly stretched right along the coast, came to be concentrated in the south. But successful efforts have been made to revive the shellfish beds in the north, although this is inevitably a gradual and ongoing process. Clear rivers and deep mountain lakes provide excellent freshwater fish, although in far lower quantities than were seen at one time.

Creamy milk, salty butter

The pastoral country of south Wales, warmed by breezes from the Gulf Stream, and with a high rainfall, has always supported large dairy herds. Even in parts of the mountainous north, however, dairy tradition exists, and some herds are kept on the lower slopes of the uplands.

Herefords were formerly the predominant breed but these days the Welsh Black is also favoured. Hardy, and mainly concentrated in the north, this is a beef cattle that can provide good-quality milk as well. Some farmers are also experimenting with other breeds.

Welsh butter is renowned for its quality. The size of a herd of cattle used to be a status symbol among farmers, so few animals were killed off for beef and the dairy herd gradually grew and grew. This naturally led to surpluses of dairy products, including butter, which had then to be well salted in order to preserve it.

Cheese, new and old

Despite its close proximity to major tourist routes and cities, large parts of Wales have somehow managed to remain largely undisturbed and undiscovered. These comprise magnificent castles, unspoilt coastline, bracken-covered auburn hillsides, hidden pastures bursting with wild flowers, and solemn grey stone houses where cheese has been made by wives and daughters for centuries. This relative isolation and the lack of past abuse to the land has enabled the organic movement to become well established in Wales.

Caerphilly, the most famous Welsh cheese, was named after the Welsh mining village where it was first made. Only lightly pressed compared with other traditional British cheeses, it had a higher moisture content and a more crumbly texture. Soaked in brine baths to seal in the moisture and slightly increase its salt content, it was an ideal cheese for miners as it replaced some of the salt lost as they toiled underground, far below the rich green pastures. That quality remains an outstanding feature of Caerphilly, even though the mining industry has shrunk to a tiny fraction of its former size.

Farmhouse Caerphilly nearly disappeared, but today there are a handful of producers making excellent Caerphilly each with its own individual style. This is part of a wider interest in cheesemaking that has seen a number of small producers appear on the scene in recent years.

Herds of dairy goats and, to a lesser extent, sheep are also found in Wales and traditional Welsh cooking relies heavily on dairy products. Cheese crops up in two simple but delicious dishes. One is Glamorgan sausages, which despite their name, contain no meat but are made of cheese, breadcrumbs, herbs and chopped onion or leek, mixed together. They are formed into sausage shapes and fried (see recipe, page 199). They used to be made with the firm white cheese of Glamorgan, now no longer produced. Welsh rabbit (or rarebit) is a traditional dish that has been adopted nationwide. There are several ways to make it, from simply toasting a slice of cheese on a piece of bread, to making a smooth, creamy cheese mixture, perhaps incorporating cream, butter or ale, pouring it on to toast and browning the top under the grill (see page 201).

Sweet mountain sheep

The mountains of the north spell sheep, which are the creatures best able to withstand the exposure to wind, rain and cold. The main traditional breed is the Welsh Mountain, which is found throughout Wales. These sheep are the smallest commonly reared in Britain and have smooth faces, bright, prominent eyes, small ears and slim, wool-free legs. The rams have curled horns. They are hardy, stocky animals, well suited to mountain life, and produce very fine, soft wool as well as marvellous meat. Other breeds have been introduced, however, so the Welsh Mountain sheep is not nearly as popular as it was at one time.

Welsh lamb is available nationwide, and a scheme of marking it makes it easy for shoppers to identify – and its quality has been recognised with the award of a PGI (see page 53). The meat is tender and lean, with a rich delicate flavour, which may have a hint of herbs if the flocks have been grazing on the patches of wild thyme and rosemary that grow in the mountains. Another distinctive type of lamb is salt marsh lamb, which picks up wonderful flavour from the salty vegetation it feeds on in its coastal grazing land.

Hill farmers aim to produce lambs no earlier than April, when the weather starts to improve and the grass begins to sprout again. Most female lambs are kept on the hills to replace older or barren ewes, which are sold to upland farmers to be kept in less harsh conditions.

Several breeds are restricted to local areas – for instance, two of the Welsh upland breeds are the black-faced Clun Forest and the Kerry Hill, which has a white face with black markings. They are less hardy than hill sheep.

Many traditional Welsh recipes feature lamb. Mutton hams were made by shepherds, who cured the hind leg of a sheep at home, using salt, sugar and spices, then hung the joint in the chimney to smoke. This is no longer done for obvious reasons. Lamb and mutton pies were a familiar part of the hiring and livestock fairs that were once commonly held throughout Wales. These can still be found in some markets, including farmers' markets (see page 57). When they are well made they are a real delicacy and well worth seeking out.

Beef cattle, which are a natural spin-off from dairy farming, are found wherever milk is produced. But in many lowland parts of South Wales herds of cattle are found alongside flocks of sheep.

As in so many other parts of the country, the poorer people's staple fare was pork, from the pig kept at the bottom of the garden. Commercial pig farming has declined in Wales, although it is still carried out in some areas and is undergoing a strong revival in response to demand for good-quality pork from superior and sometimes rare breeds.

Salt duck is a peculiarly Welsh way to treat duckling, which is rubbed thoroughly with salt and left for a day or two before cooking. This results in tender meat with a delicious flavour that is not too salty. Salt duck is not nearly as common as it once was, but may still be found in some places.

Gathered from the sands

Fine salmon are caught in the rivers Teifi, Tywi and Taf in west Wales, but their numbers have been greatly depleted. Very occasionally you may still see coracles, the traditional fisherman's craft. They are light boats, made by stretching hide or canvas over a willow framework. Salmon are also caught in the Severn estuary in special baskets, the design of which has remained the same for centuries. Some of this salmon is smoked in Wales.

The lakes and rivers also provide homes for sea trout (called sewin), brown trout, grayling and red-bellied char, although this last is something of a rarity.

Cockles are gleaned from the sands around the beautiful Gower peninsula, and also from some beaches in north Wales. They are mostly gathered by hand, a back-breaking job, which can only be done at low tide. Most of the fish

are cooked and removed from the shells before being sold. It is now relatively rare to find them sold live on the market stalls of Swansea and Cardiff.

Swansea, in common with many other coastal towns of Wales, was once a busy fishing port but now only small catches are landed there. Other sea fish caught off Wales include mullet, bass, plaice and flounder. Herrings and mackerel have been fished at Aberystwyth since medieval times, and were important at many other ports, but today the fishing industry has declined. However, the oyster and mussel beds along the Menai Straits are being revived and now produce good crops – the largest in the UK. Cardigan Bay is gradually being restocked with lobsters, after over-fishing had led to restrictions being placed on the catch. Scallops, clams and large numbers of crabs and lobster are also caught off the Welsh coast.

A food from the sea that is considered a great delicacy in Wales is laver, an edible seaweed with high vitamin and mineral content, gathered from the rocks. The seaweed is processed commercially into laverbread, a gelatinous purée. It can be eaten coated with oatmeal and fried with bacon, or made into laver sauce to eat with fish or mutton. Laver is still a popular food and of high quality.

Pick your own in the south

Fruit and vegetable growing does not lend itself to such a hilly landscape as there is in the north, but there are places where horticulture is well established. Carrots, potatoes, peas, cabbage and cauliflower are all grown in the south, with some salads and courgettes produced under glass. Early potatoes are an important crop in Gwynedd, on the Gower peninsula. and in Pembrokeshire, now part of Dyfed.

Pick-your-own farms flourish in the warmer, flatter south, particularly in Gwent and Glamorgan. Soft fruits, including strawberries, raspberries, red- and blackcurrants, gooseberries, loganberries and blackberries are all on offer. The leek is the national symbol of Wales, and features prominently in Welsh cooking – it is an ingredient in Glamorgan sausages (see opposite). And the custom of wearing a leek on 1 March, St David's Day, still survives.

Early potatoes

The mild coastal slopes of Pembrokeshire rival those of Cornwall and Kent in the race to bring the first of the early potatoes to the markets at the end of May. The earlier the crop is picked, the lighter the yield – but the higher the price that can be fetched. Delicately flavoured, these 'first earlies', available until mid-August, are ideal for salads and simple summer dishes.

Buy little and often and handle gently to avoid bruising. Scrub or scrape gently before cooking or cook in their skins in lightly salted boiling water flavoured with a sprig of fresh mint or rosemary.

Here are the main varieties of the first earlies from Pembrokeshire:

Home Guard
Creamy white flesh, more floury than other earlies. Particularly good boiled and served with plenty of butter.

Ulster Sceptre
Excellent cooking quality and waxy texture that does not crumble or break when boiled. Also good in salads or as chips.

Arran Comet
Very creamy flesh, less waxy than Ulster Sceptre, but still firm and can be cooked in the same way.

Dutch Premier
A newcomer to the British scene, Dutch Premier is gaining popularity. Pale-yellow flesh, good flavour particularly suitable for chips.

A mechanical spinner is used to bring these Pembrokeshire early potatoes to the surface of the ground, then they are gathered up and bagged by hand.

Fresh from the griddle

All over Wales, as in the north of England and Scotland, oats were the most readily available cereal, widely grown because they are not averse to the cool and wet climate. The village mill also provided wheat and barley flours, and some of these watermills are now being brought back into service to produce nourishing, stone-ground flours. Nowadays, however, they are often likely to use imported grains, as local production has declined.

Tea was always a much-loved meal in Wales, although working families could not indulge in it every day. A lot of the cooking in a Welsh cottage was done on a well-greased griddle, or bakestone, set above the hearth. All kinds of baked goods, including bread, tarts and fruit turnovers, could be produced on the bakestone by a skilled cook, who could even transform her griddle into a primitive oven by inverting a metal pot over it. This is an increasingly rare skill, sadly.

Welsh oatcakes are similar to Scottish ones, but thinner, while their pancakes, or crempog, are made with buttermilk, then well buttered and stacked up in piles, which are sliced into portions. They can also be layered with a variety of fillings, sweet or savoury. Welsh cakes (see page 261) are another type of firm griddle cake, served sprinkled with sugar and with a dab of butter in the centre.

Also on the tea table you might find scones and pikelets, and perhaps a loaf of bara brith, a spicy, speckled fruit bread, best served sliced and spread with Welsh butter. Many cakes are agreeably spicy, with cinnamon and caraway seeds being favourite flavourings. They are still commonly found in local markets.

Pure spring waters

Abundant rainfall filters down through the hills and mountains of Wales and the drinking water is bottled commercially. It is also used in the country's brewing industry.

In the 19th and early 20th centuries, Welsh brewers concentrated on low-strength beers to appease the powerful influence of the chapel and the temperance movement. It so happened that such beers also suited the large numbers of miners and steel workers who required refreshment rather than strong alcohol after their labours. With the decline of industry, the emphasis today is on premium bitters and golden ales, although dark mild still retains a following. Craft brewers – a dozen in Glamorgan alone – have brought choice and diversity to the principality, although English brewers vigorously export their beers, to the tourist areas of the north in particular.

There are also a few independent makers of mead, from fermented Welsh honey, and one of Welsh whisky. The south-facing coastal slopes of Glamorgan have a long history of viniculture; grapes have been grown there for wine since medieval times. Today a handful of vineyards in Glamorgan and Dyfed produce white wines – some of excellent quality – from German grape varieties.

THREE TOP WELSH BREWERIES

Brains, Cardiff
S A Brain dates from 1882, and in 1999 moved to the former giant Bass site next to the railway station. Its Dark is a revered Welsh mild and it also brews a strong bitter, SA, known locally as Skull Attack, with a paler version called SA Gold.

Otley, Pontypridd
Run by three brothers, Otley is a small brewery with a big range of beers, including O1, a pale, hoppy beer, Dark O, a dark mild, the tongue-in-cheek O-Garden, and a powerful O8 barley wine. A visit to their Bunch of Grapes pub, with beer-and-food matching, is a must.

Bryncelyn of Ystradgynlais
An eccentric small brewery run by people devoted to Buddy Holly. The beers include Holly Hop, Buddy Marvellous, Buddy's Delight and a Christmas beer, That'll Be the Sleigh.

FOOD FAIRS AND FESTIVALS

APRIL

LLYN AGRICULTURAL SHOW
BOTACHO WYN, NEFYN, PWLHELI, GWYNEDD

JULY

BRIDGEND SHOW, PENCOED COLLEGE, PENCOED
**ROYAL WELSH SHOW, ROYAL WELSH SHOWGROUND,
BUILTH WELLS, POWYS**

AUGUST

ANGLESEY AGRICULTURAL SHOW
MONA, NEAR LLANGEFNI, ANGLESEY
CHEPSTOW AGRICULTURAL SHOW
BROADWELL FARM, GWENT
PEMBROKESHIRE COUNTY SHOW
SHOWGROUND, WITHYBUSH, HAVERFORDWEST, DYFED
UNITED COUNTIES AGRICULTURAL AND HUNTERS SOCIETY
SHOW
SHOWGROUND, NANTYCI, DYFED
VALE OF GLAMORGAN AGRICULTURAL SHOW
FONMON CASTLE, VALE OF GLAMORGAN, SOUTH GLAMORGAN

SEPTEMBER

ABERGAVENNY FOOD FESTIVAL
HELD IN VARIOUS VENUES IN ABERGAVENNY
ABERYSTWYTH FOOD FESTIVAL
BAKER STREET, ABERYSTWYTH

NOVEMBER

ROYAL WELSH WINTER FAIR
ROYAL WELSH SHOWGROUND, BUILTH WELLS, POWYS

THE MIDLANDS

CHESHIRE
DERBYSHIRE
NOTTINGHAMSHIRE
LEICESTERSHIRE
NORTHAMPTONSHIRE
WARWICKSHIRE
HEREFORDSHIRE
WORCESTERSHIRE
SHROPSHIRE
STAFFORDSHIRE

From the fruit-laden orchards of the south to the lush dairy pastures further north, the Midlands have much to offer. Famous cheeses, prime beef and abundant produce, as well as pies and cakes, ales, cider and pure mineral water are all produced here in the heart of England.

The Midlands make a big contribution to the nation's food. Besides being home to several of Britain's major manufacturing centres, this region includes some of the richest agricultural land in the country. From the beautiful orchards of the Vale of Evesham in the south to the lush dairy pastures of Cheshire in the north, there is plenty of farming activity.

The county of Hereford and Worcester in the south has rich, red soil that supports extensive market gardens as well as allowing fruit orchards to thrive. Hops, apples, pears and plums as well as soft fruits, many types of vegetables and fine asparagus grow well in this area. Locally named Hereford cattle produce some of the best of British beef.

Moving east and north, the Shires are famed as riding and hunting country, with large rolling fields that support cattle and some sheep as well as barley, wheat and other crops.

Further north, in Cheshire and Derbyshire, both soil and climate are less suitable for fruit. Nevertheless, these are fertile areas, which benefit from being in the warmer west. Cheshire has gently rolling countryside with a mixture of grass, arable, heath and mixed farming. The heart of the county is strongly agricultural, with potatoes and milk being the main products. Cheshire is also known for its salt, which for hundreds of years was an important industry here, while Derbyshire is the big sheep-rearing county of the Midlands.

Fine, flavoursome cheeses

Dairy cattle graze the rich grass throughout the Midlands, which is one of the biggest milk-producing regions in the country. Every county has some dairy farming, but the majority of cattle are still found in the more westerly counties of Shropshire, Staffordshire, Cheshire and Derbyshire, where the warm, wet climate is perfect for producing succulent pasture.

It is hardly surprising that with such an abundance of creamy milk, the Midlands have seen the birth of many of Britain's classic traditional cheeses. The most famous of all is Stilton, which can only be produced in the three counties of Derbyshire, Leicestershire and Nottinghamshire. Stilton was brought to fame over 300 years ago by a Mrs Paulet of Leicestershire, who sold her cheeses to her brother-in-law, keeper of the Bell Inn at Stilton in Cambridgeshire. The inn was on the main London–York road, and as passing travellers soon developed a fancy for the cheese, so its reputation spread. Eventually Midlands' farmers began to make it, and now the cheese is produced by six dairies.

Other fine cheeses were made in the Midlands, but Red Leicester is the only one that survives to this day. Its reddish colour originally came from adding carrot or marigold juice to the milk, but now a natural vegetable colouring from annatto (a berry) is used. Leicester was originally made on small farms throughout the county and became popular in London during Victorian times.

Cheshire is the oldest named British cheese and is mentioned in the Domesday Book. Red Cheshire is coloured with annatto, white Cheshire is uncoloured, and blue Cheshire was made as a result of accidental rather than intentional bluing.

Derby and Sage Derby are less common than some of the others, but worth seeking out. The more mature the cheese, the better the flavour. The texture is close and flaky, the flavour mild. Sage Derby gets its distinctive colour and taste from finely chopped sage added during processing.

The region has been influenced by the cheese

THREE IMPORTANT MIDLANDS CHEESES

Stilton (7kg/15½ lb tall cylinder)
The Stilton makers in the early 1900s joined forces to protect Stilton from being copied, specifying the recipe and limiting production to Derbyshire, Leicestershire and Nottinghamshire.
Tasting notes: well matured, rich, creamy and fills the mouth; the blue is scattered like shattered porcelain; spicy, creamy and rich in flavour; mellows with age.

Red Leicester (14kg/30lb flat cylinder)
Easily identified by its deep russet colour, from annatto; it can be eaten as young as two months, but by four months it has developed a more complex flavour and firm, chewable texture.
Tasting notes: clothbound with a firm, flaky, buttery texture; marvellous, deep orange; hints of butterscotch; nutty rather than fruity; mild to medium in flavour.

Cheshire (9kg/20lb tall cylinder)
The salt marshes of Cheshire originally gave Britain's oldest cheese its unique sea-breeze freshness and character. Red Cheshire is coloured with annatto although the colour is more pale apricot.
Tasting notes: crumbly yet moist textured; savoury with a gentle, green-grass, bitter tang; slightly salty.

revolution and there are more than 40 cheesemakers making traditional and modern British cheese. These include the award-winning ewes' milk cheese Berkswell, and Shropshire Blue, made by the Stilton makers and coloured with annatto, among many others.

All sorts of fruit and veg

Worcestershire's Vale of Evesham enjoys a warm, moist climate and boasts rich, heavy soil, which is ideal for growing fruit trees. Although orchard acreage has declined somewhat, so many trees are in flower during springtime that motorists can follow the specially signposted 'Blossom Trail' that wends its way past flower-festooned orchards. Many farms specialise, growing only one or two types of fruit, although they may produce several varieties of each type. A farmer might, for instance, grow four or five varieties of eating apple, two cookers, and a couple of varieties of plum, all chosen with an eye to spreading cropping carefully through the season. In this way best use can be made of costly storage facilities.

Many types of eating apples are grown, as well as apples for cider. Bramley's Seedlings, the famous cooking apple, are widely found in Midlands' orchards and were first raised at the minster town of Southwell, Nottinghamshire, in the early 19th century. The original tree, which grew from a pip planted in the garden of Matthew Bramley's cottage, apparently still survives.

SOFT FRUITS

Soft fruits are only around for a short season, so don't hesitate when you see them. If there's a glut you might be lucky and pick up a bargain, which can be used to make jam, or stored in the freezer to be enjoyed later in the year.

Blackberries
Look for firm, dry berries that are completely black. Use on the same day. Eat them raw, or use in cooking or for jam or wine. They are good combined with apples. They freeze well. **Season:** late July to late September.

Currants
Black, red and white currants should be firm, glossy and clean, with few withered or unripe berries or empty sprigs. They will keep in the fridge for up to ten days. Eat raw, use in cooking, for jams, jellies or sauces. They can be frozen. **Season:** July to August.

Gooseberries
Choose firm, unblemished fruit. Early gooseberries are small, hard and very green and sour, suitable only for cooking. Dessert gooseberries arrive later in the season – they are larger, softer, paler in colour and sweeter. They keep well in the fridge and freeze well, too. **Season:** late May to August.

Plums also come into their own here. The Pershore Yellow Egg, an excellent plum for cooking and jam-making, was first discovered in 1822, growing wild in the woods near the little market town of Pershore. It was farmed commercially on a large scale at one time, but fewer plums are grown now and much of the acreage is planted with the more popular Victoria. However, Pershore Yellow Egg is still grown in some orchards, so look out for it in late August.

Soft fruits and berries of all kinds flourish in the Vale, and pick-your-own farms and roadside farm stalls offering strawberries, raspberries and many other fruits and vegetables are found everywhere. Gooseberries are cultivated keenly all over the Midlands, as well as further north. Pears are grown in Hereford and Worcester, mainly for perry (see 'Cider-making and Brewing', page 32), although they prefer a richer, wetter soil than apples and, as they flower earlier, are more vulnerable to frost.

Some farmers have branched out into growing more unusual crops, and herb farms have also sprung up throughout the Midlands. Many types are grown, often under glass, which helps to prolong the season as well as protecting more delicate varieties from the weather.

Travel through Leicestershire and you'll see field upon field of Brussels sprouts, still one of the nation's favourite vegetables. Root vegetables – potatoes, parsnips and turnips – are grown, as well as peas and cabbage. And, back in the Vale of Evesham, salads, runner beans and many other vegetables are farmed intensively.

Perhaps the Vale's most famous vegetable is asparagus. The stalks are thin and delicate and the flavour is excellent. Asparagus was brought here by the Romans, although it has only been cultivated commercially for 80 years. It has a short season – just six weeks – although the plants occupy the ground for the whole year, not just their own season. Harvesting has to be done by hand and, while the crop fetches a good price, many producers have chosen to use the land more economically.

First-class beef

Hereford cattle, with their characteristic white markings on the face and reddish coats, are one of the best-known breeds in Britain and are extensively reared in their home county of Hereford and Worcester. The breed is a cross between the British Red Longhorn and cattle introduced from the Low Countries in the 17th century.

Beef was not always the tender, juicy meat we enjoy today. Until the 18th century cattle were smaller and tougher than they are now, and it took the work of a Leicestershire man, Robert Bakewell, in improving breeds, to bring them up to the standard we expect today. Beef cattle nowadays have a high ratio of meat to bone. They grow faster than their forebears, and are ready for market younger, so providing more tender meat.

There are sheep in some areas, but sheep farming is not as important in the Midlands as in other parts of the country.

In spite of having such good-quality beef on the doorstep, most butchers' shops in the Midlands concentrate first and foremost on pork products. Throughout the Shires the butchers' windows are full of black puddings, home-cured bacon and hams, sausages, faggots, brawn and – last but by no means least – pork pies. The town of Melton Mowbray, in the heart of Leicestershire's fox-hunting country, is famous for its pork pies. Commercial production has gone on in Melton Mowbray since the mid-19th century and the name is now protected by a PGI (see page 53). However, other manufacturers produce the pies elsewhere, without being able to use the Melton Mowbray name.

The rolling, wooded countryside of the Shires provides cover for all sorts of game – pheasant, rabbit and hare among others. And to add spice and savour to all things meaty is Worcestershire Sauce, developed almost by accident in the 1830s by two chemists, Mr Lea and Mr Perrins, from a recipe brought back from India by the Governor of Bengal. The exact ingredients and the length of time needed for the sauce to mature in oak barrels are still secret.

Fish from rivers and lakes

With no coastline to speak of, except for the mouths of the Dee and the Mersey in Cheshire, the Midlands have to rely on other areas for supplies of sea fish. However, there is superb freshwater fish to be had. Salmon are found in the Dee and also in the Wye, although levels have been greatly reduced. Pike, brown trout and grayling are more abundant. The River Dove in Derbyshire has pure waters, which have been renowned for centuries for their valuable fishing, and both trout and grayling can still be caught here. Rutland Water in Leicestershire is a large man-made lake with a stock of excellent trout. There are also a few fish farms scattered throughout the area.

Delicious baking

Oats were the main cereal grown in Derbyshire during the 18th and 19th centuries, and local shops still sell oatcakes, although today's main arable crops are barley and winter wheat. Shops selling oatcakes also proliferate in the north of Staffordshire, where oatcakes are considered a local delicacy, much missed by those who move away from the area. The same shops often sell pikelets and crumpets too. Midlands' oatcakes are quite different from the Scottish variety, being rather like thick pancakes but made with yeast and fine oatmeal and cooked on a hot griddle.

Little cheesecakes were made in Northamptonshire to be eaten at sheep-shearing time, while the town of Shrewsbury in Shropshire has given its name to the large, flat, crisp

biscuits that have been baked there for over three centuries. They were originally flavoured with caraway seeds, and sometimes made with currants (see recipe, page 238). Perhaps the most famous baked delicacies of the region are the Bakewell Tart (see recipe, page 206) and Bakewell Pudding, both cooked with variations by different cooks but always involving jam, almonds and pastry.

Cider-making and brewing

Hereford and Worcester is second only to Kent as a major hop-growing region and the heady, yeasty scent of hops fills the lanes during early autumn. But the main drinks found here are cider and perry, made from fermented pear juice. Both are produced commercially but perry is less widely available than cider. Some farmers make single-variety ciders and perries, mainly for their own use or to sell over the gate, but most of the drinks sold commercially are made with a blend of juices from different varieties.

The abundant fruits of Hereford and Worcester are also used to make concentrated fruit juices. These contain no preservatives, sweeteners, colouring or water, and have a delicious full flavour and aroma. The emphasis is very much

NATURAL WATERS FROM THE MIDLANDS

The fine spring waters of the Midlands led to the development of spas, where people travelled for health reasons to 'take the water'. Spa towns like Buxton and Malvern boomed in Victorian times and still produce large quantities of bottled water every year.

Malvern Water
The water rises at Primeswell Spring in the Malvern Hills where the granite slopes meet the impervious rocks of the valley. Designated a 'natural mineral water' by the EEC. Available still or sparkling.

Buxton Spring Water
The water takes over 20 years to permeate through limestone and volcanic lava in the High Peak District of Derbyshire. It emerges at a temperature of 27°C from St Ann's Well in the centre of Buxton. Available still or sparkling.

Ashbourne Water
Another natural spring water from the Peak District. The water comes from an underground source in beautiful Dovedale, above the town of Ashbourne. Available still or sparkling.

on apple, and flavours include pure apple – made from Cox's and Russets – as well as apple with blackcurrant, blackberry or plum.

There are also wineries in the region, in Staffordshire, Shropshire and Worcestershire, which are among the most northerly in England.

Even though the region's brewing industry is greatly reduced since its heyday, it is still famous for its ales. These are heavily influenced by Burton-on-Trent in Staffordshire, where the sulphate-rich waters of the Trent Valley helped fashion new pale ales and India Pale Ales in the 19th century. Burton is a reduced but still influential brewing town (with a National Brewery Centre). In contrast, however, Birmingham and the Black Country remained loyal to dark mild for its legion of industrial workers. The counties of Hereford and Worcestershire vie with Kent as the major hop-growing counties of England. Farmers have developed a new style of 'hedgerow hop' that grows to half the height of conventional varieties and, as a result, is easier and cheaper to pick. And microbreweries have sprung up, some of them making distinguished ales.

THREE NOTABLE MIDLANDS' BREWERIES

Bathams, Brierley Hill, Dudley
Dating from 1877, this family-owned brewery has 11 pubs. It is best-known for its succulent and fruity Mild Ale. The brewery stands next to the main pub, the Vine Inn, known locally as the Bull & Bladder.

Burton Bridge, Burton-on-Trent
The brewery is behind the Burton Bridge inn and produces classic Burton pale ales, including XL Bitter, Bridge Bitter and the strong Thomas Sykes.

Olde Swan, Netherton, Dudley
A brew-pub first licensed in 1835 that brews Original, a straw-coloured interpretation of mild, a darker version called Dark Swan and an amber beer, Entire.

FOOD FAIRS AND FESTIVALS

EASTER MONDAY

HALLATON HARE PIE SCRAMBLING AND BOTTLE KICKING
HALLATON, LEICESTERSHIRE

JUNE

KENILWORTH SHOW
NATIONAL AGRICULTURAL CENTRE, STONELEIGH, KENILWORTH, WARWICKSHIRE
THREE COUNTIES SHOW
MALVERN, WORCESTERSHIRE

JULY

NANTWICH SHOW
DORFOLD PARK, NANTWICH

AUGUST

BAKEWELL SHOW
DERBYSHIRE

SEPTEMBER

LUDLOW MARCHES FOOD AND DRINK FESTIVAL
THE STONE FOOD AND DRINK FESTIVAL

OCTOBER

BIRMINGHAM FOOD FEST
HELD IN VARIOUS VENUES IN BIRMINGHAM
FLAVOURS OF HEREFORDSHIRE FOOD FESTIVAL
HEREFORD, HEREFORDSHIRE

THE EASTERN COUNTIES

CAMBRIDGE
ESSEX
SUFFOLK
NORFOLK
LINCOLNSHIRE

Wheat and barley, potatoes and peas, salads and soft fruits – all thrive on the rich farmlands of England's Eastern Counties. Pigs and poultry are reared, there's an abundance of game, and first-class fish and shellfish inhabit the coastal waters. The climate also encourages a good harvest of fruit for eating fresh or turning into preserves.

The Eastern Counties are the arable farmlands of Britain. More than a quarter of England's wheat and barley is grown here, and almost half the agricultural land is used for growing cereal crops. Although the soils vary from county to county – rich and peaty in the fenlands, sandier near the coasts, with belts of heath and forest throughout – the crops grown are similar. Wheat and barley, oilseed rape and sugar beet stretch for miles across broad, fertile fields. Horticulture is vital too, and the Eastern Counties help keep the nation's salad bowls and vegetable baskets filled. Important crops include sugar beets, peas, broad beans, carrots and potatoes. There are many processing and packaging plants in the region and fruit is also important, with soft-fruit farms and plenty of orchard fruits. Cattle and sheep are farmed, but pigs and poultry are more important. And then, of course, there's the sea. Stretching from the Thames Estuary in Essex, round the bulging coastline of Suffolk and Norfolk, and up to the Wash, the waters are home to a rich variety of fish and shellfish.

Keeping the balance

The soil of the Eastern Counties, coupled with the climate – relatively dry compared with the westerly grasslands – means that this is first and foremost arable land. Around three-quarters of land in the region is used for agriculture, so farmers play an essential role in managing the countryside.

Despite the presence of some cattle herds, this area was not known for its cheeses; Daniel Defoe, writing in the early 18th century, remarked that Suffolk was famous for 'the best butter and perhaps the worst cheese in England'. Fortunately for food lovers this is no longer true. F.W. Read's Lincolnshire Poacher, a superb Cheddar-style cheese, has won top awards in competitions, and an increasing number of unique and innovative cheeses, made on small farms, are now appearing in farmers' markets.

Teeming waters

The ports of Great Yarmouth and Lowestoft thrived for centuries on the herring industry. Sadly, as in other parts of the country, ecological factors including over-fishing have led to decline and the little fleets of colourful fishing boats have largely disappeared.

The herring industry bred a great tradition of making smoked products – red herrings, bloaters and kippers. Herrings preserved as 'reds' were essential in the days before refrigeration. The fish are salted for one month and then smoked until rock-hard. They have a strong, salty flavour, sometimes likened to ham, and should be soaked before use. Eat without cooking or fry. Bloaters get a short soaking in brine and are slowly smoked over oak, ungutted, for 24 hours. The flavour is mild but slightly gamey, and the flesh pale and tender. A kipper is a herring that has been split from head to tail, gutted, salted and smoked. Both types of fish can be simply grilled with butter, or poached or microwaved.

Reasonable catches of other fish are landed at ports along the coast, Lowestoft being the largest. Fish can sometimes be bought on the beach, straight from the boats, at the Suffolk coastal towns of Aldeburgh, Southwold and Dunwich.

SHELLFISH FROM THE EASTERN COUNTIES

Oysters
Portuguese and Pacific oysters are the main types. Eat raw, with a dash of lemon juice, straight from the shell. If served hot, cook lightly.
Season: September to April.

Cockles
Usually white or cream in colour, with a circular shell. Sold cooked, shelled and often preserved in brine or vinegar. **Best:** April to December.

Whelks
A brownish or greyish spiral shell, white flesh. Sold boiled, often from stalls. **Best:** February to July.

Lobsters
Usually sold boiled in the shell, which turns bright scarlet when cooked. The white flesh can be removed from the shell and used in recipes.
Season: April to November.

Shrimps
Brown and pink shrimps are caught in the Wash. Brown shrimps are greyish-brown and have no pointed 'snout'. Usually sold cooked. Shell before eating or using in recipes. **Season:** February to October.

Crabs
Brown crab is the most common variety. Sold boiled and dressed with meat removed from the shell, or undressed. Choose by weight rather than size. Can be used in recipes or eaten in salads.
Season: April to December.

Mussels
Dark blue shells, bright yellow flesh. Sold live. Steam open and serve in or out of the shell, with a sauce. **Season:** September to February.

Shellfish also thrive. Oysters and mussels are farmed in the north, for instance at Brancaster and Morston in Norfolk, while in Essex are found the native flat oysters. The Suffolk coastal town of Orford has been famous for its oysters for centuries. After being abandoned early in the 1900s the Orford beds have been revived from the 1950s onwards. Fishing boats land sole, mullet, lobster and crab from spring to autumn, cod and skate most of the year, and sprats and herring in the winter months. The Romans harvested wild natives from the Colchester oyster beds 2,000 years ago, and the beds are generally recognised as producing some of the finest oysters in the country. Other shellfish include pink and brown shrimps, caught all round the coast.

Many fishing villages have developed a speciality. In Norfolk, Cromer and Sheringham are famous for their crabs: relatively small but heavy for their size. The tiny crab boats ply dangerous waters, full of hidden rocks and dangerous tides, to bring home the catch. Lobsters are also caught off the same coast.

Mussels are cheap, plentiful and in season throughout the winter. There are beds all around the coast, especially off north Norfolk, and Lincolnshire also benefits from the clean waters of the Wash to produce sweet, plump mussels.

Cockles and whelks are a speciality in Norfolk. Stiffkey (pronounced Stookey) is known for 'Stookey Blues', large cockles with grey-blue shells, which are raked out of the sand flats at low tide. They are usually sold boiled and are best eaten well seasoned with pepper and vinegar. Another north Norfolk village, Wells-next-the-Sea, is an important fishing base for whelks. You can buy them, along with crabs and other shellfish, on the quayside.

Still on the subject of the sea, samphire is an edible sea plant that has become increasingly popular. It is commonly found around the region's coast along the shore, in marshy shallows and salty mudflats. Fleshy and succulent, it should be lightly boiled before eating.

Picked for processing

The Eastern Counties are by far the largest supplier of supermarket carrots, while almost a third of England's potato crop and half its onions are grown here. The wide, flat fields of Lincolnshire are planted with vegetables as far as the eye can see. All the most popular British vegetables are grown here, including peas, potatoes, cabbage and onions, which ripen well in the dry climate. Broad and runner beans proliferate and are used mainly for processing. And the soil and climate are ideal for producing top-quality cauliflowers and spinach.

But vegetable crops are not the region's only major contribution to the nation's tables. A quarter of the soft fruit of England and Wales is grown here, and a fifth of the orchard fruit. Every county of the region makes a special contribution to this massive harvest.

In Cambridgeshire, however, it's still a story of vegetables – onions, carrots, peas and potatoes all feature, and the celery is justly famous. But fruit gets a good look-in. There are large orchards of apples, both cooking and dessert varieties, as well as pears and plums. The area around Wisbech is a leading centre for soft fruit: you'll find strawberries, gooseberries, raspberries, red- and blackcurrants and more, at roadside stalls and pick-your-own farms.

Norfolk and Suffolk both have long agriculture histories. Again, masses of vegetables are produced, many for freezing and canning. Roots such as potatoes, carrots, parsnips and onions do particularly well, as do peas, beans, salad crops, cabbage, cauliflowers and celery. But perhaps the best-loved vegetable of the Eastern Counties is asparagus. Asparagus comes in several grades and in each one the stalks are fatter, and costlier, than the one before. Stalks of Super Extra Selected are so plump that you might only get eight to a kilo.

In Suffolk they specialise in apples. There are apples in Norfolk, too, although not the wide range of varieties grown as recently as the 1930s: most orchards are given over to

---

SALT, MUSTARD AND VINEGAR

Three of the most popular condiments come from the Eastern Counties.

Salt
Maldon Crystal Salt is harvested from a part of the Essex marshes and has been in production for 700 years. It comes in the form of large crystalline flakes and has no additives. The salty river water is first filtered and then heated so that the water evaporates, leaving behind the pure sea salt. The Maldon Crystal Salt Company is one of only four manufacturers producing salt in England.

Mustard
Jeremiah Colman created his fiery blend of brown and white mustard at a Norfolk water mill in 1814. In June the fields of East Anglia are golden with mustard, much of which goes to Colman's of Norwich for processing. Two types – brown and white – are grown. The seeds are milled and then blended. Colman's have a shop and museum in Norwich.

Vinegar
Aspall's in Suffolk make their own Cyder Vinegar from organically grown apples with no additives. The taste is a great alternative to wine vinegar for all culinary uses. Red and white wine vinegars are also made by the same firm.

FOOD FAIRS AND FESTIVALS

MARCH

TASTES OF ANGLIA FEAST EAST
CHILFORD HALL, LINTON, CAMBRIDGESHIRE

MAY

NORTH LINCOLNSHIRE REGIONAL FOOD FESTIVAL
NORMANBY HALL COUNTRY PARK, LINCOLNSHIRE

JUNE

CAKES AND ALE CEREMONY
ST MARY'S CHURCH, BURY ST EDMUNDS
THE ROYAL NORFOLK SHOW
NEW COSTESSEY, NORWICH
SUFFOLK SHOW
IPSWICH

JULY

EAST OF ENGLAND SHOW
PETERBOROUGH

SEPTEMBER

BLESSING THE WHITEBAIT CATCH CEREMONY
HELD IN SOUTHEND, THORPE BAY AND LEIGH-ON-SEA AREAS
ALDEBURGH FOOD AND DRINK FESTIVAL
SNAPE MALTINGS, SUFFOLK
EDP NORFOLK FOOD FESTIVAL
CHAPPEL BEER FESTIVAL
WAKES COLNE, ESSEX

OCTOBER

SUFFOLK HERRING FESTIVAL
MIDDLETON, SUFFOLK

DECEMBER

ROYAL SMITHFIELD SHOW
PETERBOROUGH SHOWGROUND, SUFFOLK

Cox's Orange Pippins and Bramley's Seedlings. Much soft fruit is also grown in the county.

Finally to Essex, home of the widely available Tiptree and Elsenham jams, which are made in the centre of soft fruit-growing lands. Strawberry production is particularly important and pick-your-own signs are a familiar sight. Plums, cherries and pears are also grown, many ending up in cans or as jams and preserves. The Lea Valley, which runs from Hertfordshire although Bedfordshire and Essex to the Thames, once had the largest concentration of glasshouses in the world. Although agricultural activity has decreased, it still plays an important role in the area's economy.

Talking turkey

Historically, poultry and pigs have played an important part in the economy of the Eastern Counties. Yes, you will find beef cattle and lambs here – the Red Poll, Suffolk's traditional breed of cattle, is now a rare breed but is still raised by a handful of farmers for the excellent quality of their meat. But most farmers use their land for arable farming and have little to spare for the grassy pastures required by cows and sheep.

Poultry is vitally important here. Suffolk and Norfolk are the leading areas for turkey production; chickens and ducks are farmed in great numbers, while geese and guinea fowl are also reared on farms large and small. Laying hens produce over 2 million eggs every day, and the region's farmers supply a quarter of England's table chicken. In the 17th and 18th centuries, locally bred ducks, geese and turkeys were driven to London by foot, starting their journeys in summer to arrive before Christmas.

Between them, the Eastern Counties provide a considerable proportion of home-produced pork and bacon – there is a higher density of pigs here than anywhere else in the country. Lighter pigs are sold for pork and heavier pigs for bacon.

Ham and bacon curing is a traditional East Anglian industry. Suffolk sweet-cured hams are renowned, although now rare – only three producers still make them the traditional way. They take over two months to produce, with brining followed by pickling in a liquid containing treacle, sugar, salt and beer/stout or cider, and finally five days of smoking to develop their characteristic shiny black skins. Matured for a minimum of one month after smoking, they are handsome to look at and taste marvellous. Another delightful traditional pork dish is the oddly named Huntingdon Fidget Pie, which makes use of the region's onions and apples as well as bacon (see recipe, page 118). Newmarket sausages, fairly spicy, are now made by just two butchers in the town of Newmarket.

A curious custom involving bacon is the Dunmow Flitch Trial, which has taken place in the Essex town of Great Dunmow every four years on Whit Monday since the 13th century. A flitch, or side of bacon, is given to a local married couple who can prove, to the satisfaction of a jury of six maidens and six bachelors, that they have not quarrelled or wished they were not married for 'twelvemonth and a day'!

Game is also plentiful throughout the counties. The countryside, with its fields high with wheat, its marshes, flat watery fens and the Broads, is the perfect habitat for many game birds. Pheasant scurry across the country lanes, and partridge, woodcock, quail and wild duck are common. Rabbit and hare almost overran parts of East Anglia at one point. The Denham Estate, 1,200 acres of picturesque Suffolk countryside, has Europe's largest deer herd.

Fine cakes and gingerbread

In this region, as in all parts of the country, home baking has a long tradition. There are many recipes using apples in cakes, puddings and pies. Grantham, in Lincolnshire, is famous for its white gingerbreads, which are puffed up, crunchy biscuits. This pale-coloured treat was first made in 1740 by accident when local baker William Egglestone neglected to include black treacle, which is traditionally used in gingerbread. A brown and white, spiced version of gingerbread came from Diss in Norfolk and there were other local spicy biscuits and cakes, which were sold at fairs throughout the region. They may still be found in local bakeries.

Beer, cider and wines

Norfolk is known as the grain basket of England as a result of the top-quality 'maritime' barley grown there, which is supplied to brewers throughout the country. The region is also comparatively close to London and the Southeast and as a result uses generous amounts of Kent hops in its beers. In spite of its long agricultural history, the region's beers tend to be pale and hoppy, rather than dark and malty. Brewing

BREWERIES

Adnams, Southwold, Suffolk
A classic brewery in a handsome seaside town. Bitter and Broadside are renowned, traditional bitters bursting with hop character and flavour.

Bateman's, Wainfleet, Lincolnshire
A family brewery dating from 1874, with a popular Dark Mild, a Porter and two superb bitters, XB and the stronger XXXB.

Woodforde's, Woodbastwick, Norfolk
Fast-growing craft brewery with such award-winning ales as Wherry Best Bitter, Nelson's Revenge and Norfolk Nog. Enjoy them in the Fur & Feather Inn next to the brewery.

in Norfolk was virtually destroyed by mergers and takeovers in the 1960s and 1970s but a vigorous craft brewing revival has taken place and the county now has some 30 small breweries. Best known are the region's two largest brewers, Greene King at Bury St Edmunds and Adnam's at Southwold. Look out for such classic 'country ales' as Greene King Strong Suffolk, matured in wooden vessels for up to a year, and for distinctive beers now being produced by the many newer, smaller breweries.

Cider (often spelled with a 'y') is another favourite drink in these parts, and used to be the most common thirst-quencher among farmers and country people. Traditional cider in the Eastern region comes from culinary and dessert apples, quite different from that produced in the West Country. Aspall, a Suffolk firm that has been making cyder (as they spell it) since the 18th century, had a traditional stone-trough mill in use until 1947, when their last working horse died. The Norfolk Cider Company (est. 1987) is the oldest cider maker in Norfolk, following the closure of William Gaymer and Sons, but it continues a tradition in Norfolk that stretches back to at least 1204. Apples are also used to make fine ciders that are more like apple wines, with a pale colour, delicate flavour and relatively high alcohol content.

Non-alcoholic fruit juices are also produced in a range of flavours, including grape, apple with cherry or strawberry, pear and apple, and apple and carrot. Household names such as Copella and James White reside in the region.

The great English wine revival has reached the Eastern Counties, where the climate is good for vines, with relatively sunny summers, a low rainfall and warm, late autumns. Much of the wine is still made with the Germanic grape varieties. Vineyards are scattered throughout the region, except for Lincolnshire, and many welcome visitors and sell wine on the premises.

THE NORTH

NORTHUMBERLAND
TYNE AND WEAR
DURHAM
CLEVELAND
NORTH YORKSHIRE
HUMBERSIDE
SOUTH YORKSHIRE
WEST YORKSHIRE
GREATER MANCHESTER
MERSEYSIDE
LANCASHIRE
CUMBRIA
ISLE OF MAN
CUMBERLAND

Dales and moors, hills and mountains, seas, rivers and deep lakes – the North has miles of truly glorious scenery outside its major industrial centres. And there's a wealth of good food to discover: choice lamb, celebrated cheeses, excellent fish, thirst-quenching beers and mouth-watering home-baked cakes.

The North is often thought of as being primarily an urban area, but once you leave the sprawling conurbations behind, you soon find what a large proportion is rural, encompassing many different types of unspoilt landscape and scenery of great beauty. There's plenty of good grass, to feed the region's numerous flocks of sheep and cattle herds and this emphasis on livestock means farms provide top-quality beef and lamb, as well as plenty of milk to make the famous cheeses for which the North is known.

The coastline has long played a vital role in the region's economy, and fishing is still important. Some of the best kippers in the land are smoked in the North, and people also claim that their fish and chips are second to none, with unbeatably light, crispy batter.

Northern cooking is based on dishes suitable for a hard-working community living in a bracing climate. Simple, cheap and tasty meals were designed to satisfy hearty appetites and keep working families well fed for the least possible cost. Ingenious cooks made sure that nothing was wasted and many of their dishes, which always used the best produce available locally, are still enjoyed today.

Northern cheeses

Yorkshire, Cumbria and Lancashire between them encompass huge tracts of land and a wide variety of terrain. On the lower fields, cattle are kept in large numbers and their milk is used to make butter, cream, and, of course, the excellent traditional cheeses for which the region is famous.

Lancashire is probably the most readily recognised cheese from the North. The production process is laborious but the results well worth the effort. Lancashire cheese is sometimes referred to locally as 'toaster' because it melts so well, and is often labelled 'mild' or 'tasty', depending on the strength of flavour. Try Pan Haggerty (see recipe, page 199), a delicious vegetable dish, to see for yourself.

Wensleydale, until the 1920s, always had blue veins, due to its open texture rather than by design. However, these days the white version is more common and the veined cheese is now known as Blue Wensleydale. French monks who founded the great abbeys in the Yorkshire Dales, following the Norman Conquest of 1066, first brought the recipe to this country. The North Country way to eat Wensleydale is with a slice of apple pie, gingerbread or fruit cake.

Cotherstone is another cheese, originally made by monks, which is enjoying a revival today. It is not widely available, since it is made only by a small number of producers in Yorkshire. There are several other locally produced cheeses, all of which are made on a small scale.

Not surprisingly, for a region that has so much rugged land, goats and sheep are increasingly widely farmed, and their milk is more and more used for cheeses, which now number nearly 300.

Lots of lambs and interesting offal

Huge numbers of sheep are reared on the hill farms and moorlands of the North Country. Hardy breeds are favoured so they can withstand the cold winds and bitter winters, and hill breeds are used where the terrain becomes steeper and less hospitable. The North Country Mule is a cross breed common in Cumbria, and Cheviot sheep are found on the

moors in Yorkshire. One advantage of these tough creatures is that they can survive all but the worst weather on what little they can crop from the ground and need no extra food from the farmer.

Sheep produce their lambs in spring and the youngest, most tender meat is available from June to August. Lambs born later do not reach the shops until further on in the year and have a more mature flavour. Mutton, the meat of a fully grown sheep, once staple fare throughout the country, declined in popularity for some years but is making a comeback due to demand from both chefs and home cooks. If bought in the Lakes, it will probably come from Herdwick sheep, an exceptionally hardy local breed that has become increasingly popular. Many regional dishes use lamb – Shepherd's Pie (see recipe, page 81) is one national favourite that originated in the North, and Lancashire Hot Pot (see recipe, page 80) is a popular and flavoursome way to cook lamb chops.

The hard life of the North, both in the industrial cities and among the farming communities, meant that Northerners developed a thrifty approach to food that still exists today. No part of the animal was wasted, and butchers' stalls are arrayed not just with the more usual liver, kidneys and hearts, but with other types of offal that are seldom, if ever, found further south. Tripe is very popular – there is a recipe for tripe and onions on page 143 – and brains, chitterlings (pig's intestines), lamb's fry (testicles), elder (pressed cow's udder), cow heel for enriching pies and stews, and sweetbreads are all on sale.

Black pudding is a great delicacy and the best ones are said to come from Bury. Primarily made from fresh blood and oatmeal, there are as many different variations to the texture and seasoning as there are makers. Every year the butchers compete with their French counterparts to see who can produce the best black pudding. Besides these delicacies are pressed and potted meats, jellied veal, faggots, cooked chicken, tongue and brisket, and much more. And all over Lancashire stalls sell hot meat pies, to eat there and then or take home.

Pigs, cattle and game

Bacon is traditionally prepared in the same way as it is in Scotland, with the joint rolled, so that the 'middle cut' has both streaky and back meat. York hams are cured in oak smoke and come from the meat of the Large White pig, a sizeable, sturdy breed. Over on the other side of the country, Cumberland hams, although hard to come by, are worth looking out for. They are dry-cured, salted and rubbed with brown sugar, and are usually sold unsmoked. Cumberland sausages are a delicacy that has found its way south. They contain nothing but meat, flavoured with herbs and spices, and can be up to 1.2 metres (4 feet) long.

The beef of northern England has a reputation for being juicier and tastier than that of the south. Whether or not this is true, there is no dish that signifies the best of British cooking more than roast beef, accompanied of course by Yorkshire pudding, a Northern dish that is cooked every week in thousands of homes across the country (see below). Steak and Kidney Pie (see recipe, page 99) is another much-loved dish that originates from the North.

The wild moors, mountains and dales are home to all sorts of game. There is some venison, as well as grouse, pheasant and partridge, and both venison and quail are farmed. Jugged hare is regarded as a local speciality. Derwentwater duck (see recipe, page 133) is delicious served with piquant Cumberland sauce.

Fish from sea, river and lake

With sea to both the east and west, the tradition of fishing is naturally well established in the North. Fleets from the Humberside ports trawl the North Sea mainly for white fish and many foreign vessels also use these ports. To underline the importance of the fishing industry here, the National Federation of Fish Friers, based in York, runs courses to teach people about running a fish and chip shop.

Shellfish, including crabs, lobsters and scallops, are caught in all northern waters, and tiny scallops are found off the Isle of Man. From Morecambe Bay, on the west coast, come small brown shrimps, sadly rarer now than they used to be, but still delicious eaten in the traditional way, potted with butter (see recipe page 177). There are good fish markets throughout Lancashire, where you might find hake, shrimp or herring.

A tasty herring recipe for fish stuffed and served with mustard sauce comes from Cumbria).

Fine kippers are made in Northumbria, where the venerable firm of L. Robson and Sons has its own special light cure, based on a technique originally used for salmon, which hasn't changed for more than 100 years. Few of the herrings used are caught locally, however. The Isle of Man

SUSTAINABLE FISHING

The waters around Britain once teemed with fish and shellfish, but recent decades have seen stock levels slump dramatically. Much of the decline has been caused by over-fishing, often by huge trawlers from other countries. The drive to protect and restore fish populations goes on, but in the meantime every home cook has a responsibility to avoid buying fish that are fished unsustainably. There are two excellent sources of information about this. One is the Marine Conservation Society (MCS). Their website (www.mcsuk.org) provides oversight and news about issues affecting UK fishing, and their online buying guide, at www.goodfishguide.co.uk, gives detailed advice about which fish to buy and – just as important – which to avoid. At the time of writing, 31 species got a rating of 5, meaning 'Fish to avoid' because their population levels are so low. The other source of information is the Marine Stewardship Council, which certifies fisheries all over the world that have demonstrated that their fishing practices are sustainable. You can learn more, and find out which UK fisheries are certified (12 at the time this book went to press), at their website www.msc.org.

also produces memorable kippers, and from other smokeries in the North come delicious haddock, trout, salmon and prawns.

Freshwater fish, such as trout and salmon, inhabit the Lakes and many of the rivers that flow down to the sea from the Pennines and Cheviots. As elsewhere, however, farming is a more important source of fish in the North, with trout being the most commonly produced variety.

An unusual freshwater fish that is found in the deep waters of the Lake District is the Arctic charr (or char). A relative of the salmon, charr was left behind in the inland lakes after the glacial waters of the Ice Age receded. Charr are caught with long lines, which plunge deep into the waters, weighted by bright metal spinners made of bronze, copper or even silver. It is sometimes possible to buy these fish locally.

Plentiful produce

Much of the land of the North is given over to grazing but some arable farming does go on, especially in the lower-lying areas of the drier northeast. It's not easy to grow fruit and vegetables successfully in a place where the climate is often cold and wet, although Lancashire, which has the advantage of being on the warmer west side of the Pennines, still has a large farming industry and a large proportion of fertile agricultural land. The county does well with root crops, especially potatoes, and salad vegetables, such as cucumbers, tomatoes and lettuce, which are grown under glass, but hardly any fruit is grown there. A high percentage of this abundance of fresh vegetables is consumed locally, some sold in farm shops, and the rest taken to shops and markets in the surrounding towns and cities.

Elsewhere, gooseberries and forced rhubarb are the two big fruit crops to come from the North. The 'Rhubarb Triangle' in Yorkshire produces some of the finest early rhubarb, and after years of uncertainty about its future, the industry is once again in reasonable health. Intense rivalry surrounds domestic gooseberry growing, and an annual Gooseberry Show at Egton Bridge sees a fiercely fought contest. Commercial growing centres are found in Lancashire, however, rather than Yorkshire.

The climate of the North is generally unsuitable for fruit growing, but damsons, known locally as witherslacks, are grown around Lake Windermere. These fruits have a tart flavour, but can be used very successfully for cooking, such as in Damson and Apple Tansy (see recipe, page 210).

Cakes, bakes and sweet things

Comforting cakes to cheer up chilly afternoons are a speciality of the North and a multitude of recipes come from the area, some of them with intriguing names. Singing

Hinnies, from the northeast, are made from a scone-like mixture and are so named because they sizzle on the griddle as they cook. Many recipes from the northeast feature oats, one of the staple crops grown here.

Kendal Mint Cake from the Lake District isn't a cake at all but a peppermint-flavoured sweet, which is said to be very sustaining and ideal for climbers and walkers trekking across the hills. Eccles Cakes (see recipe, page 233) are filled with a mincemeat-style mixture of dried fruits, sugar and spices, enclosed in a crisp flaky pastry crust. They come from the town of Eccles in Lancashire.

Gingerbread is popular all over the North and perhaps the most famous comes from the Lake District village of Grasmere. The Grasmere Gingerbread Shop still exists, and the cake is baked on the premises; it has been made to Sarah Nelson's secret recipe since 1855.

Rum features as a flavouring in many Lake District dishes, because the liquor was brought over in ships from the West Indies during the 18th century. Cumberland Rum Nicky (see recipe, page 209) is rather like a mince pie flavoured with rum and is a traditional dessert from the area.

Perhaps the most famous 'bake' from the North Country is Yorkshire pudding. This was originally flatter than the puffy version we know today, because the batter was cooked on an open fire beneath the spit where the joint was roasting, to catch all the delicious juices as they dripped down. Although it is often thought of purely as an accompaniment to roast beef (see recipe, page 94), in the North Yorkshire pudding is served as a pub snack with onion gravy or a meat-based filling, such as steak and kidney.

Northern brews

As this vast region covers old industrial areas along with mountains, lakes and vast swathes of agricultural land, beer had to satisfy prodigious thirsts for miners, steel and mill workers. Dark mild lingers on in a few areas, while workers in Tyneside enjoyed both an imported speciality from north of the border called Scotch Ale and the local Newcastle Brown. Social change has led to beers that are paler and more bitter in character but the generations are united by their demand for a pint with a good thick, creamy head. Micro-brewers appear like mushrooms at dawn: at the time this book went to press there were 30 in Greater Manchester, the same number in Cumbria and a total of 100 in the four quarters of Yorkshire.

One unique alcoholic drink made in the North is Lindisfarne Mead, from Holy Island off Northumberland, a drink with an ancient history. It is made from honey and, since it is known that bees have been kept in this area for many centuries, the drink was probably made by the monks who settled here 1,300 years ago. The modern winery stands opposite the ruins of the monastery.

THREE NOTABLE NORTHERN BREWERIES

Hawkshead, Staveley, Cumbria
Fast-growing craft brewery founded by ex-BBC correspondent Alex Brodie. The Beer Hall gives views of the brewery and serves all the beers, including Hawkshead Gold and Brodie's Pride.

Holt, Manchester
Traditional, no-nonsense family brewery dating from 1849, and concentrating on mild and bitter: the mild, dark and roasty, is a classic.

Timothy Taylor, Keighley, Yorkshire
On the edge of Brontë country, this family brewery, formed in 1853, draws pure brewing water from the Knowle Spring. The range includes two milds – dark and golden – and the multi-award-winning premium bitter, Landlord.

FOOD FESTIVALS

Recent decades have seen an enormous increase in the number of food festivals held throughout the country. Where food-related events used to be agricultural fairs for a particular region or county, now they are more generalised affairs featuring food stalls, cookery demonstrations, and a wide range of other activities. A few of the more prominent, long-established festivals are listed in the appropriate region. There are many others, however, and you should support those in your area as well as looking out for festivals in areas you are travelling to.

FOOD FAIRS AND FESTIVALS

EASTERTIDE

EGG DECORATING AND ROLLING COMPETITIONS
CUSWORTH HALL MUSEUM, CUSWORTH, DONCASTER, SOUTH YORKSHIRE; AVENHAM PARK, PRESTON, LANCASHIRE; AND OTHER VENUES

JULY

BLESSING THE BOATS
WHITBY, YORKSHIRE
THE GREAT YORKSHIRE SHOW
HOOKSTONE OVAL, HARROGATE, YORKSHIRE
CUMBERLAND SHOW
CARLISLE RACE COURSE, CARLISLE

AUGUST

EGTON BRIDGE GOOSEBERRY SHOW
NORTH YORKSHIRE
WIRRAL FOOD AND DRINK FESTIVAL

SEPTEMBER

FIRST FRUITS HARVEST CEREMONY
MARKET PLACE, RICHMOND, NORTH YORKSHIRE
YORK FOOD AND DRINK FESTIVAL

SCOTLAND

HIGHLAND
OUTER HEBRIDES REGION
SHETLAND
ORKNEY
GRAMPIAN
CENTRAL
TAYSIDE
FIFE
LOTHIAN
STRATHCLYDE
BORDERS
DUMFRIES AND GALLOWAY

Fine and famous foods come from this, the most mountainous region of Britain. Succulent Highland beef and tender lamb, superb salmon, mouth-watering smoked fish, firm potatoes and juicy berries are second to none, as are the traditionally baked cakes, breads and biscuits, and the world-renowned whiskies.

Scotland conjures up images of hills and mountains. Most parts, however, are low-lying and fertile, producing soft fruits and good harvests of wheat and barley. About one-third of the countryside is hostile to all but the hardiest of animals and crops, but mountain sheep and tough Highland cattle thrive in these areas. And there are plenty of fish and shellfish to be had from the seas and inland waters. Add to that the delectable products of Scottish baking and the age-old skills of distilling, and you have the picture of a country with a wealth of good food to offer.

FOOD FAIRS AND FESTIVALS

JANUARY

BURNS NIGHT SUPPERS
HELD IN VARIOUS VENUES THROUGHOUT SCOTLAND

FEBRUARY/MARCH

HIGHLAND CATTLE SHOW AND SALE
OBAN

MAY

CATRINE AGRICULTURAL SHOW
KINGENCLEUGH, NEAR MAUCHLINE
LESMAHAGOW FARMERS' SOCIETY ANNUAL SHOW
THE SHOWFIELD, BROCKETSBRAE, LANARK

JUNE

ROYAL HIGHLAND SHOW
EDINBURGH AND EXHIBITION TRADE CENTRE, INGLISTON, EDINBURGH

JULY

CAITHNESS COUNTY SHOW
RIVERSIDE, WICK, CAITHNESS
BANCHORY SHOW
KING GEORGE V PARK, BANCHORY, KINCARDINESHIRE
NEW DEER SHOW
CRAIGIEFORD PARK, ABERDEENSHIRE
Agricultural show.
PALNACKIE FLOUNDER TRAMPING WORLD CHAMPIONSHIP
PALNACKIE VILLAGE, BY DALBEATTIE, KIRKCUDBRIGHTSHIRE
SUTHERLAND AGRICULTURAL SHOW
THE LINKS, DORNOCH, SUTHERLAND

AUGUST

EAST MAINLAND AGRICULTURAL SHOW
SHOW PARK, ST ANDREWS, ORKNEY
ISLAY AGRICULTURAL SHOW
SHOWFIELD, ISLAY, ARGYLL
ORKNEY AGRICULTURAL SHOW
BIGNOLD PARK, BIGNOLD PARK ROAD, KIRKWALL, ORKNEY
PERTH AGRICULTURAL SHOW
SOUTH INCH, PERTH

SEPTEMBER

ESKDALE AGRICULTURAL SOCIETY OPEN SHOW
THE CASTLEHOLM, LANGHOLM, DUMFRIESSHIRE
KEITH HORTICULTURAL SOCIETY SUMMER SHOW
LONGMORE HALLS, BANFF ROAD, KEITH, BANFFSHIRE

OCTOBER

ABERDEEN ANGUS SHOW AND PERTH BULL SALES
THE MARKET, CALEDONIAN ROAD, PERTH

Cheesemaking revival

Dairy farming is practised in most parts of Scotland, although it is largely concentrated in the lower lands of the south, particularly in the fertile pastures of Dumfries and Galloway and Strathclyde. The most southerly islands of the Hebrides also have a climate well suited to dairying, and all these areas produce milk, butter and yogurt as well as cheese.

Considering how strongly the friendship with France influenced the Scottish language, architecture and cuisine (Scotland traded wine with France long before England), it seems strange it did not inspire cheesemaking. The crofters made their own cheese but none, with the exception of Dunlop and Crowdie – a fresh cheese rolled in oatmeal – were written into the history books until the artisan cheese revolution in the mid-1980s.

Since then cheesemaking has boomed, with around 25 producers, from the Orkneys to the Borders, making a huge diversity of cheeses. Among the best known of these modern cheeses are Isle of Mull Cheddar, Highland Blue, Blue Monday, Lanark Blue, Loch Arthur Farmhouse and Connage Dairy Brie.

A TOP SCOTTISH CHEESE

Dunlop from Ayrshire (3kg/6 ½ lb drum)
First made by Barbara Gilmour in the time of James II and named after the village where she lived, its production became a flourishing industry during the 18th and 19th centuries, only to die out again, and it was all but lost until Anne Dorward revived the recipe in the mid-1980s.
Tasting notes: like a soft Cheddar with a sweetness like butter, mild but not bland.

Fish farming – a boom industry

Fishing in Scotland has provided many communities with a livelihood over the centuries. Peterhead is the largest port, while Aberdeen is also very important. Large catches of both flat and round fish are landed, along with many other varieties of seafish. Herring is often thought of as the typical Scottish fish and still makes up the main catch of the coastal Highlands, where over half of Scottish fish are caught, but the number fished off the east coast has dwindled now because of EEC regulations. Herring are a very nutritious, oily fish, which are best cooked simply. The Scottish way is to coat them with oatmeal and fry them until they are crisp and golden.

It was during the 14th century that fishing first began to grow as an industry in the Border country. Lobster and shrimp, as well as white fish, feature in the catch here. Crabs and lobsters are caught in creels off the coast of Fife,

SMOKED FISH

Fish has been dried and smoked for many hundreds of years, probably since prehistoric times. Not only does the process preserve the fish but it also adds distinctive and complex flavours. Many varieties, including trout, mackerel and eel, are suitable for smoking, but those illustrated here are the best-known, traditional Scottish smoked fish.

Smoked salmon
Salmon is soaked in brine or dry-salted for 24 hours (although this varies from one smoker to another) to bring out the flavour, then cold-smoked over oak sawdust. Succulent, with a mild flavour. No need to cook before eating, but can be used in recipes if it is lightly cooked.

Kippers
Those from the area around Loch Fyne, on the west coast, are the best known. Herrings are split, gutted and brined, then smoked over oak for up to 12 hours. They are silvery-gold in colour. Buy whole fish, with head on. Grill, poach or microwave.

Arbroath smokies
Made first in Auchmithie, and now in Arbroath, both fishing towns of the northeast. Small haddock, heads removed, are salted for two hours, then hot-smoked in pairs over oak or beech for less than an hour. No colour is added. Can be eaten cold or grilled, or added to tarts, soups, salads or pasta.

Finnan haddock
From Findon, north of Arbroath, south of Aberdeen. The fish are split and cleaned, lightly brined, then cold-smoked for up to six hours over oak sawdust. No dye is added and the fish are a pale lemon colour. Finnan haddock must be cooked before eating; can be grilled or poached. They are the traditional fish used in ham'n'haddie. Eyemouth Pales, from the Borders, are prepared in a similar way.

while the Western Isles add more white fish to the picture, as well as excellent shellfish, including lobsters, crabs, scallops, langoustines and winkles.

Scotland also has a fine reputation for freshwater fish, from the pure waters of the deep lochs and fast-flowing rivers. Wild trout and salmon from the Tay and Tweed, caught by traditional methods, are considered among Britain's finest fish. Sadly, fish stocks are a fraction of their former size and these fish – especially salmon – are now rarities.

As wild salmon declined, the farming of salmon grew exponentially from the 1970s onwards. The fish are hatched in rivers and then transferred to fresh or seawater lochs to grow in the safety of special pens, where predators cannot harm them. The farms are found mainly in the Highlands and islands, although fish farms can be found across the rest of Scotland. Rainbow and other trout are also farmed, along with Arctic charr (or char), halibut, oysters, scallops and mussels.

Some farmed salmon and trout are turned into another of Scotland's finest foods – smoked fish. Smoking is also used to treat herrings and haddock. The traditions of smoking go back hundreds of years, when it was an important method of storing fish for long periods. Smoked fish feature in some of Scotland's most famous dishes, including Cullen Skink (see recipe, page 75). Salting fish was the method of preservation used before smoking, and it is still done on the islands and the northern coastline.

Meat from moor and mountain

Scottish beef and lamb are renowned for their excellence throughout the world. The Aberdeen Angus breed of beef cattle was first developed in the northeast of Scotland in the early 19th century. These animals have a good proportion of lean to fat and, although they are relatively small, yield a good weight for their size. The meat is lightly marbled with fat, which makes it tender, juicy and full of flavour. Other breeds include the Galloway and the Highland Shorthorn. Cattle are usually bred on hill and upland farms, then brought to maturity on the lush lowlands. The Highlands and islands have some of the best grazing in Europe, with the rich summer pastures of Orkney, Islay and Kintyre. Orkney beef, from milk-fed calves, is marketed as such, and can sometimes be found in other parts of the country.

Sheep are particularly well suited to life on the rough Scottish slopes. The Black-faced breed grazes on heather, which gives the meat a specially sweet and delicious flavour. These sheep do not lamb until June and the young are allowed to mature until the following year. Cheviots, bred in the Border hills and the lower lands of the north, are known for their wool as well as their meat. The Shetland breed, which inhabits the islands of the same name and goes back to Neolithic times, is hardy, lean and small. It feeds on grass, heather and seaweed, which give the flesh a gamey and unique flavour.

Haggis is probably the best-known Scottish meat dish although it is not widely consumed by the Scots themselves. It is made principally of minced lungs parcelled in a sheep's gut, like a big spicy sausage, and is traditionally served with great ceremony on Burns Night – 25 January. Haggis is sometimes sold without a casing, already sliced, for frying or grilling.

SCOTTISH GAME

The term 'game' describes wild birds and animals that are shot for sport during a specified season. The meat has a strong flavour and needs to be properly hung.

Venison
The meat of the deer. Marinate, then roast, casserole or use in pies and pâtés. **Season:** wild deer are in season from summer through to winter. Venison from deer farms is available all year and is every bit as good as wild.

Red grouse
The red grouse is found only in Scotland. It feeds on berries and young heather and has a fine, subtle flavour. Serve roasted or in pies or stews. Shooting starts on the 'glorious 12th' of August and goes on until 10 December.

Pheasant
Pheasants have rich, tender flesh and can be roasted or casseroled. **Season:** 1 October to 1 February.

Hare
Hares can be roasted, jugged or casseroled. **Season:** 1 August to the last day of February.

Hens, turkeys and pigs are all produced in quantity in Lothian, and some of the best pork and bacon comes from Ayrshire, although Aberdeenshire bacon, too, is renowned.

Scotland is also well known for the abundance of game that inhabits the moors and forests of the country. Roe and fallow deer, and the more common red deer, are found wild throughout the Highlands, as well as being farmed. Red grouse is the finest game bird, while hare, pheasant and many other types of game bird are also bagged in large numbers.

Late and early ripeners

Scotland produces two-thirds of British raspberries, and fine fruits they are, with an intensity of flavour that is unsurpassable because of prolonged daylight and cool temperatures in summer to ensure slow growing. Fruit farming is centred on Tayside, around Blairgowrie, and stretches south to Lothian and north to the shores of the Moray Firth. A good percentage of the crop is canned or made into jam.

BERRIES

England is catching up with Scotland on the quantity of soft fruit production, but the Scots would say that their berries have the finest concentration of flavour, due to slow ripening.

Loganberries
A cross between a raspberry and an American dewberry, loganberries are mainly used for canning. Larger, darker and softer than raspberries, with a sharp flavour. First raised in the late19th century.
Season: early July to late August.

Raspberries
Grown on canes. Eat raw, or use in jams, tarts and desserts. Store in the fridge and use as soon as possible after purchase. Can be frozen successfully.
Season: end June to October.

Strawberries
Can be grown under glass or plastic, or outdoors. Eat raw or use in desserts or jams. Store in a cool place and use quickly: they do not keep well. Can be frozen but become mushy when thawed.
Season: June to October.

Tayberries
A cross between a blackberry and a raspberry. Large, conical and bright deep purple, with a rich flavour. Easy to pick, although the canes are thorny.
Season: early July to mid-August.

Other soft fruits, such as tayberries, gooseberries, strawberries and black- and redcurrants, do well in the Scottish climate. They take longer to ripen than in the south and so come into season later. The raspberry-growing regions also produce peas, beans, potatoes and other roots, which are sold at pick-your-own farms and farm shops as well as being sent to market.

Potatoes are a common crop in Scotland, which produces some of the earliest earlies in the country. The Borders grow oil-seed rape, used for cooking oils and cattle fodder, as well as peas, turnips and potatoes; the latter two are combined in Neeps and Tatties as the classic accompaniment to haggis (see recipe, page 191). Lothian produces excellent leeks, while in the Clyde valley they specialise in plums and salad greens. The Scottish climate is very suitable for hardier herbs, such as coriander, dill, fennel, parsley, mint, marjoram and thyme (which is indigenous to Scotland). Research is being done with a view to large-scale farming of these varieties in the future.

Tea-time feasts

The delights of Scottish baking are renowned. There are many Scots who feel that no day is complete unless they have baked something for tea-time, and hardly any town or village, however small, is without at least one baker where everything is made on the premises. Each region has its own specialities.

Oats are the most important cereal, because they can withstand poor soils and harsh weather, and oatmeal features widely in baking as well as in the traditional Scottish breakfast dish, porridge, and its uncooked equivalent, brose. Oatcakes are thin, crisp biscuits that go well with cheese.

High tea is the time to savour many of Scotland's best-known baked goods. Dundee Cake, rich and topped with almonds, is one of the most famous (see recipe, page 226). Scones of all kinds – griddle, or drop scones, oven, potato ('tattie') – are ubiquitous (see recipes, pages 256 and 255), as are Scotland's famous shortbread (see recipe, page 243) and crumpets (see recipe, page 260).

Scottish ales

Whisky is not the only Scottish drink – Scottish beers have improved greatly in quality. In the past they were dark and low in hops: they were known as 'liquid porridge' to some people and as Scottish Burgundy to supporters of the Auld Alliance with France. Production was confined to the central belt, as barley grown further north was suitable for whisky-making but not brewing. Beers were known as Light and

THREE TOP SCOTTISH BREWERIES

Caledonian, Edinburgh
Its Deuchar's IPA is Scotland's leading cask beer, pale and with a fine peppery hop note from English Goldings hops.

Belhaven, Dunbar
This ancient brewery on the coast concentrates in the main on processed keg beers but its 80 Shilling is considered the classic of the style with a remarkable gooseberry fruit note.

Traquair House, Innerleithen
Scotland's oldest inhabited house, visited by Mary Queen of Scots and Prince Charles Edward Stuart, has a restored medieval brewhouse where strong Traquair House Ale and Jacobite Ale are brewed. Unmissable.

Heavy – similar to mild and bitter – and were also designated as 60, 70 and 80 Shilling Ales, using a 19th-century form of invoicing. Change came when it was found that the brewing waters of Alloa and Edinburgh were similar to those of Burton-on-Trent, and as a result pale ales for export boosted the fortunes of the brewers. Today Scottish beer is a blend of traditional ales and more English-style bitters with a robust hop character. The country is well served by craft breweries from the Borders to Orkney and Shetland.

What else but whisky?

Scotch whisky, generally regarded as among the finest anywhere, is arguably the most famous British export in the realm of food and drink.

Whisky has been distilled in Scotland for many hundreds of years, although it has only existed as a commercial concern since the mid-19th century. The name comes from the ancient Gaelic 'uisge beatha', meaning 'water of life'.

There are two basic types of Scotch whisky: Single Malt and Single Grain. Single Malt means that the whisky has been produced at a single distillery from only water and malted barley (germinated with water then dried) using batch distillation in pot stills. Single Grain may contain other cereals, malted or unmalted, and it can be produced by continuous distillation rather than in pot stills. Both types can be used to make Blended Scotch Whisky, in which the products of different distilleries are combined – as many as 50 different Single Malts or Single Grains in a single bottle of Blended. Blended Scotch doesn't have the pronounced individual character that makes Single Malt so highly prized by connoisseurs, but it achieves consistency year after year and the best examples are distinguished whiskies in their own right.

In the 19th century there were hundreds of distilleries in Scotland; today there are just under 100, most of them owned by large drinks companies. Despite the reduction in numbers, there is still a staggering variety in the whiskies produced here. The country's distilleries are traditionally divided into five producing regions: Speyside, Highlands, Lowlands, Islay and Campbeltown. The largest number of distilleries is found in Speyside, around half of Scotland's total. Highlands is much larger in area but has fewer distilleries, which include those on the islands of Arran, Lewis, Mull, Orkney and Skye. The southerly Lowlands region has a dozen or so, while Islay has a dense population of distilleries: eight at the time this book went to press. Campbeltown has just two working distilleries.

Much has been said about the local qualities that give Single Malts their special character: the water used, salt from sea breezes infiltrating the air in the barrels where the whisky is matured, and especially the use of peat. In fact, most whisky experts believe that the way the whisky is made has more to do with its flavour than local environmental influences. For this reason, it is very hard to speak of a defined 'style' in any of Scotland's whisky regions. One possible exception is Islay, all of whose whiskies are made from malt dried over peat fires. But this technique is used elsewhere, so 'peaty' whiskies are not unique to Islay.

SCOTCH WHISKY

Any selection of Scotland's best whisky producers is inevitably a highly subjective list. No two whisky aficionados will assemble identical lists of their favourites. Each of the distilleries listed here produces different 'expressions': whiskies aged for a particular time and sometimes in different types of oak barrel. Seven to ten years old is usually the minimum, but some can be aged for 30–35 years or even longer. The number refers to the minimum age of the whisky in the bottle, and greater age does not necessarily mean that the whisky is 'better'; this is a matter of personal preference. Where a single year is named on the label, e.g., The Glenlivet 1976, it means that all the whisky was distilled in that year. Note: some of the finest and most unusual bottles of Scottish whisky are sold by independent bottlers, who buy barrels from the distilleries, age them on their own premises, and bottle them when they see fit.

Speyside
Balvenie (founded 1892), Glenfarclas (founded 1836), Macallan (founded 1824)

Highland
Ardmore (founded 1898), Clynelish (founded 1819), Old Pulteney (founded 1826)

Islay
Ardbeg (founded 1794), Caol Ila (founded 1846) Lagavulin (founded 1816)

Island
Highland Park, Orkney (founded 1798), Talisker, Isle of Skye (founded 1830), Isle of Jura (founded 1810)

Lowland
Auchentoshan (founded 1823), Glenkinchie (founded 1837)

Campbeltown
Glen Scotia (founded 1832), Springbank (founded 1828)

PDOS AND PGIS

The EU grants special protected status to foods of special merit. There are two principal designations – Protected Designation of Origin (PDO) and Protected Geographical Indication (PGI). PDO covers 'agricultural products and foodstuffs which are produced, processed and prepared in a given geographical area using recognised know-how'. PGI covers 'agricultural products and foodstuffs closely linked to the geographical area. At least one of the stages of production, processing or preparation takes place in the area'.

The criteria for PDO status are more demanding, as the food must be traditionally produced entirely within a specific area – and its unique qualities must be considered possible to attain only within that area. PGIs are less confining, as the production need take place only partly within a specific area.

When this book went to press, the following PDOs and PGIs had been given to British foods.

Beer
Kentish Ale (PGI)
Kentish Strong Ale (PGI)
Rutland Bitter (PGI)

Cheeses
Beacon Fell Traditional
Lancashire (PDO)
Bonchester (PDO)
Buxton Blue (PDO)
Dorset Blue (PGI)
Dovedale (PDO)
Exmoor Blue (PGI)
Single Gloucester (PDO)
Staffordshire Cheese (PDO)
Stilton – Blue (PDO)
Stilton – White (PDO)
Swaledale (PDO)
Swaledale Ewes' Cheese
(PDO)
Teviotdale (PGI)
West Country Farmhouse
Cheddar (PDO)

Cider and cider spirits
Gloucestershire Cider (PGI)
Gloucestershire Perry (PGI)
Herefordshire Cider (PGI)
Herefordshire Perry (PGI)
Somerset Cider Brandy (PGI)
Worcestershire Cider (PGI)
Worcestershire Perry (PGI)

Cream
Cornish Clotted Cream (PDO)

Fish and shellfish
Arbroath Smokie (PGI)
Whitstable Oysters (PGI)
Scottish Farmed Salmon (PGI)
Traditional Grimsby Smoked
Fish (PGI)
Cornish Sardines (PGI)

Fresh meat and offal
Isle of Man Manx Loaghtan
Lamb (PDO)
Orkney Beef (PDO)
Orkney Lamb (PDO)
Scotch Beef (PGI)
Scotch Lamb (PGI)
Shetland Lamb (PDO)
Welsh Beef (PGI)
Welsh Lamb (PGI)

Meat products
Melton Mowbray Pork Pie (PGI)
Traditional Cumberland
Sausage (PGI)

Fruit, vegetables and cereals
Jersey Royal Potatoes (PDO)
Yorkshire Forced Rhubarb (PDO)

NORTHERN IRELAND

FERMANAGH
ARMAGH
DOWN
ANTRIM
LONDONDERRY
TYRONE

Creamy milk and butter, top-quality meat, excellent ham and bacon, and rivers and seas teeming with fish give Northern Ireland its reputation for fine, simple food. The ubiquitous potato, cooked in all manner of ways, is always mouth-wateringly good. And to savour afterwards, there's the incomparable smoothness of Irish whiskey.

A diet based on simple things sustained the people here for centuries. Milk, butter and cream, fish and meat, home-baked breads and cakes, and above all potatoes, dug straight from the crumbly, black soil and cooked in their skins to keep all the goodness in – these were, and often still are, the culinary mainstays. It has been said that no one in Northern Ireland is more than three generations from the land, and given those close links with farming it is not surprising that home cooking and baking remain important aspects of domestic life in Northern Ireland. Simple, unfussy cooking using natural, wholesome products of Northern Ireland's most important industry, agriculture, is the basis of the cuisine in this part of the United Kingdom.

The region's best-known dish, Irish stew, was originally made with young kid, but now uses lamb or mutton (see recipe, page 83). More and more lamb is being produced here, and high-quality beef cattle are also reared on an increasingly important scale. And, of course, the countryside provides perfect cover for all types of game, feathered and furred.

Potatoes and food from the land

Think of Ireland and you think of potatoes, a staple crop and an important part of the economy since the 17th century. The eating varieties grown here include the Dunbar Standard, Pentland Dell and Kerr's Pinks. Traditionally, they were – and still are – cooked in every possible way. There are potato soups, cakes, breads, pies and pancakes. One of the standard traditional potato dishes, Boxty, combines cooked and grated raw potato with flour and baking powder. It's usually made as a dough, which is then cooked on a bakestone or griddle, but can also be turned into a kind of batter and fried like a pancake.

If Kent is the Garden of England, then Armagh is the Orchard of Ireland, and indeed it is sometimes called the Orchard County. There are dozens of fruit orchards, mostly growing apples, especially Bramley's Seedlings. Other produce includes cabbage and, perhaps surprisingly, cultivated mushrooms, much of which find their way across the water not just to the UK but to other international markets.

Meaty matters

Northern Ireland is a nation of meat-lovers, and pig and cattle farming are important industries. Ulster's Landrace and Large White pigs supply a large proportion of the UK's bacon, most processed by the Wiltshire cure (see page 13) and some by traditional methods such as the Ulster Roll, which uses dry salt. Delicious Belfast hams, brined and then smoked over peat fires, have been produced for over a hundred years. Although large-scale production is economically vital, the region also supports smaller farms that work closely with local butchers, which still exist in abundance. Indeed, sometimes the butchers sell meat from their own farms.

A land of milk and cream

Northern Ireland's famous 'soft' climate encourages rich grass to grow and so the cattle are never short of good grazing. The people there enjoy the natural goodness of dairy products and consume more milk and butter per head every year than their counterparts across the water. There is no great tradition of cheesemaking, however, and all but a handful of cheeses are made in big modern creameries. The best known is Fivemiletown Creamery, which makes block Cheddar alongside some interesting soft goat cheeses and a range of Camembert-style cheeses.

Prolific waters

The rivers and lakes of Northern Ireland are alive with fish – the whole area is an angler's delight. Brown trout, sea trout, salmon, perch and pike are all caught in abundance. From Lough Neagh, the biggest lake in the British Isles, come eels, which are often smoked. The River Mourne is one of the best salmon rivers, but it's almost impossible to choose between so many superb fishing waters.

Out to sea there's more fish – mackerel, plaice, cod, skate and lobster are brought ashore all around the coast. Prawns, herring and other species are landed from the fishing fleet at Portavogie. Pubs often sell reasonably priced shellfish dishes and there are many different types of locally smoked fish to sample. Oysters are commercially grown in Strangford's unpolluted waters and are available all year round.

Home for high tea

Nearly every little town has its home bakery and the shelves are laden with farls, a type of potato cake – the word means a 'fourth part' of a round cake, and the loaves are shaped like triangles, with one rounded side. Soda bread (see recipe, page 251) is ever-popular, with its crisp crust and moist crumb. It was originally cooked on a griddle over a peat fire. Potato bread is widely made and although good cold is even better fried in bacon fat for breakfast.

High tea is a favourite meal, the table groaning with home-baked cakes and breads. Barm brack, a yeasted fruit bread (see recipe, page 251), is delicious sliced and buttered.

A toast to fine whiskey

You're never far from a pub or bar in Ireland, and whiskey was being made here long before it arrived across the water. Old Bushmills Distillery, situated on the Antrim coast, was granted, in 1608, the very first licence to distil whiskey. Local barley and water from St Columb's Rill are still used in production. But a strong, smooth liquor called poitín, or poteen, was being discreetly made in these parts for hundreds of years before that – and who's to say that the ancient tradition of illicit distilling has died out even today?

Northern Ireland ales

Some independent brewing goes on in Northern Ireland. Hilden Brewery in County Antrim makes strong, hoppy, distinctive bitter as well as other beers, which are mostly available locally.

FARMERS' MARKETS

One of the greatest developments in British food shopping of recent years has been the increasing number of farmers' markets. Of course, farmers have always sold their produce locally in market squares and other public places, but the farmers' market as known nowadays has a much shorter history: the first was started in Bath in 1997. Now the movement is huge. There are about 750 markets calling themselves farmers' markets in the UK. Of these, around 250 are certified by FARMA (the National Farmers' Retail & Markets Association, www.farma.org.uk), which imposes selection criteria including local production, attendance at the stall by a principal representative of the producer, and use of materials grown, reared or caught locally. Certified markets represent just over one-third of the total number of farmers' markets, but over half of the total annual turnover of farmers' markets, which was in the region of £250 million per annum when this book went to press.

FOOD FAIRS AND FESTIVALS

MARCH

HORSE PLOUGHING MATCH AND
HEAVY HORSE SHOW
FAIR HEAD, BALLYCASTLE

MAY

BALMORAL SHOW
BALMORAL, BELFAST

AUGUST

OUL' LAMMAS FAIR
BALLYCASTLE

SEPTEMBER

HARVEST FAIR
NEWTOWNARDS, CO. DOWN (HELD SINCE 1613)

OCTOBER/NOVEMBER

INTERNATIONAL PLOUGHING CHAMPIONSHIPS
KEARNEY, PORTAFERRY, CO. DOWN

THE
RECIPES

SOUPS & STARTERS

Cock-a-Leekie Soup

Scotland A traditional Scottish soup dating back hundreds of years, named after the boiling chicken and leeks which form its base. The traditional recipe includes prunes, but if you don't like prunes these can easily be left out.

Serves 8 • Preparation 30–40 minutes • Cooking time 1 hour 20 minutes

1.4kg (3lb) oven-ready chicken, including giblets if available
2 onions, roughly chopped
2 carrots, roughly chopped
2 celery sticks, roughly chopped
1 bay leaf
25g (1oz) butter
900g (2lb) trimmed leeks, sliced
125g (4oz) ready-to-eat dried prunes, sliced
salt and ground black pepper
freshly chopped flat-leafed parsley to garnish

For the dumplings

125g (4oz) self-raising flour, plus extra to dust
50g (2oz) shredded suet
2 tbsp freshly chopped flat-leafed parsley
2 tbsp freshly chopped thyme

Nutrition per serving
280 cals | 4g fat (1g sats) |
40g carbs | 0.2g salt

1 Put the chicken into a pan in which it fits quite snugly, then add the chopped vegetables, bay leaf and chicken giblets. Pour in 1.7 litres (3 pints) water and bring to the boil, then reduce the heat, cover and simmer gently for 1 hour.

2 Meanwhile, melt the butter in a large pan. Add the leeks and fry gently for 10 minutes or until softened.

3 Remove the chicken from the pan and leave until cool enough to handle. Strain the stock and put to one side. Strip the chicken from the bones and shred roughly. Add to the stock with the prunes and softened leeks.

4 Make the dumplings. Mix the flour, suet and chopped herbs in a bowl with salt and pepper, then add sufficient cold water to make an elastic dough. With floured hands, lightly shape the dough into 2.5cm (1in) balls. Bring the soup just to the boil and season well. Reduce the heat, add the dumplings and cover the pan with a lid. Simmer for 15–20 minutes until the dumplings are light and fluffy. Serve the soup sprinkled with chopped parsley.

.COOK'S TIP.

Make the stock a day ahead, if possible, then cool overnight. The following day, remove any fat from the surface.

Scotch Broth

Scotland This is really two meals in one: a starter and a main course. The beef flavours the stock and is removed before serving. Later, you divide up the meat and serve it with mashed potatoes, swedes or turnips.

Serves 8 • Preparation 15 minutes • Cooking time 2 hours

1 piece marrow bone, about 350g (12oz)
1.4kg (3lb) piece beef skirt (ask your butcher for this)
300g (11oz) broth mix (to include pearl barley, red lentils, split peas and green peas), soaked according to the pack instructions
2 carrots, finely chopped
1 parsnip, finely chopped
2 onions, finely chopped
¼ white cabbage, finely chopped
1 leek, trimmed and finely chopped
½ tbsp salt
2 tbsp freshly chopped flat-leafed parsley
ground black pepper

Nutrition per serving
173 cals | 2g fat (trace sats) | 35g carbs | 2.3g salt

1 Put the marrow bone and beef skirt into a 5.7 litre (10 pint) stock pot and add 2.6 litres (4½ pints) cold water – there should be enough to cover the meat. Bring the water to the boil. Remove any scum from the surface with a spoon and discard. Reduce the heat to low, add the broth mix and simmer, partially covered, for 1½ hours, skimming the surface occasionally.

2 Add the carrots, parsnip, onions, cabbage, leek and another 600ml (1 pint) cold water. Cover to bring to the boil quickly, then reduce the heat and simmer for 30 minutes.

3 Remove the marrow bone and piece of beef from the broth. Add a few shreds of beef to the broth, if you like. Season the broth well with the salt and some pepper, and stir in the chopped parsley. Ladle into warmed bowls and serve hot.

London Particular

The Southeast In the past, London was blanketed regularly in thick fogs known as 'pea-soupers', which is how this delicious soup got its great name.

Serves 8 (as a starter) • Preparation 10 minutes • Cooking time 1 hour 20 minutes

15g (½oz) butter
50g (2oz) streaky bacon rashers, rind removed, chopped
1 onion, roughly chopped
1 carrot, diced
1 celery stick, chopped
450g (1lb) split dried peas
2.3 litres (4 pints) chicken or ham stock
4 tbsp natural yogurt
salt and ground black pepper
chopped grilled bacon and croûtons to garnish

1 Melt the butter in a large pan. Add the bacon, onion, carrot and celery and cook for 5–10 minutes until beginning to soften.
2 Add the peas and stock and bring to the boil, then cover and simmer for 1 hour until the peas are soft.
3 Allow to cool slightly, then whiz in batches in a blender or food processor until smooth.
4 Return the soup to the pan. Season to taste, add the yogurt and reheat gently. Serve hot, garnished with chopped grilled bacon and croûtons.

Nutrition per serving
235 cals | 5g fat (2g sats) |
36g carbs | 1.3g salt

Simple Vegetable Soup

The North This hearty soup can make a meal in itself; use any other orange or light-coloured vegetables firm enough not to disintegrate during cooking.

Serves 4 • Preparation 10 minutes • Cooking time 40 minutes

1 or 2 onions, finely chopped
2 tbsp oil, or 1 tbsp oil and 25g (1oz) butter
1 or 2 garlic cloves, crushed (optional)
450g (1lb) chopped mixed vegetables, such as leeks, potatoes, celery, fennel, canned tomatoes and parsnips (chopped finely or into larger dice for a chunky soup)
1.1 litres (2 pints) vegetable stock

1 Fry the onions in the oil, or oil and butter, until soft, then add the garlic, if you like.
2 Add the chopped mixed vegetables and the stock. Bring to the boil, then simmer for 20–30 minutes until the vegetables are tender.
3 Leave chunky, partially purée or blend until smooth, if you like. Reheat and serve.

Nutrition per serving
114 cals | 6g fat (1g sats) |
13g carbs | 1.5g salt

Leek and Potato Soup

The North Northumberland has a proud tradition of leek-growing and is famous for its giant specimens. But giant leeks are not required here.

Serves 4 • Preparation 10 minutes • Cooking time 45 minutes

25g (1oz) butter
1 onion, finely chopped
1 garlic clove, crushed
550g (1¼ lb) leeks, trimmed and chopped
200g (7oz) floury potatoes, peeled and sliced
1.3 litres (2¼ pints) hot vegetable stock
crème fraîche and chopped chives to garnish

Nutrition per serving
117 cals | 6g fat (4g sats) |
13g carbs | 0.1g salt

1 Melt the butter in a pan over a gentle heat, then cook the onion for 10–15 minutes until soft. Add the garlic and cook for a further 1 minute. Add the leeks and cook for 5–10 minutes until softened. Add the potatoes and toss together with the leeks.
2 Pour in the hot stock and bring to the boil, then reduce the heat and simmer the soup for 20 minutes or until the potatoes are tender.
3 Leave the soup to cool a little, then whiz in batches in a blender or food processor until smooth.
4 To serve, reheat the soup gently. Ladle into warmed bowls and garnish with crème fraîche and chives.

Carrot and Coriander Soup

Countrywide A nourishing, simple soup with a vibrant colour, this is equally good as a quick lunch or as a starter for a dinner party.

Serves 6 • Preparation 15 minutes • Cooking time about 30 minutes

40g (1½ oz) butter
175g (6oz) trimmed leeks, sliced
450g (1lb) carrots, sliced
2 tsp ground coriander
1 tsp plain flour
1.1 litres (2 pints) vegetable stock
150ml (¼ pint) single cream
salt and ground black pepper
coriander leaves, roughly torn, to serve

Nutrition per serving
140 cals | 11g fat (7g sats) |
10g carbs | 0.2g salt

1 Melt the butter in a large pan. Add the leeks and carrots and stir, then cover the pan and cook gently for 7–10 minutes until the vegetables begin to soften but not colour.
2 Stir in the ground coriander and flour and cook, stirring, for 1 minute.
3 Add the stock and bring to the boil, stirring. Season with salt and pepper, then cover the pan and simmer for about 20 minutes or until the vegetables are tender.
4 Leave the soup to cool a little, then whiz in batches in a blender or food processor until quite smooth. Return to the pan and stir in the cream. Adjust the seasoning and reheat gently; do not boil.
5 Ladle into warmed bowls, scatter with torn coriander leaves and serve.

Marinated Mackerel

The West Marinating in lemon juice and seasonings is a good way to deal with an oily fish like mackerel. Served cold with brown bread and butter, it makes a delicious luncheon dish for a summer's day.

Serves 4 • Preparation 20 minutes, plus marinating • Cooking time 25 minutes

4 mackerel, about 350g (12oz) each, cleaned
3 onions: 1 finely chopped, 2 finely sliced
3 garlic cloves, crushed
1 lemon, sliced, and the juice of 1 lemon
3 tbsp olive oil
1 red pepper, seeded and finely sliced into rings
5 black peppercorns
2 bay leaves
150ml (¼ pint) white wine vinegar
salt and ground black pepper

Nutrition per serving
560 cals | 39g fat (13g sats) | 12g carbs | 1.2g salt

1 Rinse the mackerel and pat dry with kitchen paper. Put into a large, shallow container and sprinkle inside and out with the chopped onion, a little salt and one-third of the garlic. Scatter the lemon slices over, then pour the lemon juice over and season generously with pepper. Cover and leave to marinate in the fridge for at least 2 hours.

2 Heat 1 tbsp of the oil in a frying pan, add the sliced onions and fry over a low heat for 5 minutes to soften, stirring regularly. Add the remaining garlic and the red pepper and cook for a further 3 minutes.

3 Add the peppercorns, bay leaves, wine vinegar and 150ml (¼ pint) water. Bring to the boil, then simmer for 10 minutes or until the liquid is reduced by one-third. Set aside.

4 Drain the mackerel. Heat the remaining 2 tbsp of oil in a large, heavy-based frying pan. Add the mackerel and fry for 8–10 minutes, turning as needed, until the fish is tender and lightly browned.

5 Return the mackerel to a shallow dish and pour the vinegar and pepper mixture over it. Serve warm, or cool and chill.

•COOK'S TIP•

This dish is best prepared a day ahead to allow the flavours to mingle. To serve warm the next day, microwave on full power for about 3 minutes.

Chunky Pâté with Port

Countrywide This chunky pâté with a hint of alcohol is a perennial favourite. Port became very popular in England during the Anglo-French wars of the 18th century, when, deprived of French wines, many English shippers imported it from Portugal and gave their names to the blends.

Serves 8 • Preparation 25 minutes, plus setting • Cooking time about 1½ hours, plus cooling

350g (12oz) boneless belly pork, rind removed, roughly chopped
1 large skinless chicken breast, about 150g (5oz)
225g (8oz) chicken livers, trimmed
1 large duck breast, about 200g (7oz), skinned and chopped into small pieces
125g (4oz) rindless streaky bacon rashers, diced
1 tbsp freshly chopped rosemary
2 tbsp green peppercorns
salt and ground black pepper
3 tbsp port or brandy
crusty bread to serve

To finish
a few bay leaves
2 tsp powdered gelatine
150ml (¼ pint) white port or sherry

Nutrition per serving
344 cals | 22g fat (8g sats) |
3g carbs | 0.7g salt

1 Preheat the oven to 170°C (150°C fan oven) mark 3. Coarsely mince the belly pork in a food processor, retaining some small chunks. Mince the chicken breast in the processor, then mince the chicken livers.
2 Mix all the meats together in a large bowl with the port or brandy, 1 tsp salt, some pepper, the chopped rosemary and green peppercorns.
3 Pack the mixture into a 1.1 litre (2 pint) terrine and stand in a roasting tin containing 2.5cm (1in) boiling water. Cover with foil and cook in the oven for 1 hour.
4 Remove the foil and arrange a few bay leaves on top of the pâté. Cook for a further 30 minutes or until the juices run clear when the pâté is pierced in the centre with a sharp knife or skewer.

5 Drain the meat juices into a small bowl and leave to cool. Skim off any fat, then sprinkle over the gelatine and leave until softened. Stand the bowl in a pan of gently simmering water until the gelatine has dissolved. Stir in the port or brandy. Make up to 450ml (¾ pint) with water, if necessary.
6 Pour the jellied liquid over the pâté and chill until set. Store the pâté in the fridge for up to two days. Serve with crusty bread.

Duck Terrine with Apple, Apricot and Brandy

Countrywide This impressive terrine is not difficult to prepare but to allow its flavour to develop, do leave enough time for the initial marinating and then chilling after it has been cooked. Pickles and bread make a good addition to the chutney.

Serves 15 • Preparation 1½ hours, plus marinating • Cooking time 2¼–2½ hours, plus chilling

50g (2oz) stoned prunes, roughly chopped (see Cook's Tip)
50g (2oz) ready-to-eat dried apricots, roughly chopped (see Cook's Tip)
6 tbsp brandy
350g (12oz) turkey breast fillet, cut into 2.5cm (1in) cubes
800g (1lb 12oz) duck breasts, skinned – there should be 500g (1lb 2oz) meat
a few fresh thyme sprigs
50g (2oz) butter
225g (8oz) shallots or onions, roughly chopped
350g (12oz) eating apples, peeled, cored and chopped
225g (8oz) minced pork
2 tbsp freshly chopped thyme
1 medium egg, beaten
50g (2oz) shelled pistachio nuts
½ tsp salt
ground black pepper

Nutrition per slice
189 cals | 9g fat (3g sats) |
6g carbs | 0.3g salt

1 The day before, put the prunes and apricots into a bowl with 4 tbsp of the brandy, cover and leave to soak overnight. Put the turkey and duck in a roasting tin at separate ends, sprinkle with the thyme sprigs and the remaining brandy, then cover and leave to marinate in the fridge overnight.

2 Heat the butter in a pan. Add the shallots and cook for 10 minutes or until soft. Stir in the apples, then cover and cook for 5–10 minutes until soft. Set aside to cool.

3 Preheat the oven to 180°C (160°C fan oven) mark 4. Remove the turkey from the marinade and put into a food processor with the apple mixture and the minced pork. Whiz to a rough purée, then combine with the chopped thyme, egg, marinated fruits and the pistachio nuts. Season well with the salt and a good grinding of pepper.

4 Remove the duck from the marinade and put between sheets of grease-proof paper. Flatten gently with a rolling pin until 1cm (½ in) thick.

5 Baseline a 1.1 litre (2 pint) terrine or loaf tin with greaseproof paper or foil. Put a duck breast in the base of the terrine to cover it evenly with no gaps. Spread half the stuffing over it, then repeat the process, finishing with a layer of duck.

6 Cover with foil and put into a roasting tin. Add enough hot water to come three-quarters of the way up the sides of the terrine and cook in the oven for 2–2¼ hours until the juices run clear when tested with a skewer. Transfer to a wire rack, cover with a weighted board and, when cool, leave to chill for 6 hours or overnight.

7 Run a knife around the terrine and turn out on to a board. Remove the greaseproof paper and carve into thin slices. Serve with a red onion chutney.

•COOK'S TIP•

Try this with other dried fruit, such as dried cherries. You'll need 125g (4oz) in place of the prunes and apricots. Slicing this terrine, and any other terrine, is always easiest using a serrated knife.

Chicken and Vegetable Terrine

Countrywide This is a lovely summery dish to make when young vegetables are at their best.
It goes well with fresh tomato sauce and can be garnished beautifully with fresh rocket leaves
to make a stunning chilled starter.

Serves 8 • Preparation 40 minutes, plus chilling • Cooking time 1 hour 2 minutes, plus chilling

900g (2lb) chicken joints
1 small slice white bread, crusts
removed
450ml (¾ pint) double cream, chilled
1 small bunch of watercress
125g (4oz) small young carrots
125g (4oz) French beans, trimmed and
stringed
275g (10oz) peas in the pod, shelled
75g (3oz) small, even-sized button
mushrooms
200g (7oz) can artichoke hearts,
drained
butter to grease
salt and ground black pepper
rocket leaves to garnish (optional)

For the sauce
225g (8oz) ripe tomatoes, skinned and
quartered (see Cook's Tip)
125ml (4fl oz) vegetable oil
50ml (2fl oz) white wine vinegar
75ml (2½ fl oz) tomato purée

Nutrition per serving
616 cals | 54g fat (23g sats) |
8g carbs | 0.6g salt

.COOK'S TIP.

To skin tomatoes, plunge them into
boiling water for 30 seconds, then
refresh in cold water. Cut lightly into
the skin, then peel it away. To
remove the seeds, halve the tomato
and scoop out the seeds with a
spoon or cut out with
a small, sharp knife.

1 Cut all the chicken flesh away from the
   bones; discard the skin and any fat.
   Finely mince the chicken with the
   bread. Chill for 30 minutes. Stir
   the cream, a little at a time, into the
   chicken mixture with salt and pepper
   to taste.
2 Trim the watercress and discard the
   coarse stalks. Stir one-third of the
   chicken mixture into the watercress.
   Cover both bowls and chill for
   2 hours.
3 Preheat the oven to 170°C (150°C
   fan oven) mark 3. The careful
   preparation of vegetables is essential
   to the final presentation. Cut the
   carrots into neat matchstick pieces,
   2.5cm (1in) by 3mm (⅛in). Cut
   the beans into similar-length pieces.
   Blanch the carrots, beans and peas for
   2 minutes in separate pans of boiling
   water. Drain. Trim the mushroom stalks
   level with the caps. Cut the mushrooms
   across into slices 5mm (¼in) thick.
   Dice the artichoke hearts into 5mm
   (¼in) pieces.
4 Grease a 1.1 litre (2 pint) lidded
   terrine and base-line with a rectangular
   piece of greaseproof paper, and
   grease the top of the paper. Take half
   the watercress and chicken mixture
   and spread it evenly over the bottom
   of the terrine. Arrange the carrots in
   neat crossways lines over
   the top, then spread one-quarter of
   the chicken mixture carefully over
   the carrots.

5 Lightly seasoning the vegetables with
   salt and pepper as they are layered,
   sprinkle the peas over the chicken
   mixture in the dish and put another thin
   layer of chicken mixture on top. Next,
   put the mushrooms in crossways lines
   and top with the remaining watercress
   and chicken mixture. Arrange the
   artichokes on top, cover with half the
   remaining chicken mixture, arrange the
   beans in crossways lines and cover
   with the remaining chicken mixture.
6 Put a double sheet of greased
   greaseproof paper on top and cover
   tightly with the lid. Put the terrine in a
   roasting tin and add enough hot water
   to come halfway up the sides of the
   terrine. Cook in the oven for 1 hour
   or until firm.
7 Cool a little, drain off any juices,
   then invert the terrine on to a serving
   plate. Cool, then chill for 1 hour
   before serving.
8 Meanwhile, make the sauce. Purée
   the tomatoes in a blender or food
   processor with the oil, vinegar, tomato
   purée and seasoning. Rub through
   a sieve. Chill lightly before serving,
   then garnish with some rocket leaves,
   if you like.

Cheese Ramekins

The West More substantial than a soufflé, this flavoursome dish is also a good way of using up odd leftovers of different cheeses.

Serves 4 • Preparation 10 minutes • Cooking time 10–15 minutes

50g (2oz) Double Gloucester cheese, grated
50g (2oz) Cheshire cheese, grated
4 tbsp single cream or milk
50g (2oz) cooked ham, finely chopped
50g (2oz) fresh wholemeal breadcrumbs
few drops of Worcestershire sauce
a pinch of ground mixed spice
butter to grease
2 medium eggs, separated
salt and ground black pepper

Nutrition per serving
224 cals | 14g fat (8g sats) |
10g carbs | 1.4g salt

1 Preheat the oven to 200°C (180°C fan oven) mark 6. Put the cheeses into a bowl, then beat in the cream or milk, the ham, breadcrumbs, Worcestershire sauce and mixed spice. Season to taste. Grease four ramekins and stand them on a baking sheet.
2 Beat the egg yolks into the mixture. Whisk the egg whites until stiff, then fold into the mixture.
3 Spoon into the ramekin dishes and cook in the oven for 10–15 minutes until golden and risen. Serve at once.

Scotch Woodcock

Scotland This salty, savoury dish (not made with woodcock) was popular in Victorian and Edwardian days, when it was served at the end of a meal.

Serves 2 • Preparation 5 minutes • Cooking time 5 minutes

2 large slices wholemeal bread
butter
Gentleman's Relish or anchovy paste for spreading
4–6 tbsp milk
2 medium eggs
a pinch of cayenne pepper
50g can anchovies, drained

Nutrition per serving
317 cals | 19g fat (8g sats) |
18g carbs | 3.5g salt

1 Toast the bread, remove the crusts and spread with butter. Cut in half and spread with Gentleman's Relish or anchovy paste.
2 Melt a knob of butter in a pan. Whisk together the milk, eggs and cayenne pepper, then pour into the pan and stir slowly over a gentle heat until the mixture begins to thicken. Remove from the heat and stir until creamy.
3 Divide the mixture between the anchovy toasts and top with thin strips of anchovy fillet, arranged in a criss-cross pattern.

Seafood Cocktail

Countrywide A variation on the prawn cocktail, this was one of the most popular starters during the 1960s and 1970s and is now enjoying a revival. The dish can be as simple or as exotic as you like, depending on which shellfish you choose.

Serves 4 • Preparation 15 minutes

½ iceberg lettuce, shredded
175g (6oz) cooked peeled prawns or shrimps, flaked white crab meat or lobster meat, thawed if frozen
cucumber slices, capers or lemon wedges to garnish

For the dressing
2 tbsp mayonnaise
2 tbsp tomato ketchup
2 tbsp natural yogurt
squeeze of lemon juice or a dash of Worcestershire sauce
salt and ground black pepper

1 Line four small glasses with the shredded lettuce.
2 To make the dressing, put the mayonnaise into a bowl and mix with the tomato ketchup, yogurt and lemon juice or Worcestershire sauce. Season with salt and pepper to taste.
3 Combine the shellfish and dressing and pile the mixture into the glasses.
4 Garnish each glass with cucumber slices, capers or lemon wedges and serve immediately.

Nutrition per serving
110 cals | 7g fat (1g sats) |
3g carbs | 2.5g salt

•COOK'S TIP•

If you have to make this an hour or so in advance, store in the fridge (before garnishing), but bring to room temperature before serving.

Smoked Salmon Parcels

Countrywide Scottish smoked salmon and scallops combine in this luxurious starter. Served with tangy coriander dressing, the parcels will be admired not only for their elegant presentation but also for their wonderful taste.

Serves 8 • Preparation 35 minutes • Cooking time 5–6 minutes

8 large scallops or 24 small queen scallops with corals attached, about 300g (11oz) total weight
2 large ripe avocados, stones removed and peeled
1 large garlic clove, crushed
6 small spring onions, finely chopped
1 green chilli, seeded and chopped (see Cook's Tip)
1½ tbsp grapeseed oil
grated zest and juice of 1 lime, plus extra to squeeze
8 large slices smoked salmon, about 400g (14oz) total weight and 23cm (9in) in length
salt and ground black pepper
rocket leaves and lime wedges to serve

For the coriander dressing
25g (1oz) fresh coriander sprigs
1 small garlic clove, crushed
50ml (2fl oz) grapeseed oil
1 tbsp lime juice

Nutrition per serving
209 cals | 12g fat (2g sats) |
3g carbs | 2.3g salt

1 To make the coriander dressing, put all the ingredients into a blender and whiz until smooth.

2 To make the parcels, remove any tough membranes from the scallops and season with salt and pepper. Put them into a steamer and cook for about 5 minutes or until the flesh is just white. Alternatively, put the scallops on a heatproof plate, cover with another plate and steam over a pan of simmering water for about 3 minutes on each side. Drain and set on kitchen paper to cool.

3 Put the avocados, garlic, spring onions, chilli, oil and lime zest and juice into a bowl. Mash the avocados with a fork, mix well and season with salt and pepper.

4 Lay the salmon on a worksurface, put a large scallop or two small ones on each slice and spoon some avocado mixture on top. Roll the salmon around the filling. Put the parcels on serving plates and squeeze a little lime juice over them. Drizzle with the coriander dressing and serve with rocket and lime wedges.

•COOK'S TIPS•

Chillies vary enormously in strength, from quite mild to blisteringly hot, depending on the type of chilli and its ripeness. Taste a small piece first to check it's not too hot for you.

Be extremely careful when handling chillies not to touch or rub your eyes with your fingers, as they will sting. Wash knives immediately after handling chillies for the same reason. As a precaution, use rubber gloves when preparing them if you like.

Cullen Skink

Scotland This classic fish and potato soup is good and filling. The word 'skink' means stock or broth, but the strong flavour of the fish means water or milk can be used for the liquor, so there's no need to make fish stock. For a smoother, less traditional soup, whiz the soup in a blender.

Serves 4 (as a main meal soup) • Preparation 10 minutes • Cooking time 1½ hours

1 Finnan haddock, weighing about
350g (12oz), skinned
1 medium onion, chopped
600ml (1 pint) milk
700g (1½lb) potatoes
a knob of butter
salt and ground black pepper
freshly chopped flat-leafed parsley to
garnish
crusty bread to serve

Nutrition per serving
309 cals | 6g fat (4g sats) |
40g carbs | 1g salt

1 Put the haddock into a medium pan, just cover it with about 900ml (1½ pints) boiling water and bring to the boil again. Add the onion, cover and simmer for 10–15 minutes until the haddock is tender. Drain off the liquid and reserve.

2 Remove the bones from the haddock and flake the flesh, then set aside. Return the bones and strained stock to the pan with the milk. Cover and simmer gently for a further hour.

3 Meanwhile, peel and roughly chop the potatoes, then cook in lightly salted boiling water until tender. Drain well, then mash.

4 Strain the liquid from the bones and return it to the pan with the flaked fish. Add the mashed potato and the butter and stir well to give a thick creamy consistency. Adjust the seasoning and garnish with parsley. Serve with crusty bread.

•COOK'S TIP•

Ask the fishmonger to skin the
haddock for you.

LAMB

Minted Lamb Burgers with Cucumber

Countrywide Lamb and mint were made for each other, and the flavours marry perfectly in these quick burgers. When buying cucumbers, feel the stalk end and only buy if it is firm. Don't peel the cucumber, as both appearance and flavour are improved if the skin is left on.

Serves 4 • Preparation 15 minutes • Cooking time 30 minutes

450g (1lb) minced lamb
1 small onion, finely chopped
125g (4oz) fresh breadcrumbs
finely grated zest of ½ lemon
1 medium egg, beaten
3 tbsp freshly chopped mint
2 tbsp plain flour
½ cucumber, cut into 5cm (2in) long wedges
6 spring onions, trimmed and cut into 1cm (½in) pieces
200ml (7fl oz) lamb or chicken stock
1 tbsp dry sherry
salt and ground black pepper
boiled new potatoes to serve

Nutrition per serving
374 cals | 17g fat (7g sats) |
28g carbs | 1.6g salt

1 Mix the lamb, onion, breadcrumbs and lemon zest with the egg and 1 tbsp of the chopped mint. Season. Shape into eight burgers with floured hands, then completely coat in the flour.
2 Dry-fry the burgers in a large, heavy-based non-stick frying pan for about 6 minutes, until lightly browned, turning once. Add the cucumber and spring onions.
3 Pour in the stock and sherry, then add the remaining mint and salt and pepper to taste. Bring to the boil, cover and simmer gently for about 20 minutes or until the meat is tender. Skim off any excess fat before serving and taste and adjust the seasoning. Serve with boiled new potatoes.

Lamb Chops with Crispy Garlic Potatoes

Countrywide The perfect mid-week supper, tender lamb chops and garlicky potatoes. As an alternative to green beans, try some steamed broccoli or spinach. The garlic-infused olive oil is easy to make and adds a lovely flavour to the chops.

Serves 4 • Preparation 10 minutes • Cooking time 20 minutes

2 tbsp Mint Sauce (see page 182)
8 small lamb chops
3 medium potatoes, peeled and cut
into 5mm (¼ in) slices
2 tbsp Garlic-infused Olive Oil
(see Cook's Tip)
1 tbsp olive oil
salt and ground black pepper
steamed green beans to serve

Nutrition per serving
835 cals | 45g fat (19g sats) |
22g carbs | 0.7g salt

1 Spread the mint sauce over the lamb chops and leave to marinate while you prepare the potatoes.
2 Cook the potatoes in a pan of lightly salted boiling water for 2 minutes or until just starting to soften. Drain, tip back into the pan and season, then add the garlic oil and toss to combine.
3 Meanwhile, heat the olive oil in a large frying pan and fry the chops for 4–5 minutes on each side until just cooked, adding a splash of boiling water to the pan to make a sauce. Remove the chops and sauce from the pan and keep warm.
4 Add the potatoes to the pan and fry over a medium heat for 10–12 minutes until crisp and golden. Divide the potatoes, chops and sauce among four warmed plates and serve with green beans.

•COOK'S TIP•

Garlic-infused Olive Oil
Gently heat 2 tbsp olive oil with 1 sliced garlic clove for 5 minutes. Discard the garlic and use immediately. Do not store.

Oxford John Steaks with Caper Sauce

The Southeast A speciality of the butchers in Oxford's indoor market, Oxford John is the local name for a lamb leg steak. It's a very tender cut.

Serves 4 • Preparation 5 minutes • Cooking time about 25 minutes

4 lamb leg steaks, about 175g (6oz) each
25g (1oz) butter
1 tsp plain flour
300ml (½ pint) lamb or beef stock
2 tbsp drained capers
1 tbsp vinegar from the capers
salt and ground black pepper
potatoes and green beans to serve

Nutrition per serving
455 cals | 28g fat (13g sats) |
1g carbs | 1.4g salt

1 Season the lamb steaks to taste. Heat the butter in a frying pan and fry the steaks gently for 10–15 minutes, turning occasionally, until browned on both sides. Remove from the pan with a slotted spoon and transfer to a warmed dish.
2 Stir to loosen any sediment on the bottom of the pan, then stir in the flour and cook for 1–2 minutes. Gradually add the stock, stirring all the time, then cook until the sauce thickens, boils and is smooth. Add the capers and vinegar and simmer for 1–2 minutes.
3 Return the lamb steaks to the pan and simmer for 5 minutes or until the lamb is cooked to your liking. Serve hot with potatoes and green beans.

Lancashire Hotpot

The North Easy to prepare, this traditional dish could be left to cook in the oven on a low heat all day, ready to feed the hungry workers at dinner.

Serves 4 • Preparation 20 minutes • Cooking time 2½ hours

12 lamb cutlets
2 medium onions, sliced
2 large carrots, sliced
leaves from 2 thyme sprigs
750ml (1¼ pints) hot lamb stock
450g (1lb) potatoes, peeled and sliced
25g (1oz) butter
salt and ground black pepper
pickled red cabbage to serve

Nutrition per serving
653 cals | 48g fat (24g sats) |
29g carbs | 1.4g salt

1 Preheat the oven to 180°C (160°C fan oven) mark 4. Put a layer of cutlets into a large lidded casserole. Cover with a layer of onions and carrots and a sprinkling of thyme, and season well. Repeat with the remaining lamb, onions, carrots and thyme.
2 Pour in enough hot stock to almost cover the meat. Top with an overlapping layer of potatoes. Season, cover and cook in the oven for 2 hours.
3 Increase the oven temperature to 230°C (210°C fan oven) mark 8. Remove the lid and dot the top of the casserole with knobs of butter. Continue cooking for 30 minutes, uncovered, or until the potatoes are golden brown. Serve with pickled red cabbage.

Shepherd's Pie

The North Controversy surrounds this simple, traditional dish. Some hold that it is shepherd's pie when made with lamb and cottage pie when made with beef – and vice versa. Some say it should be made with raw meat, others with cooked. This tasty version is made with lamb.

Serves 4 • Preparation time 20 minutes • Cooking time about 1 hour

2 tbsp sunflower oil
450g (1lb) minced lamb
1 large onion, chopped
50g (2oz) mushrooms, sliced
2 carrots, chopped
2 tbsp plain flour
1 tbsp tomato purée
1 bay leaf (optional)
300ml (½ pint) lamb or vegetable stock
(see Cook's Tip)
700g (1½lb) potatoes, peeled and cut
into large chunks
25g (1oz) butter
60ml (2¼ fl oz) milk
50g (2oz) Cheddar cheese, crumbled
(optional)
salt and ground black pepper

Nutrition per serving
513 cals | 27g fat (11g sats) |
44g carbs | 0.6g salt

1 Heat half the oil in a large pan and brown the mince over a medium to high heat – do this in batches, otherwise the meat will steam rather than fry. Remove with a slotted spoon on to a plate.

2 Turn the heat to low and add the remaining oil. Gently fry the onion, mushrooms and carrots for 10 minutes or until softened. Stir in the flour and tomato purée and cook for 1 minute. Return the meat to the pan and add the bay leaf, if you like. Pour in the stock and bring to the boil, then cover and simmer on a low heat for 25 minutes.

3 Preheat the oven to 200°C (180°C fan oven) mark 6. Cook the potatoes in lightly salted boiling water for 20 minutes or until tender. Drain and leave to stand in the colander for 2 minutes to steam dry. Melt the butter and milk in the potato pan and add the cooked potatoes. Mash until smooth.

4 Spoon the lamb mixture into a 1.7 litre (3 pint) casserole dish. Remove the bay leaf and check the seasoning. Cover with the mashed potato and sprinkle the cheese over, if you like. Bake for 15–20 minutes until bubbling and golden. Serve immediately with green vegetables.

•COOK'S TIP•

You can use 1 lamb or vegetable stock cube dissolved in 300ml (½ pint) boiling water.

Gloucestershire Squab Pie

The West You'd be forgiven for thinking this dish might contain young pigeons, otherwise known as squabs, but this pie has always been made with lamb. If you can buy it locally the flavour will be delicious, set off by the sharp apple and spices.

Serves 4 • Preparation 30 minutes, plus chilling • Cooking time 1 hour, 35 minutes

225g (8oz) plain flour, plus extra to
dust
50g (2oz) butter
50g (2oz) lard
700g (1½lb) lamb neck fillets, sliced
into 12 pieces
1 large cooking apple, peeled, cored
and sliced
450g (1lb) onions, thinly sliced
¼ tsp ground allspice
¼ tsp freshly grated nutmeg
150ml (¼ pint) lamb or beef stock
milk to glaze
salt and ground black pepper

Nutrition per serving
805 cals | 48g fat (23g sats) |
56g carbs | 1g salt

1 Put the flour and a pinch of salt into a bowl. Rub in the butter and lard until the mixture resembles fine breadcrumbs. Mix in enough cold water to form a firm dough. Knead lightly until smooth, then chill until required.

2 Preheat the oven to 200°C (180°C fan oven) mark 6. Put half the lamb in the bottom of a 900ml (1½ pint) pie dish. Arrange half the apple slices and half the onion slices over the top. Sprinkle on the allspice and nutmeg and season to taste. Repeat the layers, then pour in the stock.

3 Roll out the pastry on a lightly floured surface slightly larger all round than the pie dish. Brush the rim of the dish with water, then lift the pastry lid over the filling and press the edge down lightly on to the rim to seal. Use any pastry trimmings to decorate.

4 Brush the pastry with milk and cook in the oven for 20 minutes. Reduce the oven temperature to 180°C (160°C fan oven) mark 4 and cook for a further 1¼ hours. Cover the pastry if it shows signs of becoming too brown. Serve hot.

•COOK'S TIP•

Once you've prepared the apple, place the slices in some water with lemon juice added, to prevent discoloration, while you prepare the onions. Drain before use.

Lamb and Barley Stew

The Southeast Lamb from the Weald of Kent is particularly tasty, while pearl barley is a good bulking ingredient to use in stews and casseroles.

Serves 6 • Preparation 15 minutes • Cooking time 2½ hours

2 tbsp plain wholemeal flour
1.4kg (3lb) boned leg or shoulder of lamb, trimmed of fat and cubed
3 streaky bacon rashers, rind removed
25g (1oz) butter
2 medium onions, chopped
2 medium carrots, sliced
125g (4oz) turnip or swede, diced
2 celery sticks, diced
2 tbsp pearl barley
2 tsp mixed freshly chopped herbs, such as thyme, rosemary, parsley, basil
300ml (½ pint) lamb or beef stock
salt and ground black pepper
freshly chopped flat-leafed parsley to garnish

Nutrition per serving
536 cals | 28g fat (12g sats) |
14g carbs | 1.2g salt

1 Season the flour with salt and pepper, then toss the lamb in the flour.
2 Dry-fry the bacon in a large flameproof casserole until the fat runs. Add the butter and the lamb and fry until browned all over, stirring. Using a slotted spoon, remove the lamb and bacon from the casserole and set aside.
3 Add the onions, carrots, turnip or swede and celery to the casserole and fry for 5–10 minutes until beginning to brown.
4 Return the lamb to the casserole, add the pearl barley and herbs and pour in the stock. Bring to the boil, then cover and simmer for 2 hours, stirring occasionally to prevent sticking, until the lamb is tender.
5 Serve hot, sprinkled with chopped parsley.

Irish Stew

Northern Ireland A traditional dish originally made with mutton, and cooked in a pot hanging over a turf fire. These days lamb is the usual choice.

Serves 4 • Preparation 15 minutes • Cooking time about 2¼ hours

700g (1½ lb) middle neck lamb cutlets, fat trimmed
2 onions, thinly sliced
450g (1lb) potatoes, peeled and thinly sliced
1 tbsp freshly chopped flat-leafed parsley, plus extra to garnish
1 tbsp dried thyme
300ml (½ pint) lamb stock
salt and ground black pepper

Nutrition per serving
419 cals | 20g fat (9g sats) |
24g carbs | 0.6g salt

1 Preheat the oven to 170°C (150°C fan oven) mark 3. Layer the meat, onions and potatoes in a deep casserole dish, sprinkling some herbs and seasoning between each layer. Finish with a layer of potato, overlapping the slices neatly.
2 Pour the stock over the potatoes, then cover with greaseproof paper and a lid. Cook for about 2 hours or until the meat is tender.
3 Preheat the grill. Take the lid off the casserole and remove the paper. Put under the grill and brown the top of the potatoes. Sprinkle with parsley and serve immediately.

Parson's Venison

Countrywide Not venison at all, but a leg of lamb given a richer, fuller flavour reminiscent of game. The boned joint is stuffed with a savoury mushroom mixture, then marinated and cooked in a heady concoction of wine and port, seasoned with spices.

Serves 6 • Preparation 10 minutes, plus marinating • Cooking time 2¼–2½ hours

25g (1oz) butter
1 small onion, finely chopped
125g (4oz) mushrooms, chopped
125g (4oz) cooked ham, chopped
2 tbsp snipped fresh chives
1.8–2kg (4–4½lb) leg of lamb, boned

For the marinade
200ml (7fl oz) dry red wine
75ml (2½fl oz) port
6 juniper berries, crushed
¼ tsp ground allspice
3 tbsp red wine vinegar
1 bay leaf
¼ tsp freshly grated nutmeg
salt and ground black pepper

Nutrition per serving
662 cals | 41g fat (19g sats) |
3g carbs | 1.4g salt

1 Melt half the butter in a pan, add the onion and mushrooms and cook, stirring frequently, until the onion is soft but not browned. Stir in the ham and chives and season to taste. Leave to cool.

2 Season the lamb inside and out with pepper, then spread the onion mixture over the inside. Roll up tightly and tie securely. Put in a large glass bowl or casserole.

3 Mix all the ingredients for the marinade. Pour over the lamb, cover and leave in a cool place for 24 hours, turning occasionally.

4 The next day, preheat the oven to 180°C (160°C fan oven) mark 4. Remove the meat from the marinade, drain and dry. Reserve the marinade. Melt the remaining butter in a flameproof casserole. Add the meat and brown on all sides over a medium to high heat.

5 Pour in the marinade and bring almost to the boil, then cover and cook in the oven for 1¾–2 hours until the meat is tender, basting occasionally with marinade.

6 Transfer the meat to a warmed plate. Skim the fat from the surface of the liquid, then boil rapidly until syrupy. Remove the bay leaf, adjust the seasoning and serve with the meat.

Boned and Stuffed Shoulder of Lamb

Countrywide A shoulder of lamb is more economical than a leg, and when combined with this fruit and nut stuffing will prove a winner for Sunday lunch. Boned shoulders of lamb are available in most supermarkets, or ask your butcher to bone the meat for you.

Serves 6 • Preparation 20 minutes, plus cooling • Cooking time 1¾ hours

2 large slices white bread, crusts
removed and discarded
a few fresh thyme sprigs
a few fresh parsley sprigs
50g (2oz) shelled pistachio nuts
175g (6oz) ready-to-eat pitted prunes
50g (2oz) ready-to-soak dried apricots
50g (2oz) butter
225g (8oz) onions, finely chopped
¼ tsp freshly ground nutmeg
1.4kg (3lb) boned shoulder or leg
of lamb
150ml (¼ pint) red wine
salt and ground black pepper
fresh herbs to garnish

Nutrition per serving
616 cals | 34g fat (15g sats) |
22g carbs | 0.8g salt

1 Put the bread, the leaves from the thyme and parsley and the nuts into a food processor and whiz for about 1 minute or until finely chopped. Transfer to a bowl. Put 50g (2oz) of the prunes into the processor with the apricots and chop finely. Stir into the crumb mixture.

2 Heat the butter in a small pan. Add the onions and sauté until soft and transparent, stirring from time to time. Stir into the crumb mixture with the nutmeg and seasoning. Mix well and leave to cool.

3 Preheat the oven to 200°C (180°C fan oven) mark 6. Unroll the shoulder of lamb. Spoon the stuffing into the lamb, roll up again and tie at regular intervals. Don't worry if a little of the stuffing begins to ooze out.

4 Put the lamb into a dry roasting tin and cook in the oven for about 1½ hours, basting occasionally. Test with a fine skewer. If the meat juices are pink, the lamb is slightly underdone. Cook for a little longer if you prefer it well done. Put the lamb into a warm serving dish, cover and keep warm.

5 Drain off most of the fat from the roasting tin, then add the wine and 300ml (½ pint) water. Bring to the boil, scraping all the sediment off the bottom of the pan. Sieve into a small pan. Add the remaining prunes and simmer for about 5 minutes. Adjust the seasoning and serve with the sliced lamb. Garnish with fresh herbs.

Roast Leg of Lamb with Rosemary

Countrywide A favourite for Sunday lunch throughout Britain. Buy the best meat you can to ensure great flavour and texture. For centuries lamb has had religious connotations and is often served at Easter and Passover.

Serves 8 • Preparation 15 minutes • Cooking time 1½ hours, plus resting

2.5kg (5½ lb) leg of lamb
4 rosemary sprigs
½ tbsp oil
4 garlic cloves, cut into slivers
4 anchovy fillets, roughly chopped
4 oregano sprigs
1 large onion, thickly sliced
1 lemon, cut into 6 wedges
salt and ground black pepper
vegetables to serve

Nutrition per serving
601 cals | 39g fat (17g sats) |
1g carbs | 1.3g salt

1 Take the lamb out of the fridge 1 hour before roasting. Pat the skin dry with kitchen paper.

2 Preheat the oven to 220°C (200°C fan oven) mark 7. Cut the rosemary into smaller sprigs. Rub the oil over the lamb. Cut small slits all over the meat, then insert the garlic slivers, rosemary sprigs, anchovy pieces and the leaves from two oregano sprigs into the gaps. Season well.

3 Put the onion slices into the bottom of a roasting tin just large enough to hold the lamb. Top with the remaining oregano, then put in the meat, fat side up (the onions must be covered to prevent them burning). Tuck lemon wedges around the meat.

4 Put the lamb into the oven and reduce the oven temperature to 190°C (170°C fan oven) mark 5. Roast for 15 minutes per 450lb (1lb) for pink meat, or longer if you like it more cooked.

5 Transfer the lamb to a board, cover with foil and leave to rest for 30 minutes before carving. Carefully pour (or skim) off the fat from a corner of the roasting tin, leaving the sediment behind. Put the tin on the hob over a medium heat and pour in 300–450ml (½ –¾ pint) vegetable water (or meat stock). Stir thoroughly, scraping up the sediment, and boil steadily until the gravy is a rich brown colour. Serve the lamb with the gravy and vegetables.

Get Ahead
• Prepare the lamb to the end of step 3 up to 2 hours ahead.
• To use, complete the recipe.

•COOK'S TIP•

The lamb is served pink here, but allow an extra 20–30 minutes if you prefer your meat more cooked.

Couscous-crusted Lamb

Countrywide Do take the trouble to trim the racks of lamb before you cook them – it will make all the difference to the appearance of the finished dish. Alternatively, ask your friendly butcher to do the work for you.

Serves 6 • Preparation 15 minutes • Cooking time about 20 minutes

75g (3oz) couscous
3 racks of lamb, excess fat trimmed off
25g (1oz) each dried cranberries and
pistachios, finely chopped
2 medium eggs
1½ tsp wholegrain mustard
1½ tsp dried mint
salt and ground black pepper

Nutrition per serving
493 cals | 28g fat (12g sats) |
10g carbs | 0.9g salt

1 Put the couscous into a bowl and pour 125ml (4fl oz) boiling water over it. Cover with clingfilm and set aside for 10 minutes.
2 Meanwhile, trim any membrane from the lamb racks, scrape the bones clean using a small knife and pat the meat dry. Put the lamb racks on to a baking tray.
3 Preheat the oven to 200°C (180°C fan oven) mark 6. Use a fork to fluff up the couscous, then stir in the cranberries, pistachios, eggs, mustard, mint and some seasoning. Press a third of the crust on top of the meat on each lamb rack.
4 Cook the lamb for 15–20 minutes for pink meat, or longer if you prefer it more well done. Transfer the racks to a board, cover with foil and leave to rest for 5 minutes before carving and serving.

FREEZING TIP

To freeze, prepare to the end of step 3 up to one month ahead. Wrap the baking tray well in clingfilm, then freeze.

To use, thaw the lamb overnight in the fridge, unwrap and complete the recipe to serve.

BEEF & VEAL

Stuffed Topside of Beef

Countrywide Topside of beef is a good cut for braising or pot-roasting. Marinating and stuffing the joint adds moisture to this lean meat. Served with crunchy roast potatoes and a selection of vegetables, it will be a winner for Sunday lunch or dinner.

Serves 6 • Preparation 35 minutes, plus marinating • Cooking time 1–1¼ hours, plus resting

1.4kg (3lb) topside or top rump of beef
1 tbsp balsamic vinegar
2 tbsp white wine vinegar
3 tbsp olive oil
3 tbsp freshly chopped marjoram or thyme
2 red peppers, cored, seeded and quartered
75g (3oz) fresh spinach, cooked and well drained
75g (3oz) pitted black olives, chopped
50g (2oz) smoked ham, chopped
75g (3oz) raisins or sultanas
salt and ground black pepper
roast potatoes and vegetables to serve

Nutrition per serving
535 cals | 29g fat (10g sats) |
13g carbs | 1.4g salt

1 Make a deep cut along the beef to create a pocket and put the joint into a dish. Combine the vinegars, oil, marjoram or thyme and some black pepper. Pour over the beef and into the pocket. Marinate in a cool place for 4–6 hours, or overnight.

2 Grill the peppers, skin side up, under a hot grill until the skins are charred. Cool in a covered bowl, then remove the skins.

3 Squeeze the excess water from the spinach, then chop and put into a bowl with the olives, ham and raisins or sultanas. Mix well and season with salt and pepper.

4 Preheat the oven to 190°C (170°C fan oven) mark 5. Line the pocket of the beef with the peppers, keeping back two pepper quarters for the gravy. Spoon the spinach mixture into the pocket and spread evenly. Reshape the meat and tie at intervals with string. Put the beef into a roasting tin just large enough to hold it and pour the marinade over it.

5 Roast for 1 hour for rare beef, or 1¼ hours for medium-rare, basting from time to time. Put the beef on a board, cover with foil and leave to rest in a warm place while you make the gravy.

6 Skim off the excess fat from the roasting tin. Put the tin on the hob and bring the pan juices to the boil. Add 125ml (4fl oz) water and bubble for 2–3 minutes. Finely chop the remaining pepper pieces and add to the gravy.

7 Carve the beef and serve with the gravy and roast potatoes, and vegetables of your choice.

Roast Rib of Beef

Countrywide Think of Olde England and it brings to mind huge ribs of beef on laden tables in banqueting halls – quintessentially British, this roast is one of the best known British dishes around the world. Yorkshire Puddings are a must.

Serves 8 • Preparation 5 minutes • Cooking time 2½ hours, plus resting

2-bone rib of beef, about 2.5–2.7kg
(5½–6lb)
1 tbsp plain flour
1 tbsp mustard powder
150ml (¼ pint) red wine
600ml (1 pint) beef stock
600ml (1 pint) water
salt and ground black pepper
thyme sprigs to garnish
Yorkshire Puddings (see page 94),
roasted root vegetables and a green
vegetable to serve

Nutrition per serving
807 cals | 53g fat (24g sats) |
2g carbs | 0.5g salt

1 Preheat the oven to 230°C (210°C fan oven) mark 8. Put the beef, fat side up, in a roasting tin just large enough to hold the joint. Mix the flour and mustard together in a small bowl and season with salt and pepper, then rub the mixture over the beef. Roast in the centre of the oven for 30 minutes.

2 Move the beef to a lower shelf, near the bottom of the oven. Reduce the oven temperature to 220°C (200°C fan oven) mark 7 and continue to roast the beef for a further 2 hours, basting occasionally.

3 Put the beef on a carving dish, cover loosely with foil and leave to rest while you make the gravy. Skim off most of the fat from the roasting tin. Put the roasting tin on the hob, pour in the wine and boil vigorously until very syrupy. Pour in the stock and, again, boil until syrupy. Add the vegetable water and boil until syrupy. There should be about 450ml (¾ pint) gravy. Taste and adjust the seasoning.

4 Remove the rib bone and carve the beef. Garnish with thyme and serve with the gravy and Yorkshire puddings and roasted vegetables.

•COOK'S TIP•

Buy the best quality meat you can afford. The beef should be a dark red colour, not bright red, and have a good marbling of fat.

Fillet of Beef en Croûte

The Southeast A dish for a special occasion. Sometimes called Beef Wellington, it was so-named because the finished joint was thought to resemble one of the Duke of Wellington's brown shiny military boots.

Serves 6 • Preparation 1 hour, plus soaking and chilling • Cooking time about 1 hour 20 minutes, plus resting

1–1.4kg (2¼ –3lb) fillet of beef, trimmed
50g (2oz) butter
2 shallots, chopped
15g (½ oz) dried porcini mushrooms,
(cepes) soaked in 100ml (3½ fl oz)
boiling water
2 garlic cloves, chopped
225g (8oz) flat mushrooms, finely chopped
2 tsp freshly chopped thyme, plus extra
sprigs to garnish
175g (6oz) chicken liver pâté
175g (6oz) thinly sliced Parma ham
375g ready-rolled puff pastry, thawed if frozen
plain flour to dust
1 medium egg, beaten
salt and ground black pepper
Rich Red Wine Sauce (see Cook's Tip)
to serve

Nutrition per serving
802 cals | 53g fat (15g sats) |
27g carbs | 2.4g salt

•COOK'S TIP•

Rich Red Wine Sauce
Soften 350g (12oz) finely chopped
shallots in 2 tbsp olive oil for
5 minutes. Add 3 chopped garlic
cloves and 3 tbsp tomato purée and
cook for 1 minute, then add 2 tbsp
balsamic vinegar. Simmer briskly
until reduced to almost nothing, then
add 200ml (7fl oz) red wine and
reduce by half. Pour in 600ml
(1 pint) beef stock and simmer until
reduced by one-third.

1 Season the beef with salt and pepper. Melt 25g (1oz) of the butter in a large frying pan and, when foaming, add the beef and cook for 4–5 minutes to brown all over. Transfer to a plate and leave to cool.

2 Melt the remaining butter in a pan, add the shallots and cook for 1 minute. Drain the porcini mushrooms, saving the liquid, and chop them. Add them to the pan with the garlic, the reserved liquid and the fresh mushrooms. Increase the heat and cook until the liquid has evaporated, then season with salt and pepper and add the chopped thyme. Leave to cool.

3 Put the pâté into a bowl and beat until smooth. Add the mushroom mixture and stir well until thoroughly combined. Check the seasoning. Spread half the mushroom mixture evenly over one side of the beef. Lay half the Parma ham on a length of clingfilm, overlapping the slices. Invert the mushroom-topped beef on to the ham. Spread the remaining mushroom mixture on the other side of the beef, then lay the remaining Parma ham, also overlapping, on top of the mushroom mixture. Wrap the beef in the clingfilm to form a firm sausage shape and chill for 30 minutes. Preheat the oven to 220°C (200°C fan oven) mark 7.

4 Cut off one-third of the pastry and roll out on a lightly floured surface to 3mm (⅛in) thick and 2.5cm (1in) larger all around than the beef. Prick all over with a fork. Transfer to a baking sheet and bake for 12–15 minutes until brown and crisp. Cool on a wire rack, then trim to the size of the beef and place on a baking sheet. Remove the clingfilm from the beef, brush with the egg and place on the cooked pastry.

5 Roll out the remaining pastry to a 25.5 × 30.5cm (10 × 12in) rectangle. Roll a lattice pastry cutter over it and gently ease the lattice open. Cover the beef with the lattice, tuck the ends under and seal the edges. Brush with the beaten egg, then cook for 40 minutes for rare to medium-rare, 45 minutes for medium. Leave to rest for 10 minutes before carving. Garnish with thyme sprigs and serve with Red Wine Sauce.

Classic Roast Beef with Yorkshire Puddings

The North and Countrywide This combination has been Britain's traditional Sunday lunch for hundreds of years. Originally, the pudding, cut into squares, was served with gravy before the meat to take the edge off the appetite. Today it is often served as a pub snack with onion gravy.

Serves 8 • Preparation 20 minutes • Cooking time about 1½ hours, plus resting

1 boned and rolled rib, sirloin, rump or topside of beef, about 1.8kg (4lb)
1 tbsp plain flour
1 tbsp mustard powder
salt and ground black pepper
fresh thyme sprigs to garnish
vegetables to serve

For the Yorkshire pudding
125g (4oz) plain flour
½ tsp salt
300ml (½ pint) milk
2 medium eggs

For the gravy
150ml (¼ pint) red wine
600ml (1 pint) beef stock

Nutrition per serving
510 cals | 24g fat (9g sats) |
16g carbs | 0.5g salt

1 Preheat the oven to 230°C (210°C fan oven) mark 8. Put the beef into a roasting tin, thickest part of the fat uppermost. Mix the flour with the mustard powder and salt and pepper. Rub the mixture over the beef. Roast the beef in the centre of the oven for 30 minutes.
2 Baste the beef and reduce the oven temperature to 190°C (170°C fan oven) mark 5. Cook for a further 1 hour, basting occasionally.
3 Meanwhile, prepare the Yorkshire pudding batter. Sift the flour and salt into a bowl. Mix in half the milk, then add the eggs and season with pepper. Beat until smooth, then whisk in the remaining milk.
4 Put the beef on a warmed carving dish, cover loosely with foil and leave to rest in a warm place. Increase the oven temperature to 220°C (200°C fan oven) mark 7.
5 Pour off about 3 tbsp fat from the roasting tin and use to grease 8–12 individual Yorkshire pudding tins. Heat in the oven for 5 minutes or until the fat is almost smoking. Pour the Yorkshire batter into the tins. Bake for 15–20 minutes until well risen, golden and crisp.
6 Meanwhile, make the gravy. Skim off any remaining fat from the roasting tin. Put the tin on the hob, add the wine and boil until syrupy. Pour in the stock and, again, boil until syrupy – there should be about 450ml (¾ pint) gravy. Taste and adjust the seasoning.
7 Carve the beef into slices. Garnish with thyme and serve with the gravy, Yorkshire puddings and vegetables of your choice.

Braised Beef with Chestnuts and Celery

Countrywide An unusual casserole which dates from the eighteenth century. Make it in the late autumn and winter when both celery and fresh chestnuts are available. A big bowl of fluffy mashed potatoes would be the ideal accompaniment.

Serves 6 • Preparation 25 minutes • Cooking time 2 hours 20 minutes

18 fresh chestnuts, skins split
15g (½ oz) butter
1 tbsp vegetable oil
2 bacon rashers, rind removed, chopped
900g (2lb) stewing steak, cubed
1 medium onion, chopped
1 tbsp plain flour
300ml (½ pint) brown ale
300ml (½ pint) beef stock
a pinch of freshly grated nutmeg
finely grated zest and juice of 1 orange
3 celery sticks, chopped
salt and ground black pepper
freshly chopped flat-leafed parsley to garnish

Nutrition per serving
336 cals | 16g fat (6g sats) |
12g carbs | 1.3g salt

1 Preheat the oven to 170°C (150°C fan oven) mark 3. Cook the chestnuts in simmering water for about 7 minutes. Remove from the water one at a time and peel off the thick outer skin and thin inner skin while still warm.

2 Heat the butter and oil in a flameproof casserole, add the bacon and beef in batches and cook, stirring occasionally, until browned. Remove the meat with a slotted spoon.

3 Add the onion to the casserole and fry, stirring, until softened. Drain off most of the fat. Return the meat to the casserole, sprinkle in the flour and cook, stirring, for 1–2 minutes.

4 Stir in the brown ale, stock, nutmeg, orange juice and half the zest. Season to taste. Bring to the boil, stir well to loosen the sediment, then add the chestnuts. Cover tightly with foil and a lid and cook in the oven for about 45 minutes.

5 After 45 minutes, add the celery to the casserole and cook for a further 1 hour or until the meat is tender. Serve with the remaining orange zest and the parsley sprinkled over the top.

.COOK'S TIP.

It's well worth spending the extra time needed to shell the chestnuts, as they do add a very special flavour to the finished dish.

Beef and Stout Stew

Northern Ireland The stout not only helps tenderise the beef but it also gives a rich malty flavour to this slow-cooked stew. Using a slow cooker will enable you to prepare this and get it on to cook in the morning, ready to eat in the evening.

Serves 6 • Preparation 15 minutes • Cooking time 8–10 hours on Low

1.4kg (3lb) shin of beef or braising steak, cut into 3cm (1¼in) cubes
2 tbsp seasoned plain flour
4 tbsp vegetable oil
2 medium onions, sliced
4 medium carrots, cut into chunks
225ml (8fl oz) stout
300ml (½ pint) hot beef stock
2 bay leaves
700g (1½ lb) baby potatoes, halved if large
2 tbsp freshly chopped flat-leafed parsley
salt and ground black pepper

Nutrition per serving
526 cals | 29g fat (10g sats) |
10g carbs | 0.4g salt

1 Toss the beef in the flour to coat and shake off any excess. Heat the oil in a large pan until hot. Add a handful of beef and cook until well browned. Remove with a slotted spoon, transfer to the slow cooker and repeat until all the meat is browned.

2 Add the onions and carrots to the pan and cook for 10 minutes or until browned. Add the stout, scraping the bottom of the pan to loosen the sediment, then stir in the hot stock. Add the bay leaves and potatoes and bring to the boil. Pour over the beef in the slow cooker, cover and cook on Low for 8–10 hours until the meat is tender.

3 Stir in the parsley, season to taste and serve.

Beef Pockets Stuffed with Mushrooms

Scotland Mushrooms make marvellous stuffings and are always available. Although this is originally a Scottish dish, ginger wine, an English speciality, appeals to the British palate's desire for strong positive flavours. Even this small quantity makes a significant difference to the recipe.

Serves 4 • Preparation 10 minutes • Cooking time 10–15 minutes

4 thick-cut steaks, about 175g (6oz)
each
15g (½oz) butter
175g (6oz) mushrooms, finely chopped
1 garlic clove, crushed
1 large onion, finely chopped
1 tbsp freshly chopped flat-leafed
parsley
1 tbsp ginger wine
1 tbsp fresh wholemeal breadcrumbs
1 tbsp fresh double cream
salt and ground black pepper
new potatoes and broccoli to serve

Nutrition per serving
362 cals | 19g fat (10g sats) |
8g carbs | 1g salt

1 Preheat the grill. Using a sharp, pointed knife, make a horizontal cut in each steak without cutting all the way through. Season to taste.
2 Melt the butter in a medium pan and lightly cook the mushrooms, garlic and onion for 5 minutes or until softened. Remove from the heat.
3 Add the parsley, ginger wine, breadcrumbs and cream and mix together well.
4 Generously fill the pocket of each steak with the stuffing.
5 Grill the steaks for 5–15 minutes until the meat is cooked to taste (see Cook's Tip). Serve at once with new potatoes and broccoli.

•COOK'S TIP•

Allow 5 minutes (one turn) for rare steaks; 9 minutes (three turns) for medium. For well-done, allow up to 15 minutes, increasing the time between turns to 3 minutes.

Scotch Collops

Scotland Collop is another word for escalope, the thick slice of meat off the bone which is cut across the grain. Collops may be beef, lamb or venison, as well as veal, and should always be flattened before use. This recipe really brings out the delicate flavour of the veal.

Serves 4 • Preparation 10 minutes • Cooking time 30 minutes

4 veal escalopes, about 175g (6oz) each, halved
40g (1½oz) butter
1 small onion, chopped
175ml (6fl oz) dry white wine
400ml (14fl oz) veal or chicken stock
1–2 tsp mushroom ketchup
about 1 tbsp lemon juice
2 tsp plain flour
a pinch of ground mace
salt and ground black pepper
crisp bacon rolls, fried button mushrooms, lemon twists and parsley sprigs to garnish

Nutrition per serving
309 cals | 12g fat (6g sats) |
4g carbs | 1.8g salt

1 Using a rolling pin or meat mallet, flatten each veal escalope between two sheets of greaseproof paper.
2 Melt 25g (1oz) of the butter in a large frying pan, add the veal and cook for about 2 minutes on each side. Transfer to a warmed serving plate and keep warm.
3 Add the onion to the pan and cook for about 3 minutes, stirring frequently, until softened but not browned. Stir in the wine and boil until almost evaporated. Stir in the stock, mushroom ketchup and lemon juice. Bring to the boil, then simmer until reduced to 225ml (8fl oz).

4 Work the flour into the remaining butter, then gradually whisk into the stock to thicken slightly. Season with the mace, salt and pepper, then taste and add more mushroom ketchup and lemon juice, if necessary.
5 Arrange the collops, overlapping each other, on the serving dish and spoon some sauce down the centre. Garnish with bacon rolls, mushrooms, lemon twists and parsley. Serve the remaining sauce separately.

•COOK'S TIP•

When flattening the escalope, a rolling pin will do less damage to the meat fibres than a meat mallet.

Steak and Kidney Pie

Countrywide A classic British dish, said to have originally been cooked in poorer households with the more affordable tougher cuts of meat supplemented by offal such as kidney. You can prepare this in advance and then freeze before baking.

Serves 6 • Preparation 40 minutes, plus cooling • Cooking time about 1½ hours

700g (1½ lb) stewing steak, cubed and seasoned

2 tbsp plain flour, plus extra to dust

3 tbsp vegetable oil

25g (1oz) butter

1 small onion, finely chopped

175g (6oz) ox kidney, cut into small pieces

150g (5oz) flat mushrooms, cut into large chunks

a small pinch of cayenne pepper

1 tsp anchovy essence

350g (12oz) puff pastry, thawed if frozen

1 large egg, beaten with a pinch of salt, to glaze

salt and ground black pepper

Nutrition per serving
565 cals | 36g fat (8g sats) |
26g carbs | 0.9g salt

1 Preheat the oven to 170°C (150°C fan oven) mark 3. Toss half the steak with half the flour. Heat the oil in a flameproof, non-stick casserole and add the butter. Fry the steak in batches until brown, then remove and put to one side. Repeat with the remaining steak.

2 Add the onion and cook gently until soft. Return the steak to the casserole with 200ml (7fl oz) water, the kidney, mushrooms, cayenne and anchovy essence. Bring to the boil, then cover and simmer for 5 minutes.

3 Transfer to the oven and cook for 1 hour or until tender. The sauce should be syrupy. If not, transfer the casserole to the hob, remove the lid, bring to the boil and bubble for 5 minutes to reduce the liquid. Leave the steak mixture to cool.

4 Preheat the oven to 200°C (180°C fan oven) mark 6. Put the steak and kidney mixture into a 900ml (1½ pint) pie dish. Pile it high to support the pastry.

5 Roll out the pastry on a lightly floured surface to 5mm (¼ in) thick. Cut off four to six strips, 1cm (½ in) wide. Dampen the edge of the dish with cold water, then press the pastry strips on to the edge. Dampen the pastry rim and lay the sheet of pastry on top. Press the surfaces together, trim the edge and press down with the back of a knife to seal. Brush the pastry with the glaze and score with the back of a knife. Put the pie dish on a baking sheet and cook in the oven for 30 minutes or until the pastry is golden brown and the filling is hot to the centre.

FREEZING TIP

▼ ▼ ▼ ▼ ▼ ▼ ▼ ▼ ▼

To freeze, complete the recipe but do not glaze or bake. Wrap the uncooked pie and freeze.

To use, thaw at cool room temperature overnight. Glaze the pastry and add 5–10 minutes to the cooking time, covering the pie with foil if the top starts to turn too brown.

Cottage Pie

Countrywide Originally, pies such as these were a means of using up leftover roasted meat of any kind, and the mashed potato topping made the meat go a lot further. These days minced beef is used in cottage pies, whereas lamb is used in shepherd's pies.

Serves 4 • Preparation 15 minutes • Cooking time about 1 hour

1 tbsp olive oil
1 onion, finely chopped
2 garlic cloves, crushed
450g (1lb) minced beef
1 tbsp plain flour
450ml (¾ pint) beef stock
2 tbsp Worcestershire sauce
1 medium carrot, diced
125g (4oz) button mushrooms, sliced
1kg (2¼lb) potatoes, roughly chopped
25g (1oz) butter
75ml (3fl oz) milk
salt and ground black pepper

Nutrition per serving
581 cals | 28g fat (12g sats) |
55g carbs | 1.8g salt

1 Heat the oil in a large pan, add the onion and fry over a medium heat for 15 minutes or until softened and golden, stirring occasionally. Add the garlic and cook for 1 minute.

2 Preheat the oven to 200°C (180°C fan oven) mark 6. Add the beef to the onion and garlic and, as it browns, use a wooden spoon to break up the pieces. Once it's brown, stir in the flour. Stir in the stock to the browned mince, cover the pan and bring to the boil. Add the Worcestershire sauce, carrot and mushrooms and season well with salt and pepper. Reduce the heat, cover and cook for 15 minutes.

3 Meanwhile, put the potatoes into a large pan of lightly salted water. Bring to the boil and cook for about 20–25 minutes until very soft. Drain and put back into the pan over a low heat to dry off. Mash until smooth, then beat in the butter and milk. Season with salt and pepper to taste.

4 Spoon the sauce into a 1.7 litre (3 pint) ovenproof dish, cover with the mashed potato, then cook in the oven for 20–25 minutes until piping hot and the topping is golden brown.

TRY SOMETHING DIFFERENT

To make individual pies, use four 450ml (¾ pint) shallow ovenproof dishes.

Teviotdale Pie

Scotland Originating in the Borders where good meat is taken for granted, this dish is a kind of suet pie that makes a small amount of meat go a long way. Vegetables can be incorporated with the meat under the suet crust, making it a true one-pot meal if you like.

Serves 4 • Preparation 5 minutes • Cooking time 1–1¼ hours

450g (1lb) lean minced beef
1 medium onion, chopped
300ml (½ pint) beef stock
1 tsp Worcestershire sauce
225g (8oz) self-raising flour
25g (1oz) cornflour
75g (3oz) shredded beef suet
about 300ml (½ pint) milk
salt and ground black pepper

Nutrition per serving
607 cals | 29g fat (15g sats) |
57g carbs | 2g salt

1 Put the meat into a large pan, preferably non-stick, over a medium heat and cook in its own fat until beginning to brown. Add the onion and cook for a further 5 minutes until softened.

2 Add the stock and Worcestershire sauce, season to taste and simmer for 15–20 minutes.

3 Preheat the oven to 180°C (160°C fan oven) mark 4. Put the self-raising flour, cornflour and suet into a bowl, then gradually stir in the milk to form a thick batter. Season well.

4 Put the meat into a 1.1 litre (2 pint) pie dish and cover with the batter mixture. Cook in the oven for 30–35 minutes until risen and browned.

•COOK'S TIP•

Suet is the solid white fat mainly taken from around the kidneys of animals. Shredded suet is processed suet that has been pre-grated.

Cornish Pasties

The West The Cornish pasty has been known since the 14th century, but by the 18th century it was firmly established as a Cornish food eaten by poorer working families who could only afford cheap ingredients such as potatoes, swede and onion. Meat was added later.

Serves 6 • Preparation 30 minutes • Cooking time 1¼ hours

450g (1lb) stewing steak, trimmed and cut into very small pieces
175g (6oz) potato, peeled and diced
175g (6oz) swede, peeled and diced
1 onion, chopped
1 tbsp freshly chopped thyme
1 tbsp freshly chopped flat-leafed parsley
1 tbsp Worcestershire sauce
25g (1oz) butter
1 medium egg, beaten, to glaze
salt and ground black pepper
salad to serve (optional)

For the shortcrust pastry
500g (1lb 2oz) plain flour, plus extra to dust
a pinch of salt
250g (9oz) butter, or half white vegetable fat and half butter, cut into pieces

Nutrition per serving
756 cals | 42g fat (25g sats) |
74g carbs | 1.1g salt

1 Make the pastry (see Cook's Tip). Sift the flour and salt into a bowl, add the fat and mix lightly. Using our fingertips, rub the fat into the flour until the mixture resembles fine breadcrumbs. Sprinkle 3–4 tbsp cold water evenly over the surface and stir with a round-bladed knife until the mixture begins to stick together in large lumps. If the dough seems dry, add a little extra water. With one hand, collect the dough together to form a ball. Knead lightly on a lightly floured surface for a few seconds to form a smooth, firm dough; do not over-work. Wrap in clingfilm and leave to rest in the fridge for 30 minutes before rolling out.

2 Meanwhile, put the meat into a bowl with the potato, swede and onion. Add the chopped herbs, Worcestershire sauce and seasoning, then mix well.

3 Preheat the oven to 220°C (200°C fan oven) mark 7. Divide the pastry into six and roll out each piece thinly on a lightly floured surface to a 20.5cm (8in) round. Spoon the filling on to one half of each round and top with a small knob of butter.

4 Brush the edges of the pastry with water, then fold the uncovered side over to make pasties. Press the edges firmly together to seal, then crimp them. Make a slit in the top of each pasty. Put on a baking sheet and brush the pastry with beaten egg to glaze.

5 Bake the pasties for 15 minutes. Reduce the oven temperature to 170°C (150°C fan oven) mark 3 and bake for a further 1 hour to cook the filling. Serve the pasties warm or cold with salad, if you like.

•COOK'S TIPS•

To make the pastry in a food processor, put the flour and salt into the processor bowl with the butter. Whiz until the mixture resembles fine crumbs, then add the water. Process briefly, using the pulse button, until the mixture just comes together in a ball. Knead lightly on a lightly floured surface for a few seconds to form a smooth, firm dough; do not over-work. Wrap in clingfilm and leave to rest in the fridge for 30 minutes before rolling out.

Shortcrust pastry can be stored in the fridge for up to three days, or frozen.

Veal and Ham Pie

The Midlands and The North Traditionally a British picnic food, this pie is made with hot water crust pastry, which is strong and durable enough to enclose the heavy filling without collapsing. It makes a perfect lunch, served with a green salad.

Serves 8 • Preparation 45 minutes, plus cooling and chilling • Cooking time about 3½ hours, plus cooling and chilling

3 or 4 small veal bones
1 small onion
1 bay leaf
4 black peppercorns
700g (1½ lb) diced pie veal
225g (8oz) diced cooked ham
1 tbsp freshly chopped flat-leafed parsley
grated zest and juice of 1 lemon
1 tbsp salt
½ tsp pepper
150ml (¼ pint) milk and 150ml (¼ pint) water mixed
150g (5oz) lard
450g (1lb) plain flour, plus extra to dust
1 medium egg, hard-boiled
1 medium egg, beaten
salad to serve

Nutrition per serving
617 cals | 37g fat (14g sats) |
45g carbs | 2g salt

1 Put the bones, onion, bay leaf and peppercorns into a pan and cover with water. Simmer for 20 minutes, then boil to reduce the liquid to 150ml (¼ pint). Strain and cool. Base-line a 20.5cm (8in) springform cake tin.

2 Mix together the diced veal, diced ham, parsley, lemon zest and juice, 1 tsp salt and the pepper.

3 Bring the milk and water and the lard to the boil in a pan, then gradually beat it into the flour and remaining salt in a bowl. Knead for 3–4 minutes.

4 Roll out two-thirds of the pastry on a lightly floured surface and mould into the springform cake tin. Cover and chill for 30 minutes. Keep the remaining pastry covered. Preheat the oven to 220°C (200°C fan oven) mark 7.

5 Spoon half the meat mixture and 2 tbsp cold jellied stock into the pastry case. Put the hard-boiled egg in the centre and cover with the remaining meat mixture and 2 more tbsp cold jellied stock. Roll out the remaining pastry to make a lid and put on top of the meat mixture, sealing the pastry edges well. Decorate with pastry trimmings and make a hole in the centre. Glaze with the beaten egg.

6 Bake for 30 minutes. Cover loosely with foil, reduce the oven temperature to 180°C (160°C fan oven) mark 4 and bake for a further 2½ hours. Cool.

7 Warm the remaining jellied stock until liquid, then pour into the centre hole of the pie. Chill the pie, then unmould and serve with salad.

•COOK'S TIP•

If you have no bones available for stock, use 2 tsp gelatine to 300ml (½ pint) stock.

Veal Blanquette

The Southeast Veal is a delicate, tender meat which is not fatty. It should look moist and be a good deep pink colour. This simple recipe provides a creamy sauce that enhances the flavour of the meat without masking it.

Serves 4 • Preparation 15 minutes • Cooking time 1¼ hours

700g (1½lb) pie veal, trimmed and cubed
2 medium onions, chopped
2 medium carrots, sliced
squeeze of lemon juice
1 bouquet garni (1 bay leaf, a few fresh parsley and thyme sprigs)
25g (1oz) butter
3 tbsp plain flour
1 medium egg yolk
2–3 tbsp single cream
salt and ground black pepper
4–6 streaky bacon rashers, rind removed, rolled and grilled, and freshly chopped flat-leafed parsley to garnish

Nutrition per serving
475 cals | 26g fat (12g sats) |
18g carbs | 2g salt

1 Put the meat, onions, carrots, lemon juice, bouquet garni and seasoning into a large pan with enough water to cover. Cover the pan and simmer gently for about 1 hour or until the meat is tender.
2 Strain off the cooking liquid, reserving 600ml (1 pint), and keep the meat and vegetables warm.
3 Melt the butter in a pan, stir in the flour and cook gently for 1 minute. Remove from the heat and gradually stir in the reserved liquid. Return to the heat, slowly bring to the boil and continue cooking, stirring, until the sauce thickens.
4 Adjust the seasoning, remove from the heat and when slightly cooled stir in the egg yolk and cream. Add the meat and vegetables and reheat without boiling for 5 minutes. Serve garnished with the bacon rolls and chopped parsley.

·COOK'S TIP·

A blanquette (from the French for white) is a stew, normally with pale meats such as veal or lamb, but the meats are not browned first.

PORK

Apricot and Gin-glazed Gammon

Countrywide Gammon and pineapple is a bit of a cliché, but these steaks are cooked in gin and topped with apricot butter. A quick and easy dish to do on the barbecue, or you can cook them under the grill.

Serves 4 • Preparation 10 minutes, plus marinating • Cooking time 6 minutes

4 tbsp gin
6 tbsp apricot jam
4 x 225g (8oz) gammon steaks
75g (3oz) butter, softened
2 tbsp freshly chopped flat-leafed parsley, plus extra sprigs to garnish
50g (2oz) ready-to-eat dried apricots, finely chopped
lemon juice
ground black pepper
Paprika Potatoes (see Cook's Tip) to serve

Nutrition per serving
710 cals | 43g fat (19g sats) |
20g carbs | 7g salt

1 Mix the gin and jam together and cover the gammon steaks with the mixture. Set aside for 10 minutes, or cover and chill overnight. Mix together the butter, parsley and apricots with lemon juice to taste. Season with pepper, cover and chill.
2 Preheat the barbecue or grill. Cook the gammon steaks for 2–3 minutes on each side, then serve immediately, topped with the apricot butter, garnished with parsley sprigs, and with paprika potatoes.

•COOK'S TIP•

Paprika Potatoes
Cut 550g (1¼ lb) scrubbed potatoes into wedges and cook in a pan of boiling water for 5 minutes. Drain and rinse, then toss in 3 tbsp olive oil, 2 tbsp paprika and plenty of salt and pepper. Barbecue or grill for 10 minutes or until golden and cooked through.

Pot Roast of Pork and Red Cabbage

The Eastern Counties Pork shoulder is an economical cut that is good for pot roasting. Cabbage and apple are traditional accompaniments to pork. Here they are cooked with the meat and take on a delicious flavour from the juices.

Serves 4 • Preparation 10 minutes • Cooking time about 2 hours

3 tbsp red wine vinegar
450g (1lb) red cabbage, shredded
225g (8oz) cooking apple, peeled,
cored and sliced
1 tbsp demerara sugar
1 tbsp plain flour
700g (1½lb) boneless pork shoulder,
rind removed
salt and ground black pepper
freshly chopped flat-leafed parsley
to garnish
mashed potatoes to serve

Nutrition per serving
458 cals | 29g fat (9g sats) |
16g carbs | 1g salt

1 Preheat the oven to 190°C (170°C fan oven) mark 5. Bring a large pan of water with 1 tbsp of the vinegar to the boil. When boiling, add the cabbage and bring back to the boil, then drain well.

2 Put the apple slices and the cabbage in a casserole just wide enough to hold the pork joint.

3 Add the sugar, the remaining vinegar and the flour. Season to taste and stir together well.

4 Slash the fat side of the joint several times and sprinkle with salt and pepper. Put on top of the cabbage and cover the casserole.

5 Cook in the oven for 1¾ hours or until the pork is tender. Serve the pork sliced on a warmed serving plate, surrounded by cabbage. Garnish with chopped parsley and serve the remaining cabbage in a serving dish, with mashed potatoes.

Cumberland Glazed Baked Gammon

Countrywide A ham is the leg of a pig that is cured separately and sold cooked. However, this recipe uses a gammon joint, which is cured as part of the whole side of the pig and sold uncooked. The dish makes an eye-catching centrepiece for a party table.

Serves 16 • Preparation 30 minutes • Cooking time 3½ –4¼ hours

4.5kg (10lb) smoked gammon joint, on the bone
2 celery sticks, roughly chopped
1 onion, quartered
1 carrot, roughly chopped
1 tsp black peppercorns
1 tbsp cloves
75g (3oz) redcurrant sprigs

For the Cumberland glaze
grated zest and juice of ½ lemon and ½ orange
4 tbsp redcurrant jelly
1 tsp Dijon mustard
2 tbsp port
salt and ground black pepper

Nutrition per serving
406 cals | 21g fat (7g sats) |
4g carbs | 6.3g salt

1 Put the gammon into a large pan. Add the celery, onion, carrot and peppercorns. Cover the meat and vegetables with cold water and bring to the boil, then simmer, covered, for 2¾–3½ hours, or allowing 15–20 minutes per 450g (1lb) plus 15 minutes. Lift the gammon out of the pan. Preheat the oven to 200°C (180°C fan oven) mark 6.

2 Meanwhile, make the glaze. Heat the lemon and orange zests and juices, redcurrant jelly, mustard and port in a pan to dissolve the jelly. Bring to the boil and bubble for 5 minutes or until syrupy. Season with salt and pepper to taste.

3 Remove the gammon rind and score the fat in a diamond pattern. Put the gammon into a roasting tin, then stud the fat with the cloves. Spoon the glaze evenly over the gammon joint.

4 Roast the gammon for 40 minutes, basting the meat with any juices.

Add the redcurrant sprigs 10 minutes before the end of the cooking time. Serve the gammon hot or cold, carved into thin slices, with the redcurrant sprigs.

Crisp Roast Pork with Apple Sauce

Countrywide Crunchy crackling is an important part of the meal when serving roast pork. Choose good-quality meat and score the skin only down to the fat – this will allow the fat to bubble up and baste the skin as it's cooking.

Serves 6 • Preparation 30 minutes, plus standing • Cooking time 2 hours, plus resting

1.6kg (3½ lb) boned rolled loin of pork
olive oil
1kg (2¼ lb) cooking apples
1–2 tbsp granulated sugar
1 tbsp plain flour
600ml (1 pint) chicken stock or dry cider
salt and ground black pepper
roast potatoes and green vegetables to serve (optional)

Nutrition per serving
769 cals | 50g fat (18g sats) |
22g carbs | 0.4g salt

1 Score the pork skin, sprinkle generously with salt and leave at room temperature for 1–2 hours.

2 Preheat the oven to 220°C (200°C fan oven) mark 7. Wipe the salt off the skin, rub with oil and sprinkle again with salt. Core and roughly chop the apples, then put half into a small roasting tin, sit the pork on top and roast for 30 minutes. Reduce the oven temperature to 190°C (170°C fan oven) mark 5 and roast for a further 1½ hours or until cooked.

3 Meanwhile, put the remaining apples into a pan with the sugar and 2 tbsp water, cover with a tight-fitting lid and cook until just soft. Put this sauce into a small serving dish.

4 Remove the pork from the tin and leave to rest. Skim off most of the fat, leaving about 1 tbsp and the apples in the tin. Stir in the flour until smooth, then stir in the stock or cider and bring to the boil. Bubble gently for 2–3 minutes, skimming if necessary. Taste and adjust the seasoning. Strain the sauce through a sieve into a jug, pushing through as much of the apple as possible. Slice the pork and serve with the sauce, gravy, roast potatoes and green vegetables, if you like.

Belly of Pork with Cider and Rosemary

Countrywide Belly is an increasingly popular cut of pork, and relatively inexpensive. The best cut is the thicker part of the belly, as it is leaner and sometimes more tender. Here it's combined with cider, garlic and rosemary.

Serves 8 • Preparation 30 minutes, plus cooling and chilling • Cooking time about 4½ hours

2kg (4½ lb) piece pork belly roast, on the bone
500ml bottle medium cider
600ml (1 pint) hot chicken stock
6–8 fresh rosemary sprigs
3 fat garlic cloves, halved
2 tbsp olive oil
grated zest and juice of 1 large orange and 1 lemon
3 tbsp light muscovado sugar
25g (1oz) softened butter, mixed with 1 tbsp plain flour (beurre manié, see page 124)
salt and ground black pepper
mixed vegetables to serve

Nutrition per serving
694 cals | 52g fat (19g sats) |
9g carbs | 0.5g salt

1 Preheat the oven to 150°C (130°C fan oven) mark 2. Put the pork, skin side up, in a roasting tin just large enough to hold it. Add the cider, hot stock and half the rosemary. Bring to the boil on the hob, then cover with foil and cook in the oven for 4 hours. Leave to cool in the cooking liquid.

2 Strip the leaves from the remaining rosemary and chop. Put into a pestle and mortar with the garlic, oil, orange and lemon zest, 1 tsp salt and 1 tbsp of the sugar. Pound for 3–4 minutes to make a rough paste.

3 Remove the pork from the tin (keep the cooking liquid), slice off the rind from the top layer of fat and set aside. Score the fat into a diamond pattern and rub in the rosemary paste. Cover loosely with clingfilm and chill until required.

4 Preheat the grill. Pat the rind dry with kitchen paper and put it fat side up on a foil-lined baking sheet. Cook under the hot grill, about 10cm (4in) away

from the heat, for 5 minutes. Turn it over, sprinkle lightly with salt, then grill for 7–10 minutes until crisp. Cool, then cut the crackling into rough pieces.

5 Make the gravy. Strain the cooking liquid into a pan. Add the orange and lemon juice and the remaining 2 tbsp sugar, bring to the boil and bubble until reduced by half. Whisk the butter mixture into the liquid and boil for

4–5 minutes until thickened. Set aside.

6 When almost ready to serve, preheat the oven to 220°C (200°C fan oven) mark 7. Cook the pork, uncovered, in a roasting tin for 20 minutes or until piping hot. Wrap the crackling in foil and warm in the oven for the last 5 minutes of the cooking time. Heat the gravy on the hob. Carve the pork into slices and serve with the crackling, gravy and vegetables.

Somerset Honeyed Pork Stew

The West Pork lends itself to sweet sauces with a touch of tartness which counteract the rich flavour of the meat. Pork and honey go particularly well together. Try to buy Somerset or other regional honey, which has a strong flavour and scent that recalls the flowers on which the bees have feasted.

Serves 4–6 • Preparation 10 minutes, plus soaking • Cooking time 1½–1¾ hours

450g (1lb) lean belly pork, rind removed, boned and cut into chunky cubes
225g (8oz) dried black-eyed or haricot beans, soaked overnight in cold water
1 tbsp clear honey
600ml (1 pint) chicken stock
300ml (½ pint) apple juice
1 medium onion, stuck with a few whole cloves
1 bouquet garni (1 bay leaf, a few fresh parsley and thyme sprigs)
3 medium carrots, sliced
2 leeks, trimmed and sliced
2 celery sticks, sliced
2 tbsp Worcestershire sauce
1 tbsp tomato purée
salt and ground black pepper
crusty bread to serve

Nutrition per serving
396 cals | 6g fat (2g sats) |
49g carbs | 1.9g salt

1 Cook the pork in a flameproof casserole over a brisk heat until the fat runs.

2 Drain the beans and add to the pork with the honey, stock, apple juice, onion and bouquet garni. Slowly bring to the boil, then cover and simmer for 1 hour or until the beans are just becoming tender.

3 Add the carrots, leeks and celery to the casserole with the Worcestershire sauce and tomato purée and season to taste. Continue simmering for a further 15–30 minutes until the beans are really tender. Discard the bouquet garni. Serve with crusty bread.

Toad in the Hole

The North/Countrywide The origins of the name of this dish are varied, but the recipe has been around for centuries. Filling and economical, it's a quick and easy supper dish. Use good-quality sausages for best results.

Serves 2 • Preparation 10 minutes • Cooking time 25–30 minutes

125g (4oz) plain flour, sifted _2oz_
2 large eggs, lightly beaten _1_
150ml (¼ pint) semi-skimmed milk _75ml_
2 tbsp oil _1_
4 pork sausages _2_
salt and ground black pepper
steamed carrots and broccoli or green
beans to serve

Nutrition per serving
571 cals | 31g fat (8g sats) |
57g carbs | 2.6g salt

1 Preheat the oven to 220°C (200°C fan oven) mark 7. Put the flour into a bowl, make a well in the centre and pour in the eggs and milk. Whisk the batter thoroughly and season it well with salt and pepper.
2 Put the oil and sausages in a 1 litre (1¾ pint) shallow ovenproof dish and cook in the oven for 10 minutes, turning once or twice.
3 Add the batter to the dish and continue to cook for 15–20 minutes until the batter is puffy and a rich golden colour all over. Serve immediately, with steamed carrots and broccoli or green beans.

Bacon Chops with Gooseberry Sauce

The Midlands Hard, early season gooseberries are perfect for this dish. Look for thick prime back bacon chops, good for gentle braising.

Serves 4 • Preparation 5 minutes • Cooking time 30 minutes

1 tbsp soft brown sugar
1 tsp mustard powder
4 bacon chops, about 175g (6oz) each
15g (½oz) butter
1 large onion, chopped
150ml (¼ pint) vegetable stock
125g (4oz) gooseberries, topped and tailed
ground black pepper
boiled shredded red cabbage to serve

Nutrition per serving
461 cals | 30g fat (13g sats) |
9g carbs | 6.8g salt

1 Mix together the sugar and mustard with pepper to taste and rub into both sides of the bacon chops.
2 Melt the butter in a large frying pan or flameproof casserole. Cook the onion for 2 minutes, then add the bacon chops, half the stock and the gooseberries. Simmer gently for 15 minutes.
3 Remove the chops. Put the onions and gooseberries in a blender or food processor and whiz until smooth.
4 Return the chops and purée to the pan with the remaining stock. Simmer gently for 10 minutes or until the chops are tender and cooked through. Serve at once with boiled shredded red cabbage.

Pork Chops with Mustard Sauce

The West Country This area is renowned for its pork. It's important to use spare-rib chops for this recipe, as loin chops won't be tender enough.

Serves 6 • Preparation 15 minutes • Cooking time 30 minutes

25g (1oz) butter
6 spare-rib pork chops, trimmed of fat
700g (1½lb) onions, chopped
700g (1½lb) trimmed leeks, chopped
1 garlic clove, crushed
900ml (1½ pints) milk
1 bay leaf
1 fresh thyme sprig
125ml (4fl oz) double cream or crème fraîche
3 tbsp English mustard
salt and ground black pepper
flat noodles, such as tagliatelle, to serve

Nutrition per serving
503 cals | 29g fat (14g sats) |
21g carbs | 1g salt

1 Heat the butter in a flameproof casserole. When the butter is foaming, fry the chops briskly until very light golden brown, then put to one side. Add the onions and leeks and cook gently until soft. Add the garlic and cook for 30 seconds.
2 Pour in the milk and bring to the boil. Put the chops back into the casserole, add the herbs and reduce the heat, then bubble gently for 10 minutes. When the pork is tender, transfer to plates and keep warm.
3 Bubble the sauce until reduced almost to nothing, then add the cream or crème fraîche and the mustard. Season well with salt and pepper, then pour over the chops. Serve with noodles.

Pork Chops with Savoy Cabbage Mash

The West Country Savoy cabbage is a winter vegetable and when combined with creamy mash and a luscious onion gravy makes a warming dish during the colder months. It is also the perfect meal for a family Sunday lunch.

Serves 4 • Preparation 5 minutes • Cooking time 15 minutes

5 large potatoes, peeled and chopped into chunks
½ small Savoy cabbage, sliced
50g (2oz) butter
4 pork chops
300g (11oz) ready-made rich onion gravy (or make your own, see Cook's Tip)
salt and ground black pepper

Nutrition per serving
617 cals | 32g fat (13g sats) |
48g carbs | 1.9g salt

1 Put the potatoes into a pan of lightly salted water, cover and bring to the boil, then simmer for 10–12 minutes until soft. After the potatoes have been cooking for 5 minutes, add the cabbage to the pan and continue cooking. Drain the potatoes and cabbage, return to the pan and add all but a knob of the butter, then season. Mash and keep warm.

2 Meanwhile, heat a griddle pan until hot. Rub the remaining butter into each chop and season. Fry the chops for 4–5 minutes on each side until cooked through. Put on to warm plates (reserve the juices in the pan) and leave to rest for a couple of minutes.

3 Add the gravy to the pan juices and bring to the boil, then reduce the heat and simmer for 1–2 minutes. Spoon the mash on to the plates, top with the pork chops and pour the gravy over.

•COOK'S TIP•
Onion Gravy
Melt 15g (½oz) butter and fry 1 peeled and sliced red onion over a medium heat for 10 minutes or until soft and translucent. Stir in 2 tbsp plain flour and cook for 1 minute. Gradually add 450ml (¾ pint) hot beef or chicken stock, stirring the gravy until smooth. Stir in 1 tsp tomato purée and simmer for 5 minutes until thickened. Stir in 2 tbsp chopped flat-leafed parsley and season.

Likky Pie

The West This feast-day dish with leeks, puff pastry and cream, more grammatically known as Leek Pie, has a delicate subtle flavour. Traditionally made in Cornwall, its origins go back hundreds of years.

Serves 4 • Preparation 10 minutes, plus cooling • Cooking time 1½ hours

225g (8oz) leeks, trimmed and sliced
450g (1lb) lean boneless pork, cut into
2.5cm (1in) cubes
150ml (¼ pint) milk
75ml (2fl oz) double cream
2 medium eggs, lightly beaten
215g pack puff pastry, thawed if frozen
plain flour to dust
salt and ground black pepper

Nutrition per serving
458 cals | 25g fat (12g sats) |
19g carbs | 1g salt

1 Preheat the oven to 200°C (180°C fan oven) mark 6.
2 Parboil the leeks in lightly salted water for about 5 minutes. Drain well. Fill a 1.1 litre (2 pint) pie dish or ovenproof casserole with the leeks and pork. Season to taste and pour in the milk. Cover with foil and cook in the oven for about 1 hour. (Don't worry if it looks curdled.) Remove the dish from the oven. Stir the cream into the eggs, then pour into the dish. Allow the filling to cool.
3 Preheat the oven to 220°C (200°C fan oven) mark 7. Put a pie funnel (or upturned egg cup), if you have one, in the centre of the dish. Roll out the pastry on a lightly floured surface to 5cm (2in) wider than the dish. Cut a 2.5cm (1in) strip from the outer edge and use to line the dampened rim of the pie dish. Dampen the pastry rim with water, cover with the pastry lid and seal the edges well, then knock up and flute. Make a hole in the centre of the pie for the funnel and use the pastry trimmings to decorate.
4 Cook in the oven for 25–30 minutes until risen and golden brown.

Huntingdon Fidget Pie

The Eastern Counties A lovely old-fashioned recipe – no one knows how it got its peculiar name. Bacon, onions and apples are the traditional filling and the pie was originally made around harvest time to feed the hungry workers.

Serves 4 • Preparation 15 minutes, plus chilling • Cooking time about 45 minutes

250g (9oz) plain flour
125g (4oz) butter, diced
450g (1lb) back bacon, rind removed
and roughly chopped
2 medium onions, roughly chopped
350g (12oz) cooking apples, peeled,
cored and roughly chopped
1 tbsp freshly chopped flat-leafed
parsley
450ml (¾ pint) medium-dry cider
1 medium egg, beaten, to glaze
salt and ground black pepper

Nutrition per serving
526 cals | 26g fat (15g sats) |
56g carbs | 3.3g salt

1 To make the pastry, sift 225g (8oz) of the flour and a pinch of salt into a bowl. Rub in the butter until the mixture resembles breadcrumbs. Add just enough water to mix to a firm dough. Gather the dough into a ball and knead lightly. Wrap the dough in foil and chill for 30 minutes.
2 Meanwhile, combine the bacon, onions and apples in a 600ml (1 pint) pie dish. Add the parsley and season.
3 Blend the remaining flour with the cider a little at a time, then pour into the pie dish.
4 Preheat the oven to 190°C (170°C fan oven) mark 5. Roll out the pastry. Cut out a thin strip long enough to go around the rim of the pie dish. Moisten the rim with water and put the pastry strip on the rim. Press down lightly all the way around. Moisten the strip of pastry, then put the lid on top and press to seal. Crimp the edge. Make a diagonal cross in the centre almost to the edges of the dish, then fold the pastry back to reveal the filling. Brush the pastry with the egg.
5 Bake in the oven for about 45 minutes or until the pastry is golden and the filling is cooked. Serve the pie hot with a green vegetable or cold with a mixed salad.

•COOK'S TIP•

Potatoes can be added to make the dish even more sustaining. Just peel, cube and parboil, then drain and combine with the bacon, onion and apples.

Raised Pork Pie

The Midlands Melton Mowbray claims to be the originator of this succulent pork pie, which these days is made throughout the country, but their pies have PDO designation (see page 53). If you can find an old-fashioned pie mould, so much the better.

Serves 8 • Preparation 45 minutes, plus cooling and chilling • Cooking time about 3½ hours, plus cooling and chilling

3 or 4 small veal bones
1 small onion
1 bay leaf
4 black peppercorns
900g (2lb) boneless leg or shoulder of pork, cubed
¼ tsp cayenne pepper
¼ tsp ground ginger
¼ tsp ground mace
¼ tsp dried sage
¼ tsp dried marjoram
1 tbsp salt
½ tsp pepper
150ml (¼ pint) milk and 150ml (¼ pint) water mixed
150g (5oz) lard
450g (1lb) plain flour, plus extra to dust
1 medium egg, beaten
salad to serve

Nutrition per serving
617 cals | 37g fat (14g sats) |
45g carbs | 2g salt

1 Put the bones, onion, bay leaf and peppercorns into a pan and cover with water. Bring to the boil, then simmer for 20 minutes. Boil to reduce the liquid to 150ml (¼ pint). Strain and cool. Base-line a 20.5cm (8in) springform cake tin.

2 Mix the pork with the spices and herbs, 1 tsp of the salt and the pepper.

3 Bring the milk, water and lard to the boil in a pan, then gradually beat it into the flour and remaining salt in a bowl. Knead for 3–4 minutes.

4 Roll out two-thirds of the pastry on a lightly floured surface and mould into the prepared cake tin. Cover and chill for 30 minutes. Keep the remaining pastry covered. Preheat the oven to 220°C (200°C fan oven) mark 7.

5 Spoon the meat mixture and 4 tbsp cold stock into the pastry case. Roll out the remaining pastry to make a lid and put on top of the meat mixture, sealing the pastry edges well. Decorate with pastry trimmings and make a hole in the centre. Glaze with the beaten egg.

6 Bake for 30 minutes. Cover loosely with foil, reduce the oven temperature to 180°C (160°C fan oven) mark 4 and bake for a further 2½ hours. Leave to cool.

7 Warm the remaining jellied stock until liquid, then pour into the centre hole of the pie. Chill and serve with salad.

•COOK'S TIP•

If you have no bones available for stock, use 2 tsp gelatine to 300ml (½ pint) stock.

Sausage Rolls

Countrywide A favourite party food, and a quick and convenient snack, sausage rolls are universally popular. Home-made sausage rolls, made with good pastry and pure sausage meat, are well worth the effort.

Makes 28 • Preparation 25 minutes • Cooking time 30 minutes

450g (1lb) puff pastry, thawed if frozen
450g (1lb) pork sausage meat
flour to dust
milk to brush
beaten egg to glaze

Nutrition per serving
119 cals | 9g fat (2g sats) |
8g carbs | 0.4g salt

1 Preheat the oven to 220°C (200°C fan oven) mark 7. Roll out half the puff pastry on a lightly floured surface to a 40.5 × 20.5cm (16 × 8in) rectangle; cut lengthways into two strips.

2 Divide the sausage meat into four, dust with flour and form two portions into rolls, the length of the pastry. Lay a sausage-meat roll on each strip of pastry. Brush the pastry edges with a little milk, fold one side of the pastry over and press the long edges together to seal. Repeat with the remaining pastry and sausage meat. Trim the ends.

3 Brush the pastry with beaten egg to glaze and cut each roll into 5cm (2in) lengths. Make two or three slits in the top of each one.

4 Transfer to a baking sheet and cook in the oven for 15 minutes. Reduce the oven temperature to 180°C (160°C fan oven) mark 4 and cook for a further 15 minutes. Transfer to a wire rack. Serve hot or cold.

TRY SOMETHING DIFFERENT

Add 1 hot red chilli, seeded and finely chopped (see Cook's Tip, page 74), 1 tbsp freshly grated ginger and a handful of freshly chopped coriander leaves to the pork sausage meat.

Oxford Sausages

The Midlands An Oxford butcher probably created this recipe in the days when every shop sold its own special home-made sausages. These are succulent and meaty, well flavoured with herbs and lemon. They are shaped in the hands before frying, and do not have skins.

Makes about 18 • Preparation 20 minutes • Cooking time 20 minutes

450g (1lb) lean boneless pork, minced
or very finely chopped
450g (1lb) lean boneless veal, minced
or very finely chopped
350g (12oz) shredded suet
225g (8oz) fresh breadcrumbs
grated zest of ½ lemon
1 tsp freshly grated nutmeg
2 tbsp freshly chopped mixed herbs or
1 tsp dried mixed herbs
1 tsp freshly chopped sage or 1 pinch
of dried sage
1 medium egg yolk, lightly beaten
plain flour for coating
vegetable oil for shallow-frying
salt and ground black pepper
mashed potatoes and a green
vegetable or grilled bacon and
tomatoes to serve

Nutrition per serving
267 cals | 19g fat (10g sats) |
12g carbs | 0.6g salt

1 Put the minced pork and veal into a large mixing bowl and add the suet, breadcrumbs, lemon zest, nutmeg and herbs. Mix together and season to taste. Add the egg yolk to the mixture and mix well with a fork until all the ingredients are thoroughly combined and bound together.

2 With floured hands, form the mixture into sausage shapes. Coat each sausage in flour, shaking off any excess.

3 Heat a little vegetable oil in a pan and cook the sausages, turning frequently, until evenly browned and cooked through. Serve the sausages with mashed potatoes and a green vegetable as a main meal, or with grilled bacon and tomatoes for breakfast.

CHICKEN & POULTRY

Classic Roast Chicken

Countrywide A perennial favourite, roast chicken has a luxurious aroma and flavour, and it makes an excellent Sunday lunch or special meal with very little preparation. Buy the best chicken you can afford; it will repay you in flavour and texture.

Serves 5 • Preparation 30 minutes • Cooking time about 1 hour 20 minutes, plus resting

1.4kg (3lb) chicken
2 garlic cloves
1 onion, cut into wedges
2 tsp sea salt
2 tsp ground black pepper
4 fresh flat-leafed parsley sprigs
4 fresh tarragon sprigs
2 bay leaves
50g (2oz) butter, cut into cubes
salt and ground black pepper

For the stuffing
40g (1½ oz) butter
1 small onion, chopped
1 garlic clove, crushed
75g (3oz) fresh white breadcrumbs
finely grated zest and juice of 1 small lemon, halves reserved for the chicken
2 tbsp each freshly chopped flat-leafed parsley and tarragon
1 medium egg yolk

For the gravy
200ml (7fl oz) white wine
1 tbsp Dijon mustard
450ml (¾ pint) hot chicken stock
25g (1oz) butter, mixed with 25g (1oz) plain flour (beurre manié, see Cook's Tip)

Nutrition per serving
682 cals | 49g fat (21g sats) |
17g carbs | 1g salt

1 To make the stuffing, melt the butter in a pan, add the onion and garlic and fry for 5–10 minutes until soft. Cool, then add the remaining ingredients, stirring in the egg yolk last. Season well.

2 Preheat the oven to 190°C (170°C fan oven) mark 5. Put the chicken on a board, breast upwards, then put the garlic, onion, reserved lemon halves and half the salt, pepper and herb sprigs into the body cavity.

3 Lift the loose skin at the neck and fill the cavity with stuffing. Turn the bird on to its breast and pull the neck flap over the opening to cover the stuffing. Rest the wing tips across it and truss the chicken (see step 4, page 135). Weigh the stuffed bird to calculate the cooking time and allow 20 minutes per 450g (1lb), plus an extra 20 minutes.

4 Put the chicken on a rack in a roasting tin. Season with the remaining salt and pepper, then top with the remaining herbs and the bay leaves. Dot with the butter and roast, basting halfway through, until cooked and the juices run clear when the thickest part of the thigh is pierced with a skewer.

5 Put the chicken on a serving dish, cover with foil and leave to rest while you make the gravy. Pour off all but about 3 tbsp fat from the tin, put the tin over a high heat, add the wine and boil for 2 minutes. Add the mustard and hot stock and bring back to the boil. Gradually whisk in knobs of the butter mixture until smooth, then season with salt and pepper. Carve the chicken and serve with the stuffing and gravy.

.COOK'S TIP.

Beurre Manié
A beurre manié is a mixture of equal parts of softened butter and flour that has been kneaded together to form a paste. It is used to thicken sauces and stews and is whisked in towards the end of cooking, then boiled briefly to allow it to thicken.

Stoved Chicken

Scotland Sometimes also called 'stovies', this Scottish dish derives from the French *étouffer*, to cook in a closed pot, and dates from the Scottish/French links of the 17th century. It makes a filling family dish and can safely be left to its own devices; a little extra cooking will not spoil the flavour.

Serves 4 • Preparation 15 minutes • Cooking time about 2½ hours

25g (1oz) butter, plus a little extra
1 tbsp vegetable oil
4 chicken quarters, halved
125g (4oz) lean back bacon, rind removed and chopped
1.1kg (2½ lb) floury potatoes, such as King Edwards, peeled and cut into 5mm (¼ in) slices
2 large onions, sliced
2 tsp freshly chopped thyme or ½ tsp dried thyme
600ml (1 pint) chicken stock
salt and ground black pepper
snipped fresh chives to garnish

Nutrition per serving
854 cals | 45g fat (14g sats) |
55g carbs | 3g salt

1 Preheat the oven to 150°C (130°C fan oven) mark 2. Heat half the butter and the oil in a large frying pan and fry the chicken and bacon for 5 minutes or until lightly browned.

2 Layer half the potato slices, then half the onion slices in the bottom of a large casserole. Season well, add the thyme and dot with half the remaining butter.

3 Add the chicken and bacon, season to taste and dot with the remaining butter. Cover with the remaining onions and finally a layer of potatoes. Season and dot with a little more butter. Pour the stock over.

4 Cover and cook in the oven for about 2½ hours or until the chicken is tender and the potatoes are cooked, adding a little more hot stock if necessary.

5 Just before serving sprinkle with snipped chives.

Chicken Casserole

Countrywide Full of vegetables and succulent chicken, this slow-cooked casserole is healthy as well as very tasty and is sure to please all the family. It will happily sit, cooking away, for 5–6 hours while you get on with other things.

Serves 6 • Preparation 15 minutes • Cooking time 5–6 hours on Low

1 tbsp sunflower oil
1.4kg (3lb) chicken
1 fresh rosemary sprig
2 bay leaves
1 red onion, cut into wedges
2 carrots, cut into chunks
2 leeks, trimmed and cut into chunks
2 celery sticks, cut into chunks
12 baby new potatoes, halved if large
900ml (1½ pints) hot chicken stock
200g (7oz) green beans, trimmed
salt and ground black pepper

Nutrition per serving
323 cals | 18g fat (5g sats) |
17g carbs | 0.9g salt

1 Heat the oil in a large pan over a medium heat. Add the chicken and fry until browned all over. Put the chicken into the slow cooker, along with the herbs and all the vegetables except the green beans. Season well.

2 Pour in the hot stock, cover and cook on Low for 5–6 hours until the chicken is cooked through. Add the beans for the last hour, or cook separately in lightly salted boiling water and stir into the casserole once it's cooked. To test that the chicken is cooked, pierce the thickest part of the leg with a skewer – the juices should run clear.

3 Remove the chicken and spoon the vegetables into six bowls. Carve the chicken and divide among the bowls, then ladle the cooking liquid over.

.COOK'S TIP.
Omit the baby new potatoes and serve with mashed potatoes.

Cornish Caudle Chicken Pie

The West The caudle in this rich and tasty pie is the mixture of egg and cream that is poured into the filling towards the end of cooking time. Recipes for chicken served in an egg-thickened sauce have been popular for centuries. Eat this pie warm, or cold.

Serves 4 • Preparation 15 minutes, plus cooling • Cooking time 1½ hours, plus standing

15g (½ oz) butter
1 tbsp vegetable oil
1 medium onion, finely chopped
4 chicken drumsticks or thighs, skinned and boned
2 tbsp freshly chopped flat-leafed parsley
4 spring onions, trimmed and chopped
150ml (¼ pint) milk
215g pack puff pastry, thawed if frozen
plain flour to dust
150ml (¼ pint) soured cream
2 medium eggs, beaten
salt and ground black pepper

Nutrition per serving
522 cals | 37g fat (18g sats) |
27g carbs | 1g salt

1 Preheat the oven to 180°C (160°C fan oven) mark 4. Heat the butter and oil in a small frying pan, add the onion, and cover and cook over a low heat until softened but not browned. Using a slotted spoon, transfer to a 1.1 litre (2 pint) pie dish.

2 Add the chicken to the pan and cook until evenly browned. Arrange on top of the onion in a single layer. Stir the parsley, spring onions, milk and seasoning into the pan and bring gently to the boil. Simmer for 2–3 minutes, then pour over the chicken.

3 Cover with foil and cook in the oven for 30 minutes or until the chicken is tender. Remove from the oven and leave to cool.

4 Meanwhile, roll out the pastry on a lightly floured surface until about 2.5cm (1in) larger all round than the pie dish. Leave the pastry to relax while the filling is cooling.

5 Preheat the oven to 220°C (200°C fan oven) mark 7. Cut off a strip from all round the edge of the pastry. Place the strip on the rim of the pie dish, moisten with a little water, then place the pastry lid on top. Crimp the edges and make a small hole in the top. Beat the soured cream and egg together, then brush the top of the pie with a little of the mixture. Bake in the oven for 15–20 minutes until a light golden brown. Reduce the oven temperature to 180°C (160°C fan oven) mark 4.

6 Pour the remaining soured cream and egg mixture into the pie through the hole. Shake the dish to distribute the cream mixture and return the pie to the oven for 15 minutes. Remove from the oven and leave to stand in a warm place for 5–10 minutes before serving, or cool completely and serve cold.

Chicken and Bacon Pie

Countrywide In the past, poultry and game pies were elaborate affairs with a thick pastry crust that acted as a seal and was not meant to be eaten. Nowadays our pies are simpler and the pastry is very much part of them. Here, buttery puff pastry provides the lid.

Serves 4 • Preparation 30 minutes, plus cooling • Cooking time about 55 minutes

1 tbsp olive oil
4 skinless, boneless chicken breasts, cut into 2.5cm (1in) cubes
1 medium onion, sliced
1 carrot, roughly chopped
50g (2oz) smoked streaky bacon, rind removed and chopped
1 tbsp plain flour, plus extra to dust
200ml (7fl oz) chicken stock
100ml (3½ fl oz) double cream
25g (1oz) frozen peas
1½ tsp wholegrain mustard
1 tbsp freshly chopped tarragon
175g (6oz) puff pastry, thawed if frozen
1 medium egg, beaten
salt and ground black pepper

Nutrition per serving
554 cals | 34g fat (6g sats) |
24g carbs | 1.3g salt

1 Heat half the oil in a large pan, then brown the chicken in batches. Remove from the pan and put to one side. Add the remaining oil and fry the onion and carrot for 10 minutes. Add the bacon and cook for 3 minutes.
2 Stir in the flour and cook for 1 minute. Gradually add the stock, stirring well. Add the cream and return the chicken and any juices to the pan. Simmer for 5 minutes or until the chicken is cooked.
3 Add the peas, mustard and tarragon, then check the seasoning. Leave to cool a little.
4 Preheat the oven to 200°C (180°C fan oven) mark 6. Put a pie funnel, if you have one, in the centre of a 1 litre (1¾ pint) pie dish or ovenproof casserole and tip in the filling. Roll out the pastry on a lightly floured surface to make a lid and cut a slit for the pie funnel. Brush the edge of the pastry all round with the egg, then lay the

pastry, brushed side down, over the dish, press to seal and trim with a sharp knife. Brush with beaten egg and cook in the oven for 25–30 minutes until golden.

Get Ahead
• Assemble the pie, then cover and chill for up to two days.
• To use, brush with beaten egg and complete the recipe.

Chicken in Red Wine with Raisins

The Southeast This is a medieval recipe originally made with rabbit, but equally good with chicken. The spicy and sweetish sauce is used to marinate the meat and fruits before cooking – the chicken takes on a marvellous flavour and the raisins and apricots become juicy and plump.

Serves 4 • Preparation 10 minutes, plus marinating • Cooking time 50 minutes

300ml (½ pint) red wine
3 tbsp red wine vinegar
125g (4oz) seedless raisins
175g (6oz) ready-to-eat dried apricots, halved
1 tsp ground ginger
1 tsp ground cinnamon
1cm (½ in) piece fresh root ginger, peeled and grated
4 cloves
4 juniper berries, lightly crushed
4 boneless chicken breasts, with skin on, about 175g (6oz) each
2 tbsp plain wholemeal flour
15g (½ oz) butter
1 tbsp vegetable oil
300ml (½ pint) chicken stock
salt and ground black pepper
orange segments to garnish
boiled rice to serve

Nutrition per serving
535 cals | 17g fat (4g sats) |
38g carbs | 1.2g salt

1 Put the wine, vinegar, raisins, apricots, ground ginger, cinnamon, fresh ginger, cloves and juniper berries into a dish. Add the chicken breasts and spoon the liquid over them. Cover and leave to marinate in a cool place for 3–4 hours or overnight.

2 Remove the chicken from the marinade and dry with kitchen paper. Season the flour with salt and pepper, then coat the chicken in the flour. Heat the butter and oil in a large flameproof casserole, add the chicken, skin side down, and fry until lightly browned, then turn it over and fry the other side. Drain on kitchen paper.

3 Pour off any excess fat from the casserole, then stir in the chicken stock, reserved marinade and fruit and bring to the boil. Return the chicken to the casserole, cover tightly and simmer for about 30 minutes, until the chicken is tender.

4 Transfer the chicken to a warmed serving plate and keep warm. Boil the liquid until reduced and thickened, then pour over the chicken. Garnish with orange segments and serve with boiled rice.

Chicken Parcels

Countrywide These neat puff pastry pasties are filled with a lovely, spicy mixture of chicken chunks, carrots and onions. They are perfect picnic food, as they can be made in advance and eaten cold with the fingers but are also good served hot with accompanying vegetables.

Serves 4 • Preparation 10 minutes • Cooking time 30–35 minutes, plus cooling

15g (½ oz) butter
1 small onion, chopped
2 medium carrots, diced
1 tbsp plain wholemeal flour
1 tsp mild curry powder
300ml (½ pint) chicken stock
1 tsp lemon juice
225g (8oz) cooked boneless chicken, chopped
368g pack puff pastry, thawed if frozen
plain flour to dust
1 medium egg, beaten, to glaze
salt and ground black pepper
mixed salad to serve

Nutrition per serving
364 cals | 21g fat (12g sats) |
25g carbs | 1.5g salt

1 Preheat the oven to 220°C (200°C fan oven) mark 7. Melt the butter in a large pan, add the onion and carrots, cover and cook for 4–5 minutes until the onion is transparent. Stir in the flour and curry powder and cook, stirring, for 1 minute. Remove from the heat and gradually stir in the stock. Bring to the boil, stirring continuously, then simmer for 2–3 minutes until thickened.

2 Reduce the heat, add the lemon juice and chicken and season to taste. Leave to cool.

3 When the chicken mixture is cool, roll out the pastry on a lightly floured surface to a 35.5cm (14in) square. Using a sharp knife, cut into four squares.

4 Put the pastry on dampened baking sheets, then spoon the chicken mixture on to the pastry, leaving a border around the edges. Brush the edges of each square lightly with water. Fold each square in half, then seal and crimp the edges to make a parcel.

5 Make two small slashes on the top of each parcel and brush with beaten egg to glaze.

6 Cook in the oven for 15–20 minutes until the pastry is golden brown. Serve with a mixed salad.

Duck with Green Peas

The Eastern Counties In this mouthwatering recipe the vegetables are cooked around the duck and take on plenty of flavour, yet without being too fatty. If fresh peas are not in season – they are only available from June to August – you can use frozen instead.

Serves 4 • Preparation 15 minutes • Cooking time about 2½ hours

1 oven-ready duck, weighing about
2kg (4½ lb), thawed if frozen
16 pickling or small onions
50g (2oz) smoked streaky bacon
rashers, rind removed and diced
450g (1lb) shelled fresh or frozen peas
a few sprigs of fresh herbs, such as
rosemary, thyme, sage
4 tbsp chicken stock
salt and ground black pepper

Nutrition per serving
575 cals | 24g fat (7g sats) |
32g carbs | 1.5g salt

1 Preheat the oven to 180°C (160°C fan oven) mark 4. Weigh the duck, prick the skin all over with a sharp skewer or fork and rub with salt. Place the duck on a wire rack or trivet in a roasting tin and roast for 30–35 minutes per 450g (1lb).

2 Thirty minutes before the end of cooking time, take the tin out of the oven, then carefully remove the duck on its rack from the tin and put to one side. Drain off the fat from the roasting tin, transferring 2 tbsp of it to a pan and discarding the remainder. Add the onions to the pan and cook on the hob, turning frequently, until lightly browned. Add the bacon and cook for 2 minutes, until the fat starts to run.

3 If using fresh peas, blanch them for 3 minutes, refresh and drain well. Do not blanch frozen peas. Mix the peas with the onions, bacon and herbs and season to taste with pepper.

4 Stir the stock into the sediment in the roasting tin, then stir in the pea mixture. Return the duck to the roasting tin, still on the rack, put back into the oven and continue cooking for the remaining 30 minutes. Serve the duck on a large plate surrounded by the vegetables and the cooking juices.

Derwentwater Duck with Cumberland Sauce

The North Game flourishes on the moors and lakes of the North, and the wild duck of Derwentwater are especially valued for their tenderness and flavour. You can, of course, use any other duck for this recipe; the rich flesh is admirably partnered by the sweet-sharp flavour of Cumberland sauce.

Serves 4 • Preparation 10 minutes • Cooking time about 1 hour

4 duck legs
finely shredded zest and juice of
1 large orange
finely shredded zest and juice of
1 lemon
4 tbsp redcurrant jelly
2 tsp cornflour
4 tbsp port
2 tbsp brandy
salt and ground black pepper
fresh watercress sprigs and orange
slices to garnish

Nutrition per serving
451 cals | 19g fat (6g sats) |
15g carbs | 1.1g salt

1 Preheat the oven to 190°C (170°F fan oven) mark 5. Prick the duck portions all over with a sharp skewer or fork, then sprinkle with salt and pepper.
2 Put the duck portions on a wire rack over a roasting tin. Roast for 45–60 minutes until the skin is crisp and the juices run clear when the thickest part of the duck is pricked with a skewer.
3 Meanwhile, make the sauce. Put the orange and lemon juices and zests into a small pan, cover and simmer gently for 5 minutes.
4 Add the redcurrant jelly and let it dissolve slowly over a gentle heat. Mix the cornflour with the port, then stir into the sauce and bring to the boil, stirring until the sauce thickens.
5 When the duck portions are cooked put them on to a warmed serving dish and keep hot while the sauce is finished. Pour off the fat from the roasting tin, leaving the cooking juices behind, then add the brandy and stir over a gentle heat to stir in the sediment in the bottom of the tin.
6 Add the orange sauce, stir well and serve with the duck. Garnish with sprigs of watercress and orange slices.

Roast Turkey with Parsley, Sage and Thyme

Countrywide The tradition of having turkey for Christmas lunch has been around for centuries, although they were a luxury affordable by few until the beginning of the last century. However, there's no reason why this splendid bird can't be enjoyed at any time of the year.

Serves 16 • Preparation 40 minutes, plus cooling and chilling • Cooking time 3¾ hours

6.3kg (14lb) turkey
2 small red onions, cut into wedges
2 lemons, cut into wedges
6 whole garlic cloves
8 fresh thyme sprigs
8 fresh sage leaves
8 fresh flat-leafed parsley sprigs
250ml (9fl oz) olive oil
roast vegetables to serve

For the seasoning
1 tbsp whole pink peppercorns
2 tsp sea salt
2 tbsp paprika
2 tbsp celery salt

For the stuffing
4 tbsp olive oil
2 large onions, finely chopped
4 garlic cloves, crushed
150g (5oz) fresh white breadcrumbs
75g (3oz) medium cornmeal or polenta
100g (3½ oz) hazelnuts, toasted and chopped
finely grated zest of 2 lemons and juice of 1 lemon
4 tbsp freshly chopped flat-leafed parsley
4 tbsp freshly chopped sage
2 medium eggs, lightly beaten
salt and ground black pepper

Nutrition per serving
280 cals | 10g fat (2g sats) | 11g carbs | 2.2g salt

1 To make the stuffing, heat the oil in a pan. Add the onions and garlic and fry gently for 10 minutes to soften but not brown. Tip into a bowl to cool. Meanwhile, put the breadcrumbs, cornmeal or polenta, hazelnuts, lemon zest, parsley, sage and eggs into a large bowl and squeeze in the lemon juice. Add the cooled onion and garlic and season with salt and pepper. Stir to bind together, and leave to cool.

2 To make the seasoning, put the peppercorns, sea salt, paprika and celery salt into a mortar and pound with a pestle to crush, or whiz in a mini processor. Stand the turkey upright on a board, with the parson's nose (the rear end) facing upwards. Sprinkle the inside cavity with 1 tbsp of the peppercorn seasoning, then pack the cavity with half the onions and lemon wedges, garlic cloves, thyme and sage and all the parsley sprigs.

3 Sit the turkey with the parson's nose facing away from you. Lift up the loose skin at the neck end with one hand and, using the other, fill the cavity with handfuls of cold stuffing. Turn the turkey over on to its breast, then lift the neck flap up and over the stuffing to cover and bring the wing tips round on top.

4 Thread a trussing needle with 2m (6ft) fine string and sew the neck flap to the turkey. Push the skewer firmly through the wings, twist the string around the ends and pull to tighten so that both wings are snug against the breast. Turn the turkey over, tuck in the parson's nose, cross the legs together, then bring the string up and over the legs and wrap around tightly, finishing with a double knot to secure. Cut off any excess.

5 Pour the oil into a large roasting tin. Immerse a piece of muslin, about 60cm (24in) long, in it to coat completely, then stretch it out, with the edges overhanging the tin. Sit the turkey on top and sprinkle with the remaining peppercorn seasoning. Scatter over the remaining thyme and sage, then arrange the remaining lemon and onion wedges and the garlic cloves around the bird. Bring the muslin up and over the turkey to wrap completely, then turn it over so that it's breast side down in the tin. Over-wrap with clingfilm and leave to chill overnight in the bottom of the fridge. Remember to take it out 30 minutes before cooking so that it has time to come to room temperature.

6 Remove the muslin and keep the turkey breast side down. Preheat the oven to 180°C (160°C fan oven) mark 4. Roast the turkey for about 3¾ hours, basting occasionally to keep the flesh moist. Turn the turkey over after cooking for 1 hour 50 minutes. To check that the turkey is cooked, pierce the thickest part of the thigh with a skewer – the juices should run clear. Serve with roasted vegetables.

Turkey and Leek Crumble

Countrywide A hint of mustard gives a good tang to the crumble topping, which gets an extra-crunchy texture from porridge oats. Leeks are available for most of the year, though they may be harder to find for three months or so in high summer.

Serves 4 • Preparation 10 minutes • Cooking time 1 hour 5 minutes

75g (3oz) butter
450g (1lb) boneless turkey, skinned and cubed
150g (5oz) plain wholemeal flour
450ml (¾ pint) milk
2 tsp freshly chopped sage
450g (1lb) leeks, trimmed and sliced
125g (4oz) small button mushrooms
1 tsp mustard powder
1 tsp paprika
50g (2oz) Cheddar cheese, grated
25g (1oz) porridge oats
salt and ground black pepper

Nutrition per serving
532 cals | 26g fat (15g sats) |
37g carbs | 1.5g salt

1 Melt 25g (1oz) of the butter in a large pan, then add the turkey and fry for 5–6 minutes until lightly browned.
2 Stir in 25g (1oz) of the flour and cook for 2–3 minutes, then gradually blend in the milk. Heat, whisking continuously, until the sauce thickens, boils and is smooth. Simmer gently for 15 minutes. Season to taste.
3 Preheat the oven to 200°C (180°C fan oven) mark 6. Add the sage, leeks and mushrooms to the sauce and simmer for 10 minutes.
4 Rub the remaining butter into the remaining flour, the mustard and paprika, then stir in the cheese and oats to make a crumble mixture.
5 Pour the turkey and leek sauce into a 1.7 litre (3 pint) ovenproof serving dish. Sprinkle with the crumble mixture and cook in the oven for 25 minutes.

•COOK'S TIP•

You could use turkey legs for this recipe, which are available in most supermarkets. Skin them, then take the meat off the bone and chop into cubes.

Roast Michaelmas Goose with Apples and Prunes

Northern Ireland and the North 'Green' geese, which had fed on pasture, made a traditional feast for Michaelmas, in late September, and were less fatty than Christmas geese. It was thought that if you ate goose at Michaelmas you would have good luck for the rest of the year.

Serves 12 • Preparation 15 minutes • Cooking time 2¾–3¼ hours

4–5kg (9–11lb) oven-ready goose, with giblets, thawed if frozen
15g (½oz) butter
1 large onion, chopped
450g (1lb) ready-to-eat prunes
4 tbsp port
1 tbsp freshly chopped sage or 1 tsp dried sage
125g (4oz) fresh wholemeal breadcrumbs
6 Cox's Orange Pippin apples
300ml (½ pint) dry white wine
salt and ground black pepper
boiled or mashed potatoes and red cabbage to serve

Nutrition per serving
670 cals | 39g fat (14g sats) |
27g carbs | 1.3g salt

---

1 Preheat the oven to 200°C (180°C fan oven) mark 6. Prick the skin of the goose all over with a sharp skewer or fork and pull the inside fat out of the bird and reserve. Rub salt over the skin.

2 To make the stuffing, melt the butter in a large frying pan, add the onion and cook for 5–6 minutes until softened. Separate the goose liver from the giblets and chop finely, then add to the onion and cook gently for 2–3 minutes.

3 Remove the stones from half the prunes and discard. Chop the prunes roughly and stir into the onion with the port. Cover and simmer gently for 5 minutes. Add the sage and breadcrumbs and mix thoroughly together. Season the stuffing mixture to taste.

4 Spoon the stuffing into the neck end of the goose, then truss with strong cotton or fine string (see step 4, page 135). Weigh the bird, then put on a wire rack placed in a roasting tin. Cover the breast with the reserved fat and then with foil. Roast for 15 minutes per 450g (1lb) plus 15 minutes, basting frequently.

5 Thirty minutes before the end of the cooking time, take the tin out of the oven, then carefully remove the goose on its rack from the tin and put to one side. Drain off the fat from the tin and discard. Core the apples and cut into eighths, then add to the tin with the remaining prunes and the wine. Return the bird to the roasting tin, still on its rack. Remove the foil and the fat and cook in the oven, uncovered, for the last 30 minutes.

6 Serve the roast goose with the cooking juices and the apples and prunes. Plain boiled or mashed potatoes go well with the richness of goose. Braised red cabbage is also a traditional accompaniment.

OFFAL

Welsh Faggots

Wales Also known as 'poor man's goose' or 'savoury duck', faggots are a filling and economical dish. 'Faggot' is a corruption of *fegato*, the Italian for liver.

Serves 4 • Preparation 10 minutes • Cooking time 40 minutes

oil to grease
450g (1lb) pig's liver
2 medium onions, roughly chopped
75g (3oz) shredded beef suet
400g (14oz) fresh breadcrumbs
1 tsp finely chopped fresh sage or
½ tsp dried sage
300ml (½ pint) boiling beef stock
salt and ground black pepper
puréed dried peas to serve

Nutrition per serving
398 cals | 21g fat (11g sats) |
28g carbs | 2g salt

1 Preheat the oven to 180°C (160°C fan oven) mark 4. Generously grease a shallow ovenproof dish. Put the liver and onions into a food processor or blender and chop finely. Tip out into a bowl and stir in the suet, breadcrumbs and sage. Season to taste.

2 Roll the mixture into 12 balls and put them in the prepared dish.

3 Pour the boiling stock into the dish, cover and cook in the oven for about 30 minutes or until the juices run clear. Uncover and continue cooking for 10 minutes. Traditionally, faggots are served with a purée of dried peas.

Liver and Onions

Countrywide Calves' liver would be ideal in this dish, but it's not always easy to find and tends to be pricey. Lamb's liver also gives excellent results.

Serves 4 • Preparation 10 minutes • Cooking time 20–25 minutes

25g (1oz) butter
450g (1lb) onions, sliced or chopped
½ tsp freshly chopped sage (optional)
450g (1lb) calf's or lamb's liver, cut into thin strips
salt and ground black pepper

Nutrition per serving
204 cals | 9g fat (4g sats) |
9g carbs | 0.9g salt

1 Melt the butter in a frying pan, add the onions and fry gently until they begin to colour, then add seasoning and the sage, if using. Cover the frying pan and simmer very gently for 10 minutes or until the onions are soft.

2 Add the liver strips to the onions, increase the heat slightly and continue cooking for 5–10 minutes, stirring all the time, until the liver is just cooked. Transfer to a warmed serving dish.

Pressed Ox Tongue

Countrywide Until fairly recently, home pressing and cooking of tongue was a regular occurrence, whereas these days it's generally bought ready cooked and sliced. However, it's easy enough to do at home and one tongue will feed about a dozen people.

Serves 12 • Preparation 20 minutes, plus soaking • Cooking time about 4½ hours, plus chilling

1.6–1.8kg (3½–4lb) pickled ox tongue
1 onion, thickly sliced
1 carrot, thickly sliced
4 celery sticks, thickly sliced
2 tbsp wine vinegar
2 bay leaves
12 black peppercorns
1 tsp powdered gelatine

Nutrition per serving
301 cals | 23g fat (8g sats)
28g carbs | 4g salt

1 A day in advance of cooking, scrub and rinse the tongue under cold water. Put into a large bowl, cover with cold water and leave to soak overnight.

2 Drain the tongue, then roll into a neat shape and secure with a skewer. Wrap in a single thickness of muslin, tying both ends together. Put the tongue into a large pan, cover with cold water, bring to the boil and boil for 1 minute. Drain, rinse with cold water, then return to the pan and cover with fresh water. Add the vegetables to the pan with the wine vinegar, bay leaves and peppercorns. Bring to the boil, then cover and simmer gently for about 4 hours.

3 Lift the tongue on to a large plate, reserving the cooking liquid. Unwrap, ease out the skewer and use it to pierce the thickest piece; if it slips in easily, the tongue is cooked. If not, simmer for a little longer.

4 Put the tongue into a colander and rinse with cold water until cool enough to handle; this will help to loosen the skin. Using a sharp knife, make a shallow slit along the underside. Peel the skin off in strips, starting from the tip end. Ease out the bones and gristle lying at the base.

5 Tightly curl the warm tongue and put it into a 12.5–15cm (5–6in) deep-sided soufflé dish or a dish that the tongue fits into tightly.

6 Strain the cooking liquid, measure 600ml (1 pint) and pour into a pan. Boil rapidly to reduce to 150ml (¼ pint). Meanwhile, put 2 tbsp water into a small bowl and sprinkle in the gelatine. Leave to soak for 10 minutes, then add to the stock and stir gently to dissolve. Leave to cool.

7 Gently pour the cooled stock over the tongue. Put a small plate that will just fit inside the soufflé dish on top of the tongue. Put weights on top of the plate and chill overnight.

8 Lift the weights off the tongue and then ease off the plate. To release the tongue, run a blunt-edged knife around the inside of the dish, then immerse the base and sides in hot water for a few seconds only. Invert on to a serving plate, shaking to release the tongue. Slice the tongue thinly to serve.

Braised Oxtail

Countrywide Cook long and cook slow – that's the rule for oxtail. And all those hours spent simmering will be amply repaid when you taste the rich tender meat and juices. If you cook it the day before, the cooled fat is much easier to remove.

Serves 6 • Preparation 20 minutes • Cooking time about 4 hours

2 oxtails, about 1.6kg (3½ lb) in total, trimmed
2 tbsp plain flour
4 tbsp oil
2 large onions, sliced
900ml (1½ pints) beef stock
150ml (¼ pint) red wine
1 tbsp tomato purée
finely grated zest of ½ lemon
2 bay leaves
2 medium carrots, chopped
450g (1lb) parsnips, chopped
salt and ground black pepper
freshly chopped flat-leafed parsley to garnish

Nutrition per serving
616 cals | 35g fat (12g sats) |
16g carbs | 1.2g salt

1 Cut the oxtails into large pieces. Season the flour with salt and pepper and use to coat the pieces. Heat the oil in a large flameproof casserole and brown the oxtail pieces, a few at a time. Remove from the casserole with a slotted spoon and set aside.

2 Add the onions to the casserole and fry over a medium heat for about 10 minutes or until softened and lightly browned. Stir in any remaining flour.

3 Stir in the stock, red wine, tomato purée, lemon zest and bay leaves. Season with salt and pepper. Bring to the boil, then return the oxtail to the casserole and lower the heat. Cover and simmer very gently for 2 hours.

4 Skim off the fat from the surface, then stir in the carrots and parsnips. Re-cover the casserole and simmer very gently for a further 2 hours or until the oxtail is very tender.

5 Skim off all the fat from the surface, then check the seasoning. Serve scattered with chopped parsley.

•COOK'S TIP•
Oxtail contains a modest amount of meat and often plenty of firm white fat, although the fat can be trimmed before cooking. It also releases generous amounts of gelatine, which helps to enrich dishes.

Lancashire Tripe and Onions

The North Tripe is the stomach lining of a cow, pig, sheep or ox and is high in protein and low in fat. It should always be sold dressed and parboiled. Years ago there were a great many specialist tripe shops, but these days very few remain.

Serves 4 • Preparation 20 minutes • Cooking time about 2¼ hours

450g (1lb) dressed tripe, washed
225g (8oz) shallots
600ml (1 pint) milk
a pinch of freshly grated nutmeg
1 bay leaf
25g (1oz) butter
3 tbsp plain flour
salt and ground black pepper
freshly chopped flat-leafed parsley
to garnish
crusty bread to serve

Nutrition per serving
240 cals | 10g fat (5g sats) |
20g carbs | 1g salt

1 Put the tripe into a pan and cover with cold water. Bring to the boil, then drain and rinse under cold running water. Cut into 2.5cm (1in) pieces.
2 Put the tripe, shallots, milk, seasoning, nutmeg and bay leaf into the rinsed-out pan. Bring to the boil, then cover and simmer for about 2 hours or until tender. Strain and keep to one side 600ml (1 pint) of the liquid. Discard the bay leaf.
3 Melt the butter in a pan, stir in the flour and cook gently for 1 minute, stirring. Remove the pan from the heat and gradually stir in the reserved cooking liquid. Bring to the boil and continue to cook, stirring, until the sauce thickens.
4 Add the tripe and shallots and reheat. Check the seasoning and sprinkle with chopped parsley. Serve with bread.

Braised Kidneys in Port

Countrywide Tender lambs' kidneys are quick to cook and at their best when served in a richly flavoured sauce. Be sure to snip out the white core from each kidney half – use sharp kitchen scissors for best results.

Serves 4 • Preparation 10 minutes • Cooking time 35 minutes

25g (1oz) butter
1 medium onion, sliced
125g (4oz) mushrooms, sliced
8 lamb's kidneys, skinned, halved and cored
3 tbsp plain flour
150ml (¼ pint) port
150ml (¼ pint) chicken stock
1 tbsp freshly chopped flat-leafed parsley
1 bouquet garni (1 bay leaf, a few fresh parsley and thyme sprigs)
salt and ground black pepper
boiled rice or mashed potatoes and a mixed salad to serve

Nutrition per serving
313 cals | 10g fat (5g sats) |
22g carbs | 1.3g salt

1 Heat the butter in a large frying pan or flameproof casserole and fry the onion for 3–4 minutes until softened. Add the mushrooms and fry for a further 3–4 minutes.

2 Stir in the kidneys and cook for 5 minutes, stirring occasionally.

3 Stir in the flour, then gradually stir in the port and stock. Slowly bring to the boil. Stir in the parsley and bouquet garni, then season to taste.

4 Cover and simmer for 15 minutes, stirring occasionally. Remove the bouquet garni and serve hot with boiled rice or mashed potatoes and a mixed salad.

Creamed Kidneys in Wine

Countrywide Use lambs' kidneys, which are the smallest available and always juicy and tender, in this very speedy dish – the cream combined with the wine creates a tasty sauce. Don't overcook the kidneys, as they will become tough.

Serves 4 • Preparation 15 minutes • Cooking time 20 minutes

25g (1oz) butter
12 lamb's kidneys, skinned, halved and cored
225g (8oz) mushrooms, sliced
3 celery sticks, diced
1 medium onion, finely chopped
25g (1oz) plain flour
300ml (½ pint) dry red wine
1 tsp mustard powder
150ml (¼ pint) double cream
salt and ground black pepper
boiled rice and a green vegetable to serve

Nutrition per serving
422 cals | 28g fat (17g sats) |
9g carbs | 1.2g salt

1 Melt the butter in a medium pan. Add the kidneys, mushrooms, celery and onion and fry gently for 10 minutes or until tender.
2 Stir in the flour and cook for 1–2 minutes. Gradually stir in the wine, mustard and salt and pepper. Cook for a further 5 minutes. Stir in the cream and gently reheat. Serve on a bed of boiled rice with a green vegetable.

Sautéed Lamb's Kidneys and Baby Onions

Countrywide Kidneys are high in protein and rich in iron, phosphorus and zinc. They have relatively little fat, although they are high in cholesterol. Avoid overcooking them, or they will toughen.

Serves 4 • Preparation 10 minutes • Cooking time 30 minutes

225g (8oz) baby onions, peeled
25g (1oz) unsalted butter
8 lamb's kidneys, skinned, halved and cored
3 tbsp balsamic vinegar
1 tbsp plain flour
300ml (½ pint) well-flavoured lamb stock
3 tbsp Madeira
salt and ground black pepper
freshly chopped flat-leafed parsley to garnish
rice to serve

Nutrition per serving
180 cals | 8g fat (4g sats) |
8g carbs | 1.6g salt

1 Add the baby onions to a pan of boiling water and blanch for 3–5 minutes; drain well.
2 Melt the butter in a sauté pan, add the onions and cook gently for 10–15 minutes until soft and browned. Increase the heat and add the lamb's kidneys, stirring and turning them for about 2 minutes or until browned. Lift out the kidneys and onions and put on to a plate.
3 Deglaze the pan with the vinegar, scraping up any sediment from the bottom of the pan, and allow almost all of the liquid to evaporate. Sprinkle in the flour and cook, stirring, over a medium heat until it begins to colour. Whisk in the stock and Madeira. Bring the sauce to the boil, then simmer until reduced and slightly syrupy. Check the seasoning.
4 Return the kidneys and baby onions to the sauce and reheat gently for 5 minutes. Scatter with plenty of chopped parsley and serve with rice.

Stuffed Hearts

The North This traditional recipe for lambs' hearts was originally called Love in Disguise, one of the many fancy names given to offal dishes to mask their origins. The fresh, zesty stuffing ingredients complement the meaty taste of their casings.

Serves 4 • Preparation 15 minutes • Cooking time 2¼ hours

4 lamb's hearts
40g (1½oz) butter
1 small onion, chopped
50g (2oz) fresh wholemeal
breadcrumbs
finely grated zest of 1 lemon
1 tbsp freshly chopped sage or ½ tsp
dried sage
a pinch of freshly grated nutmeg
1 medium egg yolk
2 tbsp plain flour
450ml (¾ pint) chicken stock
3 tbsp dry sherry
salt and ground black pepper
freshly chopped sage and grated
lemon zest to garnish
mashed potatoes and braised red
cabbage with pears (see page 184)

Nutrition per serving
692 cals | 37g fat (16g sats) |
57g carbs | 1.8g salt

1 Preheat the oven to 150°C (130°C fan oven) mark 2. Wash the hearts thoroughly under cold running water. Trim and remove any ducts.

2 Melt 15g (½ oz) of the butter in a large frying pan and lightly fry the onion for about 5 minutes or until softened. Remove from the heat and stir in the breadcrumbs, lemon zest, sage and nutmeg. Season to taste. Bind with the egg yolk and mix well.

3 Fill the hearts with the stuffing and sew up neatly with strong cotton or fine string. Coat them in the flour.

4 Heat the remaining butter in a flameproof casserole and brown the hearts well. Pour in the stock and sherry, season well and bring to the boil.

5 Cover and cook in the oven for about 2 hours or until tender. To serve, remove the hearts from the casserole

and slice. Skim the juices and pour over the hearts. Garnish with the sage and lemon zest and serve with mashed potatoes and braised red cabbage with pears.

GAME

Venison Sausages with Red Onion Marmalade

Scotland Try these gamey sausages as an alternative to pork or beef. Made from lean and healthy venison meat, they have a wonderful flavour. The jelly sauce contrasts well with the red onion marmalade.

Serves 6 • Preparation 15 minutes • Cooking time 35 minutes

12 gluten-free (100% meat) venison sausages
6 tsp redcurrant jelly

For the red onion marmalade
400g (14oz) red onions, chopped
2 tbsp olive oil
4 tbsp red wine vinegar
2 tbsp demerara sugar
1 tsp juniper berries, crushed
Colcannon (see page 189) or mashed potatoes to serve

Nutrition per serving
390 cals | 25g fat (10g sats) | 14g carbs | 0.3g salt

1 Preheat the oven to 220°C (200°C fan oven) mark 7. Put the sausages into a small roasting tin. Roast in the oven for 35 minutes, turning once.

2 After 25 minutes, spoon the redcurrant jelly over and continue to cook.

3 Meanwhile, make the red onion marmalade. Gently fry the red onions in the oil for 15–20 minutes. Add the vinegar, sugar and juniper berries and cook for a further 5 minutes or until the onions are very tender. Serve the sausages with the red onion marmalade and Colcannon or mashed potatoes.

Peppered Venison Stew

Scotland Venison is becoming more widely available with the development of deer farming, and it can be bought all year round because it can be frozen. You can use beef or lamb if venison is not available.

Serves 6 • Preparation 20 minutes • Cooking time 2¾ hours

25g (1oz) plain flour
900g (2lb) stewing venison, beef or lamb, cut into 4cm (1½ in) cubes
5 tbsp oil
225g (8oz) button onions or shallots, peeled with root end intact
225g (8oz) onion, finely chopped
4 garlic cloves, crushed
2 tbsp tomato purée
125ml (4fl oz) red wine vinegar
75cl bottle red wine
2 tbsp redcurrant jelly
1 small bunch of fresh thyme, plus extra sprigs to garnish (optional)
4 bay leaves
1 tbsp coarsely ground black pepper
6 cloves
900g (2lb) mixed root vegetables, such as carrots, parsnips, turnips and celeriac, cut into 4cm (1½ in) chunks; carrots cut a little smaller
600–900ml (1–1½ pints) beef stock
salt and ground black pepper

Nutrition per serving
540 cals | 24g fat (7g sats) |
24g carbs | 1.5g salt

---

1 Put the flour into a plastic bag, season with salt and pepper, then toss the meat in it.
2 Heat 3 tbsp of the oil in a large flameproof casserole over a medium heat and brown the meat well in small batches. Remove and put to one side.
3 Preheat the oven to 180°C (160°C fan oven) mark 4. Heat the remaining oil and fry the button onions or shallots for 5 minutes or until golden. Add the chopped onion and the garlic and cook, stirring, until soft and golden. Add the tomato purée and cook for a further 2 minutes, then add the vinegar and wine and bring to the boil. Bubble for 10 minutes.
4 Add the redcurrant jelly, thyme, bay leaves, the ground black pepper, cloves and meat to the pan, together with the vegetables and enough stock to barely cover the meat and vegetables. Bring to the boil, cover and cook in the oven for 1¾–2¼ hours until the meat is very tender. Serve hot, garnished with thyme sprigs, if you like.

FREEZING TIP

To freeze, complete the recipe to the end of step 4, without the garnish. Cool quickly and put into a freezerproof container. Seal and freeze for up to one month.

To use, thaw overnight at cool room temperature. Preheat the oven to 180°C (160°C fan oven) mark 4. Put in a flameproof casserole and add an extra 150ml (¼ pint) beef stock. Bring to the boil. Cover and reheat for 30 minutes.

Venison Escalopes with Red Wine

Scotland You can buy venison from any butcher with a game licence. Young venison is usually tender enough not to need hanging but older, tougher animals benefit from it. Your butcher can advise on this.

Serves 6 • Preparation 5 minutes, plus marinating • Cooking time 15 minutes

6 escalopes of venison cut from the haunch (leg), about 175g (6oz) each
1 small onion, finely chopped
1 bay leaf
2 fresh parsley sprigs
8 juniper berries
300ml (½ pint) dry red wine
15g (½ oz) butter
1 tbsp vegetable oil
2 tbsp redcurrant jelly
salt and ground black pepper
chips and carrots to serve

Nutrition per serving
265 cals | 8g fat (3g sats) |
4g carbs | 0.7g salt

1 Put the escalopes into a large shallow dish and sprinkle with the onion, bay leaf, parsley and juniper berries. Pour the wine over, cover and marinate in the fridge for 3–4 hours or overnight, turning the escalopes occasionally.

2 Remove the escalopes from the marinade, reserving the marinade. Heat the butter and oil in a large frying pan and fry the escalopes for 3–4 minutes on each side. Transfer to a warmed serving dish and keep warm while you make the sauce.

3 Strain the reserved marinade into the frying pan and stir to loosen any sediment. Increase the heat and boil rapidly for 3–4 minutes until syrupy. Stir in the redcurrant jelly and season the mixture to taste. Cook for 1–2 minutes, stirring, then pour over the escalopes. Serve immediately with chips and carrots.

Roast Grouse

Scotland When buying oven-ready grouse, the meat should smell fresh and the skin should be smooth, with no discoloration or dry spots. Barding the breasts with bacon helps to keep the meat moist.

Serves 4 • Preparation 10 minutes • Cooking time 40 minutes, plus resting

2 oven-ready grouse
6 streaky bacon rashers
2 tbsp vegetable oil
2 tbsp freshly chopped rosemary or thyme (optional)
salt and ground black pepper
deep-fried thinly sliced potatoes (game chips, see page 188) and parsnips or hand-cooked salted crisps and watercress to serve

Nutrition per serving
320 cals | 18g fat (4g sats) | trace carbs | 0.3g salt

1 Preheat the oven to 200°C (180°C fan oven) mark 6. Put the grouse into a large roasting tin, with enough space between them so that they can brown evenly. Cover the breast of each with bacon, then drizzle with 1 tbsp oil. Season with salt and pepper and sprinkle with herbs, if using.
2 Roast in the oven for 40 minutes or until the juices run clear when the thigh is pierced with a skewer.
3 Leave to rest in a warm place for 10 minutes before serving.
4 Serve with crisp deep-fried slices of potato and parsnip or ready-made hand-cooked crisps, plus watercress to contrast with the richness of the meat.

Pheasant with Cider and Apples

Countrywide Pheasant can have a tendency to be on the dry side if roasted, but when casseroled in cider with apples, as here, it is tender and succulent. The pheasant season is from 1st October until 31st January.

Serves 8 • Preparation 1 hour • Cooking time 1–1½ hours

2 oven-ready pheasants, about 700g
(1½ lb) each, each cut into four
portions
2 tbsp plain flour, plus extra to dust
50g (2oz) butter
4 streaky bacon rashers, rind removed
225g (8oz) onions, roughly chopped
275g (10oz) celery sticks, roughly
chopped
4 eating apples, such as Granny
Smith, cored, cut into large pieces and
tossed in 1 tbsp lemon juice
1 tbsp dried juniper berries, lightly
crushed
2.5cm (1in) piece fresh root ginger,
peeled and finely chopped
300ml (½ pint) chicken stock
2 × 440ml cans dry cider
140ml (4½ fl oz) double cream
salt and ground black pepper
fried apple wedges, thyme sprigs
and juniper berries to garnish

Nutrition per serving
463 cals | 27g fat (13g sats) |
13g carbs | 0.7g salt

---

1 Preheat the oven to 170°C (150°C fan oven) mark 3. Season each pheasant portion and dust lightly with flour. Melt the butter in a large flameproof casserole and brown the pheasant pieces in batches until deep golden brown. Remove and keep warm.
2 Put the bacon into the casserole and cook for 2–3 minutes until golden. Add the onions, celery, apples and lemon juice, juniper and ginger and cook for 8–10 minutes. Stir the flour into the vegetables and cook for 2 minutes, then add the stock and cider and bring to the boil. Return the pheasant to the casserole, cover and cook in the oven for 45 minutes–1 hour until tender.

3 Lift the pheasant out of the sauce and keep it warm. Strain the sauce through a sieve and return it to the casserole with the cream. Bring to the boil and bubble for 10–15 minutes until syrupy. Return the pheasant to the sauce and season with salt and pepper.
4 To serve, garnish the pheasant with the fried apple wedges, thyme sprigs and juniper berries.

Get Ahead
• Complete the recipe to the end of step 3, cool quickly, then cover and chill for up to two days.
• To use, bring the pheasant to the boil and reheat in the oven at 180°C (160°C fan oven) mark 4 for 20–25 minutes.

Pot-roasted Pheasant with Red Cabbage

Countrywide While pheasant is in season (see left), try this easy pot-roast. The combination of tender pheasant, piquant cabbage and tangy bacon is a winner. Pot-roasting pheasant keeps it very moist.

Serves 4 • Preparation 15 minutes • Cooking time about 1 hour

25g (1oz) butter
1 tbsp oil
2 oven-ready young pheasants, halved
2 onions, sliced
450g (1lb) red cabbage, cored and finely shredded
1 tsp cornflour
250ml (9fl oz) red wine
2 tbsp redcurrant jelly
1 tbsp balsamic vinegar
4 rindless smoked streaky bacon rashers, halved
salt and ground black pepper

Nutrition per serving
659 cals | 21g fat (12g sats) |
11g carbs | 1.4g salt

TRY SOMETHING DIFFERENT

Instead of the pheasants, use oven-ready poussins, small corn-fed chickens or small guinea fowl; put an onion wedge inside each bird before browning to impart extra flavour.

1 Preheat the oven to 200°C (180°C fan oven) mark 6. Melt the butter with the oil in a large flameproof casserole over a medium to high heat. Add the pheasant halves and brown on all sides, then remove and put to one side. Add the onions and cabbage to the casserole and fry for 5 minutes, stirring frequently, until softened.

2 Blend the cornflour with a little water to make a paste. Add to the casserole with the wine, redcurrant jelly and vinegar. Season with salt and pepper and bring to the boil, stirring.

3 Arrange the pheasant halves, skin side up, on the cabbage. Put the halved bacon rashers on top. Cover the casserole and cook in the oven for 30 minutes or until the birds are tender (older pheasants will take an extra 10–20 minutes).

4 Serve the pot-roasted pheasants and red cabbage with the cooking juices spooned over them.

Rabbit Casserole with Grainy Mustard

The Eastern Counties Rabbit is available throughout the year and is increasingly stocked in supermarkets. Wild rabbit meat is leaner and tastier than the farmed variety, with a gamey flavour. Rabbit meat is low in fat and cholesterol, making it a healthy option.

Serves 4 • Preparation 15 minutes • Cooking time 1–1½ hours

4–6 rabbit joints, about 700–900g (1½–2lb) in total
2 tbsp plain flour, plus extra to dust
2 tbsp oil
15g (½ oz) butter
2 garlic cloves, crushed
300g (11oz) shallots, halved if large
225g (8oz) carrots, thickly sliced
150ml (¼ pint) white wine
300ml (½ pint) chicken stock
3–4 tbsp wholegrain mustard
4 tbsp crème fraîche
salt and ground black pepper
chopped herbs to garnish

Nutrition per serving
410 cals | 24g fat (12g sats) |
16g carbs | 1.3g salt

1 Preheat the oven to 170°C (150°C fan oven) mark 3. Season the rabbit joints with salt and pepper, then toss in flour to coat lightly, shaking off the excess.

2 Heat the oil and butter in a large flameproof casserole and brown the rabbit joints on all sides over a high heat, in batches if necessary. Remove and set aside.

3 Reduce the heat, then add the garlic, shallots and carrots to the casserole and cook for 5 minutes. Stir in the flour and cook for 2 minutes.

4 Add the wine, stock and mustard, stir well and bring to the boil. Return the rabbit to the casserole, then put the lid on and cook in the oven for 1–1½ hours until the rabbit is very tender.

5 Using a slotted spoon, transfer the rabbit and vegetables to a warmed serving dish and keep warm.

6 If necessary, put the casserole over a high heat for a few minutes to reduce the sauce a little. Stir in the crème fraîche and check the seasoning. Pour the creamy mustard sauce over the rabbit and garnish with herbs to serve.

Poacher's Pie

The Eastern Counties Rabbit features widely in the traditional recipes of the Eastern Counties because there used to be a surplus of wild rabbits and hares, partially controlled by game shooting. If wild rabbit is not available, use farmed meat, on sale in many supermarkets.

Serves 4 • Preparation 20 minutes, plus chilling • Cooking time 1½ hours

225g (8oz) plain flour, plus extra to dust
50g (2oz) butter
50g (2oz) lard
450g (1lb) boneless rabbit, skinned and cubed
125g (4oz) streaky bacon rashers, rind removed and chopped
2 medium potatoes, peeled and sliced
1 medium leek, trimmed and sliced
1 tbsp freshly chopped flat-leafed parsley
¼ tsp mixed dried herbs
chicken stock
1 medium egg, beaten, to glaze
salt and ground black pepper

Nutrition per serving
692 cals | 37g fat (16g sats) |
57g carbs | 1.8g salt

1 Preheat the oven to 190°C (170°C fan oven) mark 5. Put the flour and a pinch of salt into a bowl and rub in the butter and lard until the mixture resembles fine breadcrumbs. Add 3–4 tbsp cold water and mix to form a firm dough. Chill for 30 minutes.
2 Fill a 1.7 litre (3 pint) pie dish with alternate layers of rabbit, bacon and vegetables, sprinkling with seasoning and herbs. Half-fill the dish with stock.
3 Roll out the pastry on a lightly floured surface to 5cm (2in) wider than the top of the dish. Cut a 2.5cm (1in) strip from the outer edge and line the dampened rim of the dish. Dampen the pastry rim and cover with the pastry lid. Trim and seal the edges. Make a hole in the centre to let the steam escape. Decorate with pastry leaves made from the trimmings and brush with beaten egg.
4 Cook in the oven for 30 minutes. Cover loosely with foil, then reduce the oven temperature to 180°C (160°C fan oven) mark 4 and cook for a further 1 hour. Serve hot.

Kentish Pigeons in a Pot with Plums

The Southeast Fruit is widely used in savoury recipes in Kent, and the delicate, slightly sharp flavour of plums goes well with game. Pigeons are widely available in early autumn, when plums are at their best.

Serves 4 • Preparation 15 minutes • Cooking time 1¾ hours

25g (1oz) butter
1 tbsp vegetable oil
4 oven-ready young pigeons
(see Cook's Tip)
2 tsp plain wholemeal flour
1 onion, chopped
2 cloves
1 tbsp freshly chopped mixed herbs,
such as rosemary, sage, thyme, or
1 tsp dried herbs
125ml (4fl oz) port
450g (1lb) purple plums, stoned and
halved
freshly grated nutmeg
salt and ground black pepper

Nutrition per serving
385 cals | 17g fat (4g sats) |
17g carbs | 1g salt

1 Preheat the oven to 170°C (150°C fan oven) mark 3. Heat the butter and oil in a large frying pan. Coat the pigeons lightly in the flour, shaking off any excess, then add to the pan and fry, turning occasionally, until lightly browned on all sides. Transfer to a flameproof casserole.

2 Stir the onion into the frying pan and fry gently until beginning to soften. Spoon over the pigeons, then sprinkle the cloves and herbs over the top.

3 Stir the port into the frying pan, bring to the boil, then pour over the pigeons. Arrange the plums over the top. Cover tightly and cook in the oven for 1½ hours or until the pigeons are tender.

4 Transfer the pigeons and plums to a warmed serving plate. Boil the juices for 2–3 minutes to thicken them and concentrate the flavour. Season to taste with salt, pepper and nutmeg, then pour over the pigeons. Serve.

•COOK'S TIP•

Pigeons are available fresh or frozen, usually plucked and oven-ready.

Gamekeeper's Pie

Scotland Similar to a shepherd's pie, this gamey pie features long, slow cooking to bring all the flavours together. Ask your butcher for venison mince or buy online. The topping of creamy mash makes this a lovely comforting dish for a cold day.

Serves 8 • Preparation 20 minutes • Cooking time 1¼ hours

2 tbsp sunflower oil
800g (1lb 12oz) minced venison
1 onion, finely chopped
1 celery stick, finely chopped
1 large carrot, grated
1 garlic clove, crushed
1½ tbsp plain flour
150ml (¼ pint) full-fat milk
2 tbsp port
150ml (¼ pint) red wine
350ml (12fl oz) hot beef or game stock
1 tbsp Worcestershire sauce
2 tsp dried juniper berries, roughly crushed
½ tbsp fresh thyme leaves
1 bay leaf
1.3kg (2lb 14oz) Desirée or similar waxy potatoes, peeled and cut into chunks
50g (2oz) butter
50–75ml (2–2½ fl oz) double cream
salt and ground black pepper
seasonal vegetables to serve

Nutrition per serving
403 cals | 17g fat (8g sats) |
34g carbs | 1g salt

1 Heat 1 tbsp oil in a large pan and brown the mince over a medium heat in batches. Remove from the pan using a slotted spoon and set aside.
2 Using the same pan, turn the heat down to low, add the remaining oil and gently fry the onion, celery and carrot for 15 minutes or until softened but not coloured. Add the garlic and fry for 1 minute. Sprinkle the flour over and cook, stirring, for 1 minute.
3 Turn the heat to medium and add the milk, 2 tbsp at a time, stirring until it is absorbed. Stir in the port and wine and simmer until thickened. Add the hot stock, Worcestershire sauce, juniper berries, thyme and bay leaf

and bring to the boil. Return the mince to the pan, cover and simmer for 45 minutes, stirring occasionally.
4 Meanwhile, bring a large pan of lightly salted water to the boil and cook the potatoes for about 15 minutes or until tender. Drain and leave to steam dry in the colander. Heat the butter and cream in a small pan. Push the potato through a potato ricer or sieve into the rinsed potato pan. Stir in enough cream and butter to make a smooth but not sloppy mash.. Check the seasoning.
5 Preheat the grill to medium. Tip the hot

venison into an ovenproof dish about 30.5 × 20.5cm (12 × 8in). Spread the mash on top and grill for 3–4 minutes until golden. Serve with seasonal vegetables.

Get Ahead
- Assemble the pie up to two days ahead, wrap the dish in clingfilm and chill. Alternatively, wrap in clingfilm and freeze for up to three months.
- To use, if frozen, thaw overnight in the fridge. Reheat at 200°C (180°C fan oven) mark 6 for 25 minutes.

FISH &
SHELLFISH

Fishcakes

Countrywide Increasingly trendy nowadays, fishcakes were originally a way of using up leftover pieces of fish and cooked potatoes. Vary the fish according to what's available, or use a mixture of smoked and unsmoked.

Serves 4 • Preparation 15 minutes • Cooking time 20 minutes

350g (12oz) fish, such as cod, haddock or coley, cooked and flaked
350g (12oz) potatoes, cooked and mashed
25g (1oz) butter
1 tbsp freshly chopped flat-leafed parsley
a few drops of anchovy essence (optional)
milk, if needed
1 medium egg, beaten
plain flour to dust
125g (4oz) fresh breadcrumbs
vegetable oil for shallow-frying
salt and ground black pepper
basil leaves to garnish
lemon wedges and salad to serve

Nutrition per serving
412 cals | 19g fat (5g sats) |
39g carbs | 1.5g salt

1 Mix the fish with the potatoes, butter, parsley, seasoning and anchovy essence, if using, binding if necessary with a little milk or beaten egg.
2 On a lightly floured board, form the mixture into a roll, then cut into eight slices and shape into flat cakes. Coat them with egg and breadcrumbs.
3 Heat the oil in a frying pan, add the fishcakes and fry, turning once, until crisp and golden. Drain well on kitchen paper. Garnish with basil and serve with lemon wedges and salad.

TRY SOMETHING DIFFERENT

▼▼▼▼▼▼▼▼▼▼

Replace the cod, haddock or coley with smoked haddock, herrings, canned tuna or salmon.

Red Mullet Baked in Paper

The West Red mullet is known as the woodcock of the sea because you can eat it all. Cooking in paper conserves all the juices, and the parcels, when opened at table, show the attractive red colour to advantage.

Serves 2 • Preparation 5 minutes • Cooking time 30 minutes

2 red mullet, about 225g (8oz) each
1 tbsp freshly chopped flat-leafed parsley
1 small onion, sliced
50g (2oz) mushrooms, chopped
finely grated zest and juice of 1 lemon
salt and ground black pepper
boiled new potatoes and broccoli to serve

Nutrition per serving
259 cals | 9g fat (0g sats) |
2g carbs | 1.1g salt

1 Preheat the oven to 180°C (160°C fan oven) mark 4. Cut two squares of greaseproof paper large enough to wrap the fish. Place the fish on top, then add the remaining ingredients. Fold the paper to make a secure parcel.
2 Place the parcels on a baking sheet and bake for 30 minutes or until the fish is tender. Serve the fish in their parcels with boiled potatoes and broccoli.

Somerset Fish Casserole

The West Cider is a flavoursome and British alternative to white wine when cooking fish. Its robust taste makes it a good partner for the stronger brill or coley suggested in the recipe. For a more pronounced cider flavour use slightly more than suggested and boil it down to the required quantity.

Serves 4 • Preparation 15 minutes • Cooking time 35 minutes

50g (2oz) plain flour
900g (2lb) haddock, cod or coley fillets, skinned and cut into 5cm (2in) chunks
65g (2½oz) butter
1 medium onion, finely chopped
300ml (½ pint) dry cider
2 tsp anchovy essence
1 tbsp lemon juice
1 eating apple
salt and ground black pepper
freshly chopped flat-leafed parsley to garnish
steamed mangetouts to serve

Nutrition per serving
401 cals | 16g fat (9g sats) |
18g carbs | 1.4g salt

1 Preheat the oven to 180°C (160°C fan oven) mark 4. Season 25g (1oz) of the flour with salt and pepper, then coat the fish chunks in the flour.

2 Melt 25g (1oz) of the butter in a medium pan and cook the onion gently for 5 minutes or until softened. Add the fish and cook for a further 3 minutes or until lightly browned on all sides. Transfer the fish and onion to a buttered ovenproof serving dish.

3 To make the sauce, add 25g (1oz) of the butter to that remaining in the pan, then add the remaining flour and cook, stirring, for 1 minute. Gradually stir in the cider, anchovy essence and lemon juice. Bring to the boil, stirring continuously, then simmer for 2–3 minutes until thick and smooth.

4 Pour the sauce over the fish and cook in the oven for 20 minutes.

5 Meanwhile, peel, core and slice the apple into rings, then fry the apple rings in the remaining butter for 1–2 minutes. Drain on kitchen paper and use to top the fish. Serve garnished with chopped parsley.

Smoked Haddock Kedgeree

Countrywide Kitchri was originally a spicy Indian dish containing onions and lentils. The British brought the recipe back from India and Anglicised it, leaving out the stronger flavourings and lentils, while adding flaked smoked fish to the rice and eggs.

Serves 4 • Preparation 10 minutes • Cooking time 20 minutes

175g (6oz) long-grain rice
450g (1lb) smoked haddock fillets
2 medium eggs, hard-boiled and shelled
75g (3oz) butter
salt and cayenne pepper
freshly chopped flat-leafed parsley to garnish

Nutrition per serving
429 cals | 20g fat (11g sats) |
38g carbs | 3.1g salt

1 Cook the rice in a pan of lightly salted fast-boiling water until tender. Drain well and rinse under cold water.

2 Meanwhile, put the haddock into a large frying pan with just enough water to cover. Bring to simmering point, then simmer for 10–15 minutes until tender. Drain, skin and flake the fish, discarding the bones.

3 Chop one egg and slice the other into rings. Melt the butter in a pan, add the cooked rice, fish, chopped egg, salt and cayenne pepper and stir over a medium heat for 5 minutes or until hot. Pile on to a warmed serving dish and garnish with parsley and the sliced egg.

Smoked Finnan Haddock with Egg Sauce

Scotland True Finnan haddocks are smoked in Findon (corrupted to Finnan), near Aberdeen, but any properly smoked haddock – brownish not bright yellow in colour – will do for this dish. A green salad would go well with this.

Serves 4 • Preparation 10 minutes • Cooking time 25 minutes

2 Finnan haddocks, about 275g (10oz) each
1 bay leaf
300ml (½ pint) milk
25g (1oz) butter
25g (1oz) plain flour
2 medium eggs, hard-boiled, shelled and finely chopped
1 tbsp freshly chopped flat-leafed parsley
ground black pepper
boiled potatoes and salad to serve

Nutrition per serving
254 cals | 10g fat (5g sats) |
8g carbs | 0.5g salt

1 Put the haddock, skin side down, in a large frying pan. Add the bay leaf and pepper to taste, then pour the milk over. Bring to the boil, then gently simmer for 10–15 minutes until tender.
2 Using a fish slice, transfer the fish to a warmed serving dish reserving the milk. Cover and keep warm.
3 Melt the butter in a pan. Add the flour and cook gently, stirring, for 1–2 minutes. Remove from the heat and gradually stir in the reserved milk. Bring to the boil, stirring constantly, then simmer for 2–3 minutes until thick and smooth. Stir in the eggs and parsley, then pour the sauce into a sauceboat or jug. Serve the fish with the sauce, boiled potatoes and a salad.

Cumberland Stuffed Herrings with Mustard Sauce

The North Mustard sauce makes a good accompaniment to the oily flesh of herrings, and English mustard has the 'bite' needed to make a good contrast with the rich fish. If herrings are unobtainable, you can use small mackerel, or if only large fish of either type are available, serve each person a half.

Serves 4 • Preparation 10 minutes • Cooking time 30 minutes

4 herrings with roe, or small mackerel,
about 225g (8oz) each, head and fins
removed, and cleaned
300ml (½ pint) milk
25g (1oz) fresh breadcrumbs
1 small onion, finely chopped
25g (1oz) butter
3 tbsp plain flour
1 tsp prepared English mustard
1 tsp white wine vinegar
salt and ground black pepper
green beans to serve

Nutrition per serving
576 cals | 37g fat (12g sats) |
18g carbs | 1.7g salt

1 Preheat the oven to 180°C (160°C fan oven) mark 4. Put the roes into a small pan with the milk. Bring to the boil, then simmer gently for 5 minutes. Strain, reserving the milk. Finely chop the roes.

2 Open out the fish on a board, inner side down, and press lightly down the middle to loosen the backbone. Gently ease the backbone away.

3 Mix together the breadcrumbs and onion and add the chopped roes. Season to taste and spread on the flesh side of the fish. Fold the fish over to enclose the stuffing. Cover and cook in the oven for 20 minutes or until tender.

4 Meanwhile, put the butter, flour and the reserved milk into a pan. Heat, whisking continuously, until the sauce thickens, boils and is smooth. Simmer for 1–2 minutes. Stir in the mustard and vinegar, adjust the seasoning and serve with the fish and green beans.

Old-fashioned Fish Pie

Countrywide A topping of mashed potato makes the fish filling in this pie go further and increases its appeal as comfort food. Fish pies can be simple affairs, or as grand as you want them to be, for example with the addition of shellfish, and a pastry topping instead of potato.

Serves 4 • Preparation 20 minutes • Cooking time 50 minutes

450g (1lb) haddock, cod or coley fillets
300ml (½ pint) milk, plus 6 tbsp
1 bay leaf
6 black peppercorns
2 onion slices
65g (2½oz) butter
3 tbsp flour
150ml (¼ pint) single cream
2 medium eggs, hard-boiled, shelled and chopped
2 tbsp freshly chopped flat-leafed parsley
900g (2lb) potatoes, cooked and mashed
1 medium egg
salt and ground black pepper

Nutrition per serving
610 cals | 28g fat (15g sats) |
56g carbs | 1.4g salt

1 Put the fish into a frying pan, pour the 300ml (½ pint) milk over it and add the bay leaf, peppercorns, onion slices and a good pinch of salt. Bring slowly to the boil, cover and simmer for 8–10 minutes until the fish flakes when tested with a fork.

2 Using a fish slice, lift the fish out of the pan and put on a plate. Flake the fish, discarding the skin and bone. Strain and put the milk to one side. Preheat the oven to 200°C (180°C fan oven) mark 6.

3 Melt 40g (1½ oz) of the butter in a pan, stir in the flour and cook gently for 1 minute, stirring. Remove the pan from the heat and gradually stir in the reserved milk. Bring to the boil slowly and continue to cook, stirring until the sauce thickens. Season.

4 Stir in the cream and fish, together with any juices. Add the chopped eggs and parsley and adjust the seasoning. Spoon the mixture into a 1.1 litre (2 pint) pie dish or similar ovenproof dish.

5 Heat the 6 tbsp milk and remaining butter in a pan, then beat into the potatoes. Season and leave to cool slightly.

6 Spoon the cooled potato into a large piping bag fitted with a large star nozzle. Pipe shell-shaped lines of potato across the fish mixture. Alternatively, spoon potato on top and roughen the surface with a fork.

7 Put the dish on a baking sheet and cook in the oven for 10–15 minutes until the potato is set.

8 Beat the egg with a good pinch of salt, then brush over the pie. Return to the oven for 15 minutes or until golden brown.

TRY SOMETHING DIFFERENT

- Stir 125g (4oz) grated Cheddar cheese into the sauce.
- Beat 125g (4oz) grated Cheddar or Red Leicester cheese into the mashed potatoes.
- Stir 175g (6oz) canned sweetcorn, drained, and ¼ tsp cayenne pepper into the fish mixture.
- Fry 125g (4oz) sliced button mushrooms in 25g (1oz) butter for 3 minutes. Stir into the fish mixture.
- Sprinkle the potato topping with 50g (2oz) mixed grated Parmesan and fresh breadcrumbs after the first 10–15 minutes.
- Cover the pie with puff pastry instead of the potatoes.

Fish and Chips

Countrywide The British national dish, fish and chips has been popular since the nineteenth century. Salt, vinegar, mushy peas and gherkins are the traditional accompaniments, but try lemon mayonnaise, below.

Serves 2 • Preparation 15 minutes • Cooking time 12 minutes

4 litres (7 pints) sunflower oil for deep-frying
125g (4oz) self-raising flour
¼ tsp baking powder
¼ tsp salt
1 medium egg
150ml (¼ pint) sparkling mineral water
2 hake fillets, about 125g (4oz) each
450g (1lb) Desirée potatoes, peeled and cut into 1cm (½ in) chips
salt, vinegar and lemon mayonnaise (see Cook's Tip) to serve

Nutrition per serving
1186 cals | 79g fat (18g sats) |
73g carbs | 3.2g salt

---

1 Heat the oil in a deep-fryer to 190°C (test by frying a small cube of bread – it should brown in 20 seconds).
2 Whiz the flour, baking powder, salt, egg and water in a food processor or blender until combined into a batter. Remove the blade from the food processor. (Alternatively, put the ingredients into a bowl and beat everything together until smooth.) Drop one of the fish fillets into the batter to coat it.
3 Put half the chips into the deep-fryer, then add the battered fish. Fry for 6 minutes or until just cooked, then remove and drain well on kitchen paper. Keep warm if not serving immediately.
4 Drop the remaining fillet into the batter to coat, then repeat step 3 with the remaining chips. Serve with salt, vinegar and lemon mayonnaise.

•COOK'S TIP•
Lemon Mayonnaise
Put 2 medium egg yolks, 2 tsp lemon juice, 1 tsp Dijon mustard and a pinch of sugar into a food processor. Season, then whiz briefly until pale and creamy. With the motor running, slowly pour in 300ml (½ pint) light olive oil through the feeder tube, in a steady stream, until the mayonnaise is thick. Add 1 tsp grated lemon zest and an additional 1 tbsp lemon juice and whiz briefly to combine. Store the mayonnaise in a screw-topped jar in the fridge. It will keep for up to three days.

Poached Salmon

Scotland This makes a good centrepiece for a party. The fish should be moist and succulent and it's worth taking the trouble to remove the bones, making it much easier to carve. You can experiment with dressing a cold salmon – add thin slices of cucumber or shelled prawns.

Serves 8 • Preparation 15 minutes • Cooking time see below

1 salmon
wine or water with lemon and a
bay leaf
salt and ground black pepper
lemon slices and chervil or flat-leafed
parsley sprigs to garnish

Nutrition per serving
675 cals | 41g fat (7g sats) |
0g carbs | 0.4g salt

1 To prepare the salmon, slit the fish along the underside between the head and rear gill opening. Cut out the entrails and discard. Rinse the fish to remove all the blood.

2 Snip off the fins and trim the tail into a neat 'V' shape. Leave the head on, if you like. Pat dry with kitchen paper and weigh the fish before cooking.

3 Fill a fish kettle or large pan with water, or a mixture of water and wine. Bring to the boil, then lower the fish into the kettle or pan. (A piece of muslin wrapped around the salmon will enable it to be lifted out.)

4 Bring the liquid back to the boil, then simmer for 7–8 minutes per 450g (1lb) if eating hot.

5 If eating cold, bring the liquid back to the boil, then cook for 5 minutes for fish under 3.2kg (7lb), 10–15 minutes for fish over 3.2kg (7lb), allow to cool completely in the liquid, then lift out and remove the skin and bones. Garnish with lemon slices and chervil or parsley sprigs.

TRY SOMETHING DIFFERENT

Salmon can also be poached in the oven. Put the fish into a deep roasting tin – it must fit snugly. Preheat the oven to 150°C (130°C fan oven) mark 2. Pour enough water, or water and wine over the fish to three-quarters cover it. Cover tightly with buttered foil. Cook in the oven allowing 10 minutes per 450g (1lb). If serving the fish hot, allow an extra 10 minutes at the end of the cooking time.

Dover Sole with Parsley Butter

The Southeast Because of its price, Dover sole is a treat, but when cooked simply, as here, it has a superb taste. It is an excellent source of low-fat protein and calcium. The buttery sauce with parsley and lemon really complements the delicate flesh.

Serves 2 • Preparation 5 minutes • Cooking time 20 minutes

2 Dover soles, about 275g (10oz) each, gutted and descaled
3 tbsp plain flour
2 tbsp sunflower oil
25g (1oz) unsalted butter
2 tbsp freshly chopped flat-leafed parsley
juice of ½ lemon
salt and ground black pepper
lemon wedges to serve

Nutrition per serving
450 cals | 25g fat (8g sats) |
16g carbs | 1.5g salt

1 Rinse the fish under cold water, then gently pat them dry with kitchen paper. Put the flour on a large plate and season with salt and pepper. Dip the fish into the seasoned flour, to coat both sides, gently shaking off the excess.

2 Heat 1 tbsp oil in a large sauté pan or frying pan and fry one fish for 4–5 minutes on each side until golden. Transfer to a warmed plate and keep warm in a low oven. Add the remaining oil to the pan and cook the other fish in the same way; put on a plate in the oven to keep warm.

3 Add the butter to the pan and melt. Turn up the heat slightly until it turns golden, then take off the heat. Add the parsley and lemon juice, then season well. Put one fish on each warmed dinner plate and pour the parsley butter over it. Serve with lemon wedges.

Trout with Almonds

Countrywide Trout are farmed throughout Great Britain and the benefits of eating oily fish are well known. This classic dish is always popular.

Serves 4 • Preparation 5 minutes • Cooking time 10–15 minutes

4 trout, gutted, with heads and tails intact
2 tbsp plain flour
65g (2½ oz) butter
50g (2oz) flaked almonds
juice of ½ lemon, or to taste
1–2 tbsp freshly chopped flat-leafed parsley
salt and ground black pepper

Nutrition per serving
450 cals | 28g fat (11g sats) |
6g carbs | 1.1g salt

1 Rinse the trout and pat dry with kitchen paper. Put the flour on a plate and season with salt and pepper. Dust the fish with the seasoned flour to coat lightly. Melt 50g (2oz) of the butter in a large frying pan. Fry the trout, two at a time, for 5–7 minutes on each side, turning once, until golden on both sides and cooked.
2 Remove the fish from the pan, drain on kitchen paper and put on a warmed serving plate; keep warm. Wipe out the pan.
3 Melt the remaining butter in the pan and fry the almonds until lightly browned. Add the lemon juice and spoon over the trout. Scatter with chopped parsley and serve immediately.

Soused Herrings

Scotland A prolific fish in Scotland, here the herrings are cooked in a pickling mixture (souse), and then eaten cold.

Serves 4 • Preparation 10 minutes • Cooking time 45 minutes, plus cooling

4 large or 6–8 small herrings, cleaned, boned, and heads and tails removed
1 small onion, sliced into rings
6 black peppercorns
1–2 bay leaves
fresh flat-leafed parsley sprigs
150ml (¼ pint) malt vinegar
salt and ground black pepper
salad to serve (optional)

Nutrition per serving
215 cals | 13g fat (3g sats) |
trace carbs | 1.1g salt

1 Preheat the oven to 180°C (160°C fan oven) mark 4. Season the fish and divide into fillets. Roll up and secure. Arrange in a shallow ovenproof dish with the onion rings, peppercorns and herbs.
2 Pour in the vinegar and enough water to almost cover the fish. Cover with greaseproof paper or foil and cook in the oven for 45 minutes or until tender.
3 Leave the herrings to cool in the cooking liquid before serving as an appetiser or with salad.

Baked Mackerel with Gooseberry Sauce

The West This delicious summer dish (available all year round if you freeze gooseberry purée) offers an interesting contrast in flavours – rich oily mackerel is offset by tangy gooseberries. Be sure to sieve the gooseberries if you want to get rid of all the pips.

Serves 4 • Preparation 10 minutes • Cooking time 25–30 minutes

15g (½oz) butter
225g (8oz) gooseberries, topped and tailed
4 mackerel, about 350g (12oz) each, cleaned and heads removed
lemon juice, to taste
1 medium egg, beaten
salt and ground black pepper

Nutrition per serving
841 cals | 61g fat (1g sats) |
5g carbs | 1.3g salt

1 Preheat the grill. Melt the butter in a medium pan and add the gooseberries. Cover tightly and cook over a low heat, shaking the pan occasionally, until the gooseberries are tender.

2 Meanwhile, season the mackerel inside and out with salt, plenty of pepper and lemon juice. Make two or three slashes in the skin on each side of the fish, then grill for 15–20 minutes, depending on size, turning once, until tender.

3 Purée the gooseberries in a blender or food processor, or press through a sieve. Pour the purée into a clean pan, beat in the egg, then reheat gently, stirring. Season to taste. Put the mackerel on warmed plates and spoon the sauce beside the fish.

Traditional Kippers

The North Kippers are split and opened-out herrings that have been lightly brined, then cold-smoked. Northumberland produces some of the finest

Serves 2 • Cooking time 5–15 minutes

2 kippers
butter, freshly chopped parsley and
toast to serve

Nutrition per serving
331 cals | 25g fat (4g sats) |
38g carbs | 3.1g salt

Three ways to cook kippers:
1 Grill the kippers for 5 minutes.
2 Alternatively, put into a jug of boiling water and leave in a warm place for 5–10 minutes.
3 You can also wrap them in foil and cook them in the oven at 190°C (170°C fan oven) mark 5 for 10–15 minutes.
4 Serve with butter, parsley and toast.

Grilled Lobster

Countrywide Prepared simply, the flavour of lobster is superb. This is a real treat for a special occasion.

Serves 2 • Preparation 20 minutes • Cooking time 15 minutes

1 killed fresh lobster, about 700g
(1½ lb) (see Cook's Tip)
25g (1oz) butter, softened, plus melted
butter to brush and serve
salt and cayenne pepper

Nutrition per serving
186 cals | 120g fat (7g sats) |
0g carbs | 1.6g salt

1 Preheat the grill. Split the lobster lengthways. Remove the head sac, which lies just behind the eyes, and discard. Remove the black coral (tomalley) and the green intestine, which lie inside the back of the shell just behind the head sac.
2 Brush the shell and flesh with melted butter and grill the flesh side for 8–10 minutes, then turn the lobster and grill the shell side for 5 minutes.

3 Dot the flesh with small pieces of softened butter, sprinkle with a little salt and cayenne pepper and serve immediately, with melted butter.

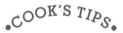

If you are able to buy a live lobster from your fishmonger, choose one that has all claws and legs intact.

To kill a lobster humanely, put it into the freezer for 5 minutes, then put it on a chopping board and hold the body firmly. Take a large chef's knife and plunge it straight down into the lobster's head, right between or just below the eyes.

Classic Dressed Crab

The Southeast/Eastern Counties This is an attractive dish using both the white and brown meat from the crab. They are in season from April to December. Dressing a crab was described by cookery writer Hannah Glasse in her 18th-century book of recipes.

Serves 2 • Preparation 30 minutes

1 medium cooked crab, about 900g
(2lb), cleaned (see Cook's Tip)
1 tbsp lemon juice
2 tbsp fresh white breadcrumbs
1 medium egg, hard-boiled
1 tbsp freshly chopped flat-leafed
parsley
salt and ground black pepper
salad leaves, and brown bread and
butter to serve

Nutrition per serving
180 cals | 8g fat (1g sats) |
5g carbs | 3g salt

1 Flake the white crab meat into
  a bowl, removing any shell or
  membrane, then add 1 tsp of the
  lemon juice and season to taste.
  Mix lightly with a fork.
2 Pound the brown crab meat in another
  bowl and work in the breadcrumbs
  and remaining lemon juice. Season
  with salt and pepper to taste.
3 Using a small spoon, put the white
  crab meat into the cleaned crab shell,
  arranging it down either side and
  piling it up well. Spoon the brown
  meat into the middle between the
  sections of white meat.
4 Chop the egg white; press the yolk
  through a sieve. To garnish the crab,
  spoon lines of chopped parsley,
  sieved egg yolk and chopped egg
  white along the 'joins' between the
  white and brown crab meat. Serve on
  a bed of salad leaves, with brown
  bread and butter.

.COOK'S TIPS.

Crab is available cooked or live, but it is better to buy a live crab and cook it at home to ensure it is perfectly fresh. Kill the crab in the same way as for lobster (see page 175).

To clean the cooked crab, put the crab on a board with the belly facing up. Twist off the legs and claws. Lift off and discard the 'apron' (tail) – long and pointed in a male, short and broad in a female. Pull the body out of the shell and remove and discard the feathery gills and grey stomach sac. Use your fingers, a crab pick or a small knife to remove the white meat. Use a spoon to scrape the brown meat from the shell.

Potted Prawns

The North Morecambe Bay is famous for its seafood, especially its prawns and shrimps. Potting the prawns preserves them under the layer of spiced butter. Use the seal of butter for spreading on the accompanying toast.

Serves 6 • Preparation 15 minutes, plus chilling • Cooking time 10 minutes

600g (1lb 5oz) cooked small prawns
250g (9oz) butter
¼ tsp ground mace
½ tsp each cayenne pepper and
freshly grated nutmeg
1 tbsp Worcestershire sauce
2 tbsp freshly chopped chives
salt and ground black pepper
6 slices white bread to serve

Nutrition per serving
466 cals | 35g fat (22g sats) |
17g carbs | 2g salt

1 Dry the prawns on kitchen paper. Clarify the butter by gently melting it in a small pan. Spoon off the white scum, then pour the clear butter into another pan, discarding any milky residue.

2 Add the mace, cayenne pepper, nutmeg and Worcestershire sauce to the clarified butter, season with salt and pepper, then heat through for 3 minutes without letting the mixture boil. Take off the heat and cool slightly. Stir in most of the chives.

3 Divide the prawns among six 100ml (3½ fl oz) ramekins and top with the flavoured butter. Sprinkle the remaining chives on top. Chill overnight.

4 Preheat the grill. Put the bread on a baking sheet and toast until golden. Cut off the crusts and slice each piece horizontally through the centre to make two slices. Toast the uncooked sides until golden. Carefully slice each piece in half diagonally and serve with the prawns.

Prawn Tartlets

Countrywide These tartlets are well worth the preparation involved. It is important to ensure that the vegetable mixture is reduced until thick or the tart filling will be watery. They are in season from April to December.

Serves 6 • Preparation 50 minutes • Cooking time 1¼–1½ hours, plus cooling

30 raw large prawns, shells on, about
400g (14oz) total weight
4 tbsp olive oil
2 shallots, finely chopped
2 garlic cloves, roughly chopped
1 bay leaf
150ml (¼ pint) brandy
150ml (¼ pint) white wine
400g can chopped tomatoes
2 tbsp freshly chopped tarragon, plus
fresh tarragon sprigs to garnish
175g (6oz) celeriac, chopped
125g (4oz) carrots, chopped
175g (6oz) leeks (white part only),
roughly chopped
2 tbsp vegetable oil
150ml (¼ pint) double cream
grated zest of ½ lemon
225g (8oz) puff pastry, thawed if frozen
1 small egg, beaten, for blind baking
salt and ground black pepper
celeriac and carrots, shredded,
blanched and dressed with lemon
juice and olive oil to serve

Nutrition per serving
489 cals | 34g fat (10g sats) |
21g carbs | 1.4g salt

1 Cook the prawns in a pan of lightly salted boiling water for 1 minute or until the shells are pink. Plunge into a bowl of cold water to cool. Remove the heads and shells and put to one side. Cover and chill the prawns.

2 Meanwhile, heat the olive oil in a large pan, add the shallots and cook gently for 5 minutes or until soft. Add the garlic, bay leaf and prawn heads and shells. Cook over a high heat for 1 minute, then add the brandy. (If you're cooking over gas, take care, as the brandy may ignite.) Allow the liquid to reduce by half, then add the wine. Bring to the boil and bubble until reduced by half, then add the tomatoes and season. Add 1 tbsp of the tarragon. Cook over a medium-low heat for 20 minutes. Put a colander over a large bowl, pour the contents of the pan into the colander and push through as much liquid as possible. Put the liquid to one side and discard the heads and shells.

3 Put the celeriac, carrots and leeks into a food processor and pulse until finely chopped. Heat the vegetable oil in a frying pan, add the vegetables and cook quickly for 2 minutes (don't allow them to colour). Add the prawn and tomato liquid and the cream, bring to the boil and bubble for 10–15 minutes until thick. Season and stir in the remaining tarragon and the lemon zest. Cool.

4 Preheat the oven to 200°C (180°C fan oven) mark 6. Roll out the pastry and line six 4cm (1½ in) diameter (at base) brioche tins. Bake blind (see Cook's Tip); cool.

5 Divide the vegetable mixture among the pastry cases and top each with five prawns. Put back in the oven for 10–15 minutes until hot to the centre. Season with pepper, garnish with tarragon and serve with a salad of finely shredded celeriac and carrots.

•COOK'S TIP•

To bake blind, prick each pastry base with a fork. Cover with foil or greaseproof paper 7.5cm (3in) larger than each tin, then spread baking beans on top. Bake for 15–20 minutes. Remove the foil or paper and beans and bake for 5–10 minutes until the pastry is light golden. When cooked and while still hot, brush the base of the pastry with a little beaten egg to seal the fork pricks and any cracks. This will prevent any filling leaking, which can make it difficult to remove the tarts from the tins.

VEGETABLE SIDE DISHES

Mint Sauce

Countrywide The classic accompaniment to roast lamb, best in spring when mint is also at its best.

Serves 4 • Preparation 10 minutes, plus standing

1 small bunch of mint, stalks removed
1–2 tsp golden caster sugar, to taste
1–2 tbsp wine vinegar, to taste

Nutrition per serving
10 cals | trace fat (0g sats) |
2g carbs | 0g salt

1 Finely chop the mint leaves and put into a bowl with the sugar. Stir in 1 tbsp boiling water and set aside for about 5 minutes to dissolve the sugar.
2 Add the wine vinegar to taste. Leave to stand for about 1 hour before serving.

Cumberland Sauce

The North A traditional accompaniment, served cold, to gammon and other rich meats. It has a sharp, fruity flavour.

Serves 4 • Preparation 10 minutes • Cooking time 10 minutes, plus cooling

finely pared zest and juice of 1 orange
finely pared zest and juice of 1 lemon
4 tbsp redcurrant jelly
1 tsp Dijon mustard
4 tbsp port
pinch of ground ginger (optional)
salt and ground black pepper

Nutrition per serving
70 cals | 0g fat (0g sats) |
15g carbs | 0.7g salt

1 Cut the citrus zests into fine julienne strips and put into a small pan. Add cold water to cover and simmer for 5 minutes, then drain.
2 Put the orange and lemon juices, citrus zests, redcurrant jelly and mustard into a pan and heat gently, stirring, until the sugar has dissolved. Simmer for 5 minutes, then add the port.
3 Allow to cool. Season with salt and pepper to taste and add a little ginger if you like.

Bread Sauce

Countrywide A traditional British sauce dating back many centuries, bread sauce is easy to make at home. Serve it with roast chicken or turkey.

Serves 8 • Preparation 10 minutes • Cooking time 15 minutes

1 onion, quartered
4 cloves
2 bay leaves
450ml (¾ pint) milk
150g (5oz) fresh white breadcrumbs
½ tsp freshly grated nutmeg, or to taste
50g (2oz) butter
200ml (7fl oz) crème fraîche
salt and ground black pepper

Nutrition per serving
210 cals | 16g fat (11g sats) |
13g carbs | 0.8g salt

1 Stud each onion quarter with a clove. Put the onion, bay leaves and milk into a pan. Heat very gently on the lowest possible heat for 15 minutes.
2 Remove the onion and bay leaves, then add the breadcrumbs, nutmeg and butter and stir to combine. Add the crème fraîche and season with salt and pepper to taste. Serve warm.

Apple Sauce

Countrywide This sauce is traditionally served with roast pork and goose, to cut the richness of the meats.

Serves 4 • Preparation 10 minutes • Cooking time 10 minutes

450g (1lb) cooking apples, such as Bramleys
2 tbsp sugar, or to taste
25g (1oz) butter

Nutrition per serving
110 cals | 5g fat (3g sats) |
17g carbs | 0.1g salt

1 Peel, core and slice the apples and put into a pan with 2–3 tbsp water. Cover and cook gently for 10 minutes, stirring occasionally, or until soft and reduced to a pulp.
2 Beat with a wooden spoon until smooth, then pass through a sieve, if you like a smooth sauce. Stir in sugar to taste and the butter. Serve warm.

Carrots with Mint and Lemon

The Eastern Counties Tender young carrots, in the shops during early spring to early summer, have a lovely sweet flavour.

Serves 4 • Preparation 15 minutes • Cooking time 15 minutes

700g (1½lb) small new carrots, trimmed and scrubbed
finely grated zest and juice of ½ lemon
1 tsp light soft brown sugar
15g (½ oz) butter
2 tbsp freshly chopped mint
salt and ground black pepper

1 Cook the carrots in lightly salted boiling water for about 10 minutes or until just tender. Drain.
2 Return the carrots to the pan with the remaining ingredients and toss together over a high heat until the butter melts. Serve at once.

Nutrition per serving
86 cals | 4g fat (2g sats) | 12g carbs | 0.5g salt

•COOK'S TIP•

Unwashed carrots, which sometimes still have their feathery foliage, keep better than those sold washed and prepacked.

Braised Red Cabbage with Pears

Countrywide A variation on the more usual red cabbage with apples, this has lots of flavour and is very good with cold meats.

Serves 6 • Preparation 15 minutes • Cooking time about 50 minutes

1 tbsp olive oil
1 red onion, halved and sliced
2 garlic cloves, crushed
1 large red cabbage, about 1kg (2¼ lb), shredded
2 tbsp light muscovado sugar
2 tbsp red wine vinegar
8 juniper berries
¼ tsp ground allspice
300ml (½ pint) vegetable stock
2 pears, cored and sliced
salt and ground black pepper
fresh thyme sprigs to garnish

1 Heat the oil in a large pan, add the onion and fry for 5 minutes. Add the remaining ingredients, except the pears, and season with salt and pepper. Bring to the boil, then cover and simmer for 30 minutes.
2 Add the pears and cook for a further 15 minutes or until nearly all the liquid has evaporated and the cabbage is tender. Serve hot, garnished with thyme.

Nutrition per serving
63 cals | 1g fat (0g sats) | 12g carbs | 0.9g salt

Baked Beetroot

Countrywide Beetroot is delicious served hot. When preparing the beetroots for cooking in the oven don't damage the skin or the colour will 'bleed' during baking. Also do not prod them with a fork to see if they are done, but instead test whether the skin slides off easily.

Serves 6 • Preparation 15 minutes • Cooking time 1¼–1½ hours

1.25kg (2lb 12oz) beetroot
15g (½ oz) butter
salt and ground black pepper
freshly chopped parsley or chives to garnish

Nutrition per serving
90 cals | 2g fat (1g sats) |
15g carbs | 0.2g salt

1 Preheat the oven to 200°C (180°C fan oven) mark 6. Trim the beetroot and carefully rinse in cold water, making sure you do not tear the skins.
2 Rub the butter over the middle of a large piece of foil. Put the beetroot on the buttered foil and season with salt and pepper. Bring the edges of the foil up over the beetroot and fold together to seal and form a parcel. Put on a baking sheet.
3 Bake for 1¼–1½ hours until the beetroot are soft and the skin comes away easily.
4 Leave for a minute or two until cool enough to handle, then rub off the skins and roughly chop, then scatter chopped parsley or chives over the beetroot to serve.

TRY SOMETHING DIFFERENT

Use baby beetroot. Roast them whole as per the method, then in step 4 rub off the skins and halve or leave whole.

Brussels Sprouts with Chestnuts and Shallots

Countrywide Brussels sprouts and chestnuts are a delicious combination, traditionally served at Christmas to accompany the turkey. Buy Brussels sprouts on the day they are needed if possible, as they will only keep for a day or two before starting to turn yellow even if in the refrigerator.

Serves 8 • Preparation 15 minutes • Cooking time 12 minutes

900g (2lb) small Brussels sprouts, trimmed
1 tbsp olive oil
8 shallots, finely chopped
200g pack peeled cooked chestnuts
15g (½ oz) butter
a pinch of freshly grated nutmeg
salt and ground black pepper

Nutrition per serving
140 cals | 5g fat (1g sats) |
8g carbs | 0.3g salt

1 Add the sprouts to a large pan of lightly salted boiling water, return to the boil and blanch for 2 minutes. Drain the sprouts and refresh with cold water.
2 Heat the oil in a wok or sauté pan. Add the shallots and stir-fry for 5 minutes or until almost tender.
3 Add the sprouts to the pan with the chestnuts and stir-fry for about 4 minutes to heat through.
4 Add the butter and nutmeg, and season generously with salt and pepper. Serve immediately.

•COOK'S TIP•

If you have to store Brussels sprouts, prepare them for cooking and keep in the fridge in a polythene bag. For convenience, blanch the Brussels sprouts ahead, then pan-fry just before serving. This helps to retain their colour and texture.

Roasted Root Vegetables

Countrywide These are high in fibre and low in fat. Try other combinations of vegetables: celeriac instead of parsnips or fennel instead of swede.

Serves 4 • Preparation 15 minutes • Cooking time 1 hour

1 large potato, peeled and cut into large chunks
1 large sweet potato, peeled and cut into large chunks
3 carrots, cut into large chunks
4 small parsnips, halved
1 small swede, cut into large chunks
3 tbsp olive oil
2 fresh rosemary and 2 fresh thyme sprigs
salt and ground black pepper

1 Preheat the oven to 200°C (180°C fan oven) mark 6. Put all the vegetables into a large roasting tin. Add the oil.
2 Use scissors to snip the herbs over the vegetables, then season with salt and pepper and toss everything together. Roast for 1 hour or until tender.

Nutrition per serving
251 cals | 10g fat (1g sats) |
39g carbs | 0.2g salt

Bubble and Squeak Cakes

The Southeast This classic dish takes its name from the sounds of cooking – the vegetables bubbling while boiled and then squeaking in the frying pan.

Makes 12 • Preparation 15 minutes, plus cooling • Cooking time 45 minutes

550g (1¼lb) old potatoes, peeled and cut into even-sized chunks
125g (4oz) butter
175g (6oz) leeks, trimmed and finely shredded
175g (6oz) green cabbage, finely shredded
plain flour to dust
1 tbsp oil
salt and ground black pepper

1 Cook the potatoes in a large pan of lightly salted boiling water until tender, then drain and mash.
2 Heat 50g (2oz) of the butter in a large non-stick frying pan. Add the leeks and cabbage and fry for 5 minutes, stirring, or until soft and beginning to colour. Combine the leeks and cabbage with the potatoes and season well with salt and pepper. Leave to cool. When cool enough to handle, mould into 12 cakes and dust with flour.
3 Heat the oil and remaining butter in a non-stick frying pan and cook the cakes for 4 minutes on each side or until they are golden, crisp and hot right through. Serve.

Nutrition per cake
130 cals | 10g fat (6g sats) |
10g carbs | 0.2g salt

Crispy Roast Potatoes

Countrywide Great roast potatoes should be crisp on the outside and fluffy inside. You need a floury potato, such as King Edward, and hot fat in the tin.

Serves 8 • Preparation 20 minutes • Cooking time 1 hour 50 minutes

1.8kg (4lb) potatoes, preferably King Edward, peeled and cut into two-bite pieces
2 tsp paprika
2–3 tbsp goose or white vegetable fat
salt

Nutrition per serving
211 cals | 6g fat (3g sats) |
37g carbs | 0.1g salt

1 Put the potatoes into a pan of lightly salted cold water. Cover and bring to the boil. Boil for 7 minutes, then drain well in a colander.
2 Sprinkle the paprika over the potatoes in the colander, then cover and shake the potatoes roughly, so they become fluffy around the edges.
3 Preheat the oven to 220°C (200°C fan oven) mark 7. Heat the fat in a large roasting tin on the hob. When it

sizzles, add the potatoes. Tilt the pan to coat, taking care as the fat will splutter. Roast in the oven for 1 hour.
4 Reduce the oven temperature to 200°C (180°C fan oven) mark 6 and roast for a further 40 minutes. Shake the potatoes only once or twice during cooking, otherwise the edges won't crisp and brown. Season with a little salt before serving.

FREEZING TIP

▼▼▼▼▼▼▼▼▼▼

To freeze, complete the recipe to the end of step 2, then cool, seal in large freezer bags and freeze for up to one month.

To use, cook from frozen, allowing an additional 15–20 minutes total cooking time.

Game Chips

Scotland These thin, crisp chips are traditionally served with game birds. Try this method for making beetroot, celeriac or parsnip chips.

Serves 4 • Preparation 10 minutes • Cooking time 1–2 minutes per batch

3 large old potatoes, peeled and sliced wafer-thin
vegetable oil to deep-fry

Nutrition per serving
225 cals | 11g fat (1g sats) |
29g carbs | 0.3g salt

1 Dry the potato slices on kitchen paper.
2 Heat enough oil for deep-frying in a large heavy-based pan (or deep-fat fryer) to 190°C (test by frying a small cube of bread – it should brown in 20 seconds).
3 Fry the potato slices in small batches for 1–2 minutes per batch until crisp and golden. Drain on kitchen paper and keep them warm while you cook the remaining chips.

Colcannon

Northern Ireland This traditional Irish dish is their version of bubble and squeak and a favourite on St Patrick's Day, in March. Inexpensive and nourishing, it was often served with boiled bacon or ham but is a warming side dish to accompany many dishes.

Serves 4 • Preparation 10 minutes • Cooking time 20 minutes

900g (2lb) potatoes, peeled and cut
into even-sized chunks
50g (2oz) butter
¼ Savoy cabbage, shredded
100ml (3½ fl oz) semi-skimmed milk
salt and ground black pepper

Nutrition per serving
310 cals | 12g fat (7g sats) |
45g carbs | 0.5g salt

1 Put the potatoes into a pan of cold lightly salted water. Bring to the boil, then partially cover the pan and simmer for 15–20 minutes until the potatoes are tender.
2 Meanwhile, melt the butter in a large frying pan. Add the cabbage and stir-fry for 3 minutes.
3 Drain the potatoes well, then tip back into the pan and put over a medium heat for 1 minute to drive off the excess moisture. Turn into a colander and cover to keep warm.
4 Pour the milk into the potato pan and bring to the boil, then take off the heat. Add the potatoes and mash well until smooth.
5 Add the cabbage and any butter from the pan and mix together. Season with salt and pepper to taste and serve.

Clapshot

Scotland This hearty root vegetable dish is eaten as an accompaniment to haggis. Turnips in Scotland and the North are known as swede in the South.

Serves 6 • Preparation 20 minutes • Cooking time 20 minutes

700g (1½ lb) potatoes, peeled and roughly chopped
700g (1½ lb) swede, roughly chopped
25g (1oz) butter
2 tbsp snipped fresh chives
salt and ground black pepper

1 Cook the potatoes and swede in lightly salted boiling water until tender, then drain well. Mash together until smooth.
2 Beat in the butter and snipped chives, then season to taste. Serve hot.

Nutrition per serving
145 cals | 4g fat (2g sats) |
26g carbs | 0.5g salt

Stump

The North This tasty vegetable purée combines three of the best of Britain's traditional root vegetables.

Serves 4 • Preparation 10 minutes • Cooking time 35 minutes

225g (8oz) carrots, sliced
225g (8oz) swede, sliced
225g (8oz) potatoes, peeled and sliced
15g (½oz) butter
150ml (¼ pint) milk
salt and ground black pepper

1 Simmer the vegetables in lightly salted water in a medium pan for 30 minutes or until soft. Drain well.
2 Mash the vegetables with the butter and milk. Reheat gently and season to taste. Serve hot.

Nutrition per serving
121 cals | 4g fat (2g sats) |
19g carbs | 0.8g salt

•COOK'S TIP•

This is a good way of using up older carrots and swede, which tend to be tough unless cooked well. You can vary the quantities if you prefer one vegetable to predominate but do include enough carrots to give an attractive colour.

Neeps and Tatties

Scotland The classic accompaniment to haggis, this dish is in fact two creamy, smooth mashes of swede and potatoes. Traditionally also served at Burns Night, 25 January. Cut both vegetables into even-sized pieces to ensure even cooking.

Serves 4 • Preparation 15 minutes • Cooking time 25 minutes

250g (9oz) swede, cut into even-sized chunks
450g (1lb) potatoes, peeled and cut into even-sized chunks
50–100g (2–3½ oz) butter
1 tbsp double cream (optional)
freshly grated nutmeg
salt and ground black pepper
haggis to serve

Nutrition per serving
276 cals | 20g fat (12g sats) |
23g carbs | 0.3g salt

1 Bring a large pan of lightly salted water to the boil, add the swede and cook for 20–25 minutes until tender. Drain and steam dry for 2 minutes.

2 Meanwhile, bring another large pan of lightly salted water to the boil, add the potatoes and cook for 15–20 minutes until tender. Drain and steam dry for 2 minutes.

3 Mash each vegetable with half the butter until smooth, adding a splash of cream, if you like. Season with nutmeg, salt and pepper. Serve with haggis.

VEGETARIAN DISHES

Cheesy Potato Pie

Countrywide Buy maincrop potatoes rather than new for this recipe. Maris Piper is particularly good for mashing, or you could use Desiree, recognisable by its red skin. Cotswold cheese, a mixture of Double Gloucester cheese and chives, gives a lovely flavour to the crisp potato topping.

Serves 4 • Preparation 10 minutes • Cooking time 50 minutes

900g (2lb) potatoes, peeled and cut into even-sized chunks
3 tbsp milk
125g (4oz) Cotswold or Cheddar cheese, grated (see Cook's Tip)
50g (2oz) butter
450g (1lb) leeks, trimmed and sliced
1 large red pepper, cored, seeded and roughly chopped
450g (1lb) courgettes, thickly sliced
225g (8oz) button mushrooms
2 tsp mild paprika
25g (1oz) plain wholemeal flour
300ml (½ pint) vegetable stock
salt and ground black pepper

Nutrition per serving
460 cals | 21g fat (12g sats) |
52g carbs | 1.7g salt

1 Preheat the oven to 200°C (180°C fan oven) mark 6. Cook the potatoes in lightly salted boiling water for 15–20 minutes until tender. Drain and mash with the milk, half the cheese and half the butter. Season to taste.

2 Meanwhile, heat the remaining butter in a large pan and fry the leeks and red pepper for 4–5 minutes until softened. Add the courgettes, mushrooms and paprika and fry for a further 2 minutes.

3 Sprinkle in the flour, then gradually add the stock and bring to the boil, stirring continuously. Cover and simmer for 5 minutes.

4 Spoon the vegetable mixture into an ovenproof serving dish and cover evenly with the cheesy potato. Sprinkle with the remaining cheese. Cook in the oven for 20–25 minutes until the top is crisp and golden brown.

•COOK'S TIP•

Some vegetarians prefer to avoid cheeses that have been produced by the traditional method, because this uses animal-derived rennet. However, most supermarkets and cheese shops now stock an excellent range of vegetarian cheeses, produced using vegetarian rennet. Always check the label when buying.

Leek and Pea Flan

Wales This attractive green flan makes excellent use of traditional Welsh leeks. Frozen peas taste just as good in it as fresh, but don't use canned ones or the flavour will be altered. Enjoy it at room temperature or cold, to take on a picnic.

Serves 4 • Preparation 15 minutes • Cooking time about 1 hour

450g (1lb) leeks, trimmed and sliced
125g (4oz) fresh or frozen shelled peas
150ml (¼ pint) milk
150g (5oz) natural yogurt
3 medium eggs
175g (6oz) plain wholemeal flour,
plus extra to dust
125g (4oz) Cheddar cheese, grated
(see Cook's Tip, page 194)
75g (3oz) butter
salt and ground black pepper

Nutrition per serving
519 cals | 31g fat (17g sats) |
38g carbs | 1.6g salt

1 Preheat the oven to 190°C (170°C fan oven) mark 5. Cook the leeks and peas in a little lightly salted water in a tightly covered medium pan until tender. Drain well.

2 Put the leeks, peas, milk and yogurt into a blender or food processor and whiz until smooth.

3 Beat 2 of the eggs into the purée and season to taste. Lightly beat the remaining egg in a small bowl.

4 Put the flour and half the cheese into a bowl. Rub in the butter until the mixture resembles fine breadcrumbs, then bind together with the remaining egg.

5 Roll out the pastry on a lightly floured surface and use to line a 23cm (9in) flan dish. Pour in the leek mixture, sprinkle the remaining cheese over the top and cook in the oven for 50–55 minutes until golden.

Farmhouse Cauliflower Soufflés

The West The distinctive flavour of cauliflower lends itself to soufflé treatment. This dish, like all soufflés, can be started and left before finishing off. If the sauce base is allowed to cool, allow about 10 minutes extra cooking time. Ensure people are ready to eat the soufflé as soon as it is done.

Serves 8 • Preparation 10 minutes, plus cooling • Cooking time 40 minutes

40g (1½ oz) butter, plus extra to grease
225g (8oz) small cauliflower florets
3 tbsp plain flour
200ml (7fl oz) milk
1 tbsp wholegrain mustard
125g (4oz) mature Farmhouse Cheddar cheese, grated (see Cook's Tip, page 194)
4 medium eggs, separated
salt and ground black pepper

Nutrition per serving
170 cals | 12g fat (6g sats) |
6g carbs | 0.7g salt

1 Preheat the oven to 180°C (160°C fan oven) mark 4. Grease eight individual ramekin dishes.
2 Put the cauliflower in a pan and just cover with lightly salted boiling water. Cover the pan and simmer until tender, then drain.
3 Meanwhile, prepare a white sauce. Put the butter, flour and milk into a saucepan. Heat, whisking continuously, until the sauce thickens, boils and is smooth. Simmer for 1–2 minutes, then add the mustard and season to taste.
4 Turn the sauce into a blender or food processor. Add the cauliflower and whiz to an almost smooth purée.
5 Turn into a large bowl and leave to cool slightly. Stir in the cheese with the egg yolks.
6 Whisk the egg whites until stiff but not dry and fold into the sauce mixture. Spoon into the dishes.
7 Cook in the oven for 25 minutes or until browned and firm to the touch. Serve at once.

Cauliflower Cheese

Countrywide The smoothness of the cheese sauce contrasts well with the slight crispness of the cauliflower. Try different cheeses, according to how strong you like the sauce – Double Gloucester is a pale mild cheese with a salty tang, whereas a strong Cheddar will give more of a bite.

Serves 2 • Preparation 5 minutes • Cooking time 20 minutes

1 cauliflower
1 quantity cheese (mornay) sauce
(see Cook's Tip)
extra grated cheese to sprinkle (see
Cook's Tip, page 194)
salt
jacket potato to serve (optional)

Nutrition per serving
383 cals | 24g fat (14g sats) |
20g carbs | 2.2g salt

1 Remove the coarse outer leaves from the cauliflower, cut a cross in the stalk end and wash the whole cauliflower under the tap.
2 Put the cauliflower into a medium pan, stem side down, then pour enough boiling water over it to come halfway up. Add a pinch of salt and cover the pan. Bring to the boil and cook for 10–15 minutes. Stick a sharp knife into the florets – they should be tender but not mushy. Preheat the grill.
3 Drain the cauliflower and put it into an ovenproof dish. Pour the cheese sauce over it, sprinkle with a little grated cheese, then grill for 2–3 minutes until golden on top. Serve on its own or with a jacket potato, if you like.

TRY SOMETHING DIFFERENT

Make this with ½ head of cauliflower and ½ head of broccoli. Cut the stems off the florets, then peel and chop them into pieces the same size as the cauliflower and broccoli florets. They will take only about 4 minutes to cook until just tender. Make as above.

•COOK'S TIP•

Mornay Sauce Pour 300ml (½ pint) semi-skimmed milk into a pan. Add 1 onion slice, 6 peppercorns, 1 mace blade and 1 bay leaf. Bring almost to the boil, remove from the heat, cover and leave to infuse for about 20 minutes, then strain. To make the roux, melt 15g (½ oz) butter in a pan, stir in 15g (½ oz) plain flour and cook, stirring, for 1 minute until cooked but not coloured. Remove from the heat and gradually pour on the infused milk, whisking constantly. Season lightly with salt, pepper and grated nutmeg. Return to the heat and cook, stirring constantly, until the sauce is thickened and smooth. Simmer gently for 2 minutes. Remove from the heat and stir 50g (2oz) finely grated Gruyère or mature Cheddar cheese and a large pinch of mustard powder or cayenne pepper into the finished sauce. Heat gently to melt the cheese, if necessary.

White Nut Roast

Countrywide This recipe makes a 'loaf' which slices well and can be served hot or cold. Any type of chopped nuts can be used for this dish, such as almonds, Brazil nuts or unsalted peanuts, and you could use a mature Cheddar instead of sage Derby or Parmesan.

Serves 8 • Preparation 20 minutes, plus cooling • Cooking time about 1 hour

40g (1½oz) butter, plus extra to grease
1 onion, finely chopped
1 garlic clove, crushed
225g (8oz) mixed white nuts, such as
Brazil nuts, macadamia nuts, pinenuts
and whole almonds, ground in a food
processor or nut mill
125g (4oz) fresh white breadcrumbs
grated zest and juice of ½ lemon
75g (3oz) sage Derby cheese or
Parmesan (see Cook's Tip, page 194),
grated
125g (4oz) cooked, peeled (or vacuum-
packed) chestnuts, roughly chopped
½ x 400g can artichoke hearts, drained
and roughly chopped
1 medium egg, lightly beaten
2 tsp each freshly chopped flat-leafed
parsley, sage and thyme, plus extra
sprigs, and some to garnish (optional)
salt and ground black pepper

Nutrition per serving
371 cals | 28g fat (9g sats) |
20g carbs | 0.8g salt

1 Preheat the oven to 200°C (180°C fan oven) mark 6. Melt the butter in a pan and cook the onion and garlic for 5 minutes or until soft. Put into a large bowl and set aside to cool.

2 Add the nuts, breadcrumbs, lemon zest and juice, cheese, chestnuts and artichokes. Season well and bind together with the egg. Stir in the herbs.

3 Put the mixture on to a large piece of buttered foil and shape into a fat sausage, packing tightly. Scatter with the extra herb sprigs and wrap in the foil.

4 Cook on a baking sheet for 35 minutes, then unwrap the foil slightly and cook for a further 15 minutes or until turning golden.

Slice and serve garnished with herb sprigs, if you like.

.COOK'S TIPS.

To freeze, complete the recipe to the end of step 3, cool, cover and freeze for up to one month.

To use, cook from frozen for 45 minutes, then unwrap the foil slightly and cook for a further 15 minutes or until turning golden.

Pan Haggerty

The North Use firm-fleshed potatoes such as Desiree, Romano or Maris Piper, as they will keep their shape and not crumble into mash.

Serves 4 • Preparation 5 minutes • Cooking time 35 minutes

25g (1oz) butter
1 tbsp vegetable oil
450g (1lb) potatoes, peeled and thinly sliced
2 medium onions, thinly sliced
125g (4oz) Cheddar or Lancashire cheese, grated (see Cook's Tip, page 194)
salt and ground black pepper

Nutrition per serving
287 cals | 17g fat (9g sats) |
25g carbs | 1.2g salt

1 Heat the butter and oil in a large heavy-based frying pan. Remove the pan from the heat and put in layers of potatoes, onions and grated cheese, seasoning well with salt and pepper between each layer, and ending with a top layer of cheese.

2 Cover and cook the vegetables gently for about 30 minutes or until the potatoes and onions are almost cooked. Meanwhile, preheat the grill.

3 Uncover and brown the top of the dish under the hot grill. Serve straight from the pan.

Glamorgan Sausages

Wales This was originally made with Glamorgan cheese, hence the name, but since this is no longer available, nowadays Caerphilly is used.

Serves 4 • Preparation 25 minutes, plus chilling • Cooking time 15 minutes

150g (5oz) Caerphilly cheese, grated (see Cook's Tip, page 194)
200g (7oz) fresh white breadcrumbs
3 spring onions, finely chopped
1 tbsp freshly chopped flat-leafed parsley
leaves of 4 thyme sprigs
3 large eggs, 1 separated
vegetable oil
salt and ground black pepper

Nutrition per serving
403 cals | 20g fat (9g sats) |
39g carbs | 1.7g salt

1 Preheat the oven to 140°C (120°C fan oven) mark 1. Mix the cheese with 150g (5oz) of the breadcrumbs, the spring onions and herbs in a large bowl. Season well.

2 Add the whole eggs plus the extra yolk and mix well to combine. Cover and chill for 5 minutes.

3 Lightly beat the egg white in a shallow bowl. Tip the rest of the breadcrumbs on to a large plate.

4 Take 2 tbsp of the cheese mixture and shape into a small sausage, about 4cm (1½in) long. Roll first in the egg white, then in the breadcrumbs to coat. Repeat to make 12 sausages in total.

5 Heat 2 tsp oil in a large heavy-based pan until hot, and fry the sausages in two batches for 6–8 minutes, turning until golden all over. Keep warm in the oven while cooking the rest. Serve with a chutney.

Cheshire Potted Cheese

The Midlands This is an excellent way to use up odd pieces of cheese. They can be grated up together. As long as the butter seal is unbroken, this mixture keeps in the fridge for several weeks. Served with a salad, it makes a light lunch.

Makes about 350g (12oz) • Preparation 10 minutes

225g (8oz) Cheshire cheese, grated
(see Cook's Tip, page 194)
about 50g (2oz) butter, softened
¼ tsp ground mace or allspice
2 tbsp sweet sherry or Madeira
melted butter for sealing
toast, fruit and celery to serve

Nutrition per serving
127 cals | 11g fat (7g sats) |
trace carbs | 0.4g salt

1 Mix the cheese with the softened butter and spice. The exact amount of butter will depend to a certain extent on how dry or moist the cheese is. Beat thoroughly. Add the sherry or Madeira and mix again.

2 When the cheese is well amalgamated with the other ingredients, put it into small pots or ramekin dishes, pressing it well down and smoothing the tops. Cover each with melted butter and store in the fridge. Remove from the fridge about 1 hour before serving. Serve spread on toast or bread with fruit and celery.

Eggy Bread

Countrywide If time allows, let the bread stand in the eggy mixture until it is all absorbed, before frying until beautifully brown and crisp.

Serves 1–2 • Preparation 5 minutes • Cooking time 10 minutes

75ml (2½ fl oz) milk
1 small egg
2 slices wholemeal bread
25g (1oz) butter
125g (4oz) Caerphilly cheese, grated
(see Cook's Tip, page 194)
2 tbsp pickle
3 pickled onions, chopped

Nutrition per serving
434 cals | 30g fat (18g sats) |
23g carbs | 2.2g salt

1 Preheat the grill. Beat together the milk and egg. Dip both slices of bread into the egg mixture, coating well on both sides.
2 Melt the butter in a large frying pan and fry the bread until golden brown on both sides. Keep warm.
3 Mix together the cheese, pickle and pickled onions. Spread the cheese mixture over the bread, then grill until golden and bubbling. Serve immediately.

Welsh Rarebit

Wales There have been variations of this dish throughout Great Britain since the 18th century, but the Welsh version has proved the most enduring.

Serves 4 • Preparation 5 minutes • Cooking time 6–8 minutes

225g (8oz) Cheddar cheese, grated (see
Cook's Tip, page 194)
25g (1oz) butter
1 tsp English mustard
4 tbsp brown ale
4 slices white bread, crusts removed
salt and ground black pepper
flat-leafed parsley sprig to garnish
tomato quarters to serve

Nutrition per serving
380 cals | 25g fat (15g sats) |
21g carbs | 1.9g salt

1 Put the cheese, butter, mustard and beer into a heavy-based pan over a low heat and stir occasionally until the cheese is melted and the mixture is smooth and creamy. Season with salt and pepper to taste.
2 Toast the bread under the grill on one side only. Turn the slices over and spread the cheese mixture on the untoasted side. Put under the grill for 1 minute or until golden and bubbling, then serve with tomato quarters and a parsley garnish.

PUDDINGS

Bread and Butter Pudding

Countrywide A Victorian nursery favourite, this inexpensive pudding has recently regained its popularity, thanks to appearing on restaurant menus.

Serves 4 • Preparation 10 minutes, plus soaking • Cooking time 30–40 minutes

50g (2oz) butter, softened, plus extra
to grease
275g (10oz) white farmhouse bread, cut
into 1cm (½ in) slices, crusts removed
50g (2oz) raisins or sultanas
3 medium eggs
450ml (¾ pint) milk
3 tbsp golden icing sugar, plus extra
to dust

Nutrition per serving
450 cals | 13g fat (5g sats) |
70g carbs | 1.1g salt

---

1 Lightly butter four 300ml (½ pint) gratin dishes or one 1.1 litre (2 pint) ovenproof dish. Butter the bread, then cut into triangles. Arrange the bread in the dish(es) and sprinkle with the raisins or sultanas.
2 Beat the eggs, milk and sugar in a bowl. Pour the mixture over the bread and leave to soak for 10 minutes. Preheat the oven to 180°C (160°C fan oven) mark 4.
3 Put the pudding(s) in the oven and bake for 30–40 minutes. Dust with icing sugar to serve.

Osborne Pudding

Countrywide A variation on bread and butter pudding, this uses brown bread spread with marmalade. The recipe has been around for centuries.

Serves 4 • Preparation 10 minutes, plus standing • Cooking time 45 minutes

4 thin slices day-old wholemeal bread
butter and orange marmalade for
spreading
50g (2oz) currants or sultanas
450ml (¾ pint) milk
2 medium eggs
1 tbsp brandy or rum (optional)
finely grated zest of 1 orange
1 tbsp light soft brown sugar
freshly grated nutmeg
custard or cream to serve

Nutrition per serving
329 cals | 14g fat (7g sats) |
42g carbs | 0.8g salt

---

1 Spread the bread with butter and marmalade, then cut into triangles. Arrange, buttered side up, in a buttered ovenproof serving dish, sprinkling the layers with the fruit.
2 Heat the milk, but do not boil. Beat the eggs with the brandy or rum, if using, and the orange zest, then gradually pour in the warm milk, stirring continuously. Pour over the bread and leave to stand for at least 15 minutes to allow the bread to absorb the milk. Preheat the oven to 180°C (160°C fan oven) mark 4.
3 Sprinkle the sugar and nutmeg on top of the pudding and bake for 30–40 minutes until set and lightly browned. Serve hot with custard or cream.

Rice Pudding

Countrywide There's nothing nicer than a lovingly made rice pudding, but do use creamy fresh milk. The orange zest adds a different flavour.

Serves 6 • Preparation 5 minutes • Cooking time 1½ hours

butter to grease
125g (4oz) short-grain pudding rice
1.1 litres (2 pints) milk
50g (2oz) golden caster sugar
1 tsp vanilla extract
grated zest of 1 orange (optional)
freshly grated nutmeg to taste

Nutrition per serving
239 cals | 8g fat (5g sats) |
34g carbs | 0.2g salt

1 Preheat the oven to 170°C (150°C fan oven) mark 3. Lightly butter a 1.7 litre (3 pint) ovenproof dish.
2 Put the rice, milk, sugar, vanilla extract and orange zest, if using, into the dish and stir everything together. Grate the nutmeg over the top of the mixture.
3 Bake the pudding in the middle of the oven for 1½ hours or until the top is golden brown.

Queen of Puddings

Countrywide A few simple ingredients combine to make this very attractive British pudding.

Serves 4 • Preparation 20 minutes, plus standing • Cooking time about 1¼ hours

4 medium eggs
600ml (1 pint) milk
125g (4oz) fresh breadcrumbs
3–4 tbsp raspberry jam
75g (3oz) caster sugar

Nutrition per serving
387 cals | 9g fat (3g sats) |
65g carbs | 1g salt

1 Separate 3 eggs and beat together the 3 egg yolks and 1 whole egg. Add to the milk and mix well. Stir in the breadcrumbs.
2 Spread the jam on the bottom of a pie dish. Pour in the milk mixture and leave for 30 minutes. Preheat the oven to 150°C (130°C fan oven) mark 2.
3 Bake in the oven for 1 hour or until set. Put the egg whites into a clean, grease-free bowl and whisk until they form stiff peaks. Fold in the sugar, then pile on top of the custard and return to the oven for a further 15–20 minutes until the meringue is set.

Almond Bakewell Tarts

The Midlands A buttery mixture flavoured with ground almonds and baked in a light, flaky pastry case is the basis of this traditional Derbyshire recipe, sometimes known as Bakewell tart, the origin of which is still secret.

Makes 6 • Preparation 25 minutes, plus chilling • Cooking time 50 minutes, plus cooling

For the sweet pastry
200g (7oz) plain flour, plus extra to dust
a pinch of salt
100g (3½ oz) unsalted butter, at room
temperature, cut into pieces
3 large egg yolks
75g (3oz) caster sugar
½ tsp vanilla extract

For the filling
125g (4oz) unsalted butter, softened
125g (4oz) caster sugar
3 large eggs
125g (4oz) ground almonds
2–3 drops almond extract
6 tbsp redcurrant jelly

For the crumble topping
25g (1oz) unsalted butter
75g (3oz) plain flour
25g (1oz) caster sugar
Plum Sauce (see Cook's Tip) to serve

Nutrition per serving
931 cals | 52g fat (24g sats) |
104g carbs | 0.8g salt

1 To make the pastry, sift the flour and salt into a mound on a clean surface. Make a large well in the centre and add the butter, egg yolks, sugar and vanilla extract. Using the fingertips of one hand, work the sugar, butter and egg yolks together until well blended. Gradually work in all the flour to bind the mixture together. Knead the dough gently on a lightly floured surface until smooth, then wrap in clingfilm and chill for at least 30 minutes before rolling out.

2 Roll out the pastry thinly on a lightly floured surface and line six 10cm (4in), 3cm (1¼in) deep tartlet tins. Chill for 30 minutes. Preheat the oven to 190°C (170°C fan oven) mark 5.

3 Bake the tartlet cases blind (see Cook's Tip page 178). Remove from the oven and leave to cool.

4 To make the filling, beat the butter and sugar together until light and fluffy. Gradually beat in 2 eggs, then beat in the remaining egg with one-third of the ground almonds. Fold in the remaining almonds and the almond extract.

5 Melt the redcurrant jelly in a small pan and brush over the inside of each pastry case. Spoon in the almond filling. Put the tarts on a baking sheet and bake for 20–25 minutes until golden and just firm. Leave in the tins for 10 minutes, then unmould on to a wire rack and leave to cool completely.

6 To make the crumble topping, rub the butter into the flour and add the sugar. Spread evenly on a baking sheet and grill until golden. Cool, then sprinkle over the tarts. Decorate with plums (see Cook's Tip) and serve with Plum Sauce.

•COOK'S TIP•
Plum Sauce
Put 450g (1lb) halved and stoned ripe plums, 50–75g (2–3oz) soft brown sugar and 150ml (¼ pint) sweet white wine into a pan with 150ml (¼ pint) water. Bring to the boil, then simmer until tender. Remove 3 plums to decorate; thickly slice and put to one side. Cook the remaining plums for about 15 minutes until very soft. Put into a food processor and whiz until smooth. Sieve, if you like, adding more sugar to taste. Leave to cool

Treacle Tart

Countrywide A very popular traditional pudding, this tart is definitely one for those with a sweet tooth. Don't serve it too hot, warm is best. Ice cream, custard or clotted cream are all good accompaniments.

Cuts into 6 slices • Preparation 25 minutes, plus chilling • Cooking time 45–50 minutes, plus cooling

For the sweet pastry
225g (8oz) plain flour, plus extra to dust
a pinch of salt
150g (5oz) unsalted butter, at room temperature, cut into pieces
1 medium egg yolk
15g (½oz) golden caster sugar

For the filling
700g (1½lb) golden syrup
175g (6oz) fresh white breadcrumbs
grated zest of 3 lemons
2 medium eggs, lightly beaten

Nutrition per slice
486 cals | 15g fat (8g sats) |
88g carbs | 1.1g salt

1 To make the pastry, sift the flour and salt into a mound on a clean surface. Make a large well in the centre and add the butter, egg yolk and sugar. Using the fingertips of one hand, work the sugar, butter and egg yolks together until well blended. Gradually work in all the flour to bind the mixture together. Knead the dough gently on a lightly floured surface until smooth, then wrap in clingfilm and chill for at least 30 minutes before rolling out.

2 Roll out the pastry on a lightly floured surface and use to line a 25.5cm (10in), 4cm (1½in) deep, loose-based fluted tart tin. Prick the base all over with a fork and chill for 30 minutes.

3 Preheat the oven to 180°C (160°C fan oven) mark 4. To make the filling, heat the syrup in a pan over a low heat until thinner in consistency. Remove from the heat and mix in the breadcrumbs and lemon zest. Stir in the beaten eggs.

4 Pour the filling into the pastry case and bake for 45–50 minutes until the filling is lightly set and golden. Allow to cool slightly. Serve warm.

TRY SOMETHING DIFFERENT

▼▼▼▼▼▼▼▼▼

For the pastry, replace half the plain flour with wholemeal flour. For the filling, use fresh wholemeal breadcrumbs instead of white.

Summer Pudding

Countrywide Bursting with colour and packed with juicy fruit, this pudding is best made when all the black and red berry fruits are in season. Strawberries, however, are best avoided, as they are too soft and will disintegrate.

Serves 8 • Preparation 10 minutes, plus chilling • Cooking time 10 minutes

800g (1lb 12oz) mixed summer berries, such as 250g (9oz) each redcurrants and blackcurrants and 300g (11oz) raspberries
125g (4oz) golden caster sugar
3 tbsp crème de cassis
9 thick slices slightly stale white bread, crusts removed
crème fraîche or clotted cream to serve

___

Nutrition per serving
173 cals | 1g fat (trace sats) |
38g carbs | 0.4g salt

___

1 Put the redcurrants and blackcurrants into a medium pan. Add the sugar and cassis. Bring to a simmer and cook for 3–5 minutes until the sugar has dissolved. Add the raspberries and cook for 2 minutes. Once the fruit is cooked, taste it – there should be a good balance between tart and sweet.

2 Meanwhile, line a 1 litre (1¾ pint) bowl with clingfilm. Put the base of the bowl on one piece of bread and cut around it. Put the circle of bread into the base of the bowl.

3 Line the inside of the bowl with more slices of bread, slightly overlapping them to prevent any gaps. Spoon in the fruit, making sure the juice soaks into the bread. Keep back a few spoonfuls of juice in case the bread is unevenly soaked when you turn out the pudding.

4 Cut the remaining bread to fit the top of the pudding neatly, using a sharp knife to trim any excess bread from around the edges. Wrap in clingfilm, weigh down with a saucer and a can and chill overnight.

5 To serve, unwrap the outer clingfilm, upturn the pudding on to a plate and remove the inner clingfilm. Drizzle with the reserved juice and serve with crème fraîche or clotted cream.

Cumberland Rum Nicky

The North This rich and sticky tart is a Northern speciality incorporating several of the exotic imports that came from Cumberland's trade with the West Indies. Dates, ginger and rum feature widely in many local dishes. This version is high in fibre.

Serves 6 • Preparation 10 minutes • Cooking time 30–35 minutes

225g (8oz) stoned dates, chopped
125g (4oz) ready-to-eat dried apricots
50g (2oz) stem ginger in syrup, drained and chopped
3 tbsp light rum
2 tbsp soft light brown sugar
350g (12oz) plain wholemeal flour, plus extra to dust
a pinch of salt
175g (6oz) butter
1 medium egg yolk, lightly beaten
a little milk
demerara sugar to decorate (optional)
natural yogurt to serve

Nutrition per serving
451 cals | 18g fat (10g sats) |
66g carbs | 0.6g salt

1 Preheat the oven to 200°C (180°C fan oven) mark 6. Grease a 25.5cm (10in) flat pie plate.
2 Mix together the dates, apricots, ginger, rum and half the light brown sugar. Leave to soak while making the pastry.
3 Put the flour and salt into a bowl and rub in 125g (4oz) of the butter until the mixture resembles fine breadcrumbs. Add the remaining sugar, then the egg yolk and enough water to bind. Knead lightly on a floured surface.
4 Roll out half the pastry on a lightly floured surface and use to line the prepared plate. Spread the pastry

with the soaked dried fruit. Dot with the remaining butter. Brush the edge of the pastry with water.
5 Roll out the remaining pastry slightly larger all round than the pie plate. Lift the pastry lid over the filling and press the edges down lightly to seal. Cut any pastry trimmings into leaves and use to decorate the pie. Brush with milk and bake for 30–35 minutes until golden brown. Sprinkle with demerara sugar, if you like. Serve hot with natural yogurt.

Damson and Apple Tansy

The North Tansies originally always included the bittersweet herb called tansy, which still lends its name to many custard and omelette-type puddings. This sweet-tart combination with Cox's apples traditionally used the Witherslack damsons, which grow south of Lake Windermere.

Serves 4 • Preparation 10 minutes • Cooking time 20 minutes

2 large Cox's Orange Pippin apples, peeled, cored and thinly sliced
225g (8oz) damsons, halved, stoned and quartered
15g (½oz) butter
40g (1½oz) sugar
a pinch of ground cloves
a pinch of ground cinnamon
4 medium eggs, separated
3 tbsp soured cream or natural yogurt, plus extra to serve

Nutrition per serving
226 cals | 12g fat (5g sats) |
24g carbs | 0.3g salt

1 Preheat the grill. Put the apples, damsons, butter and half the sugar into a large frying pan. Cook over a gentle heat, until the fruit is softened, stirring continuously. Stir in the cloves and cinnamon, then remove from the heat.

2 Beat the egg yolks with the cream or yogurt and stir into the fruit. Whisk the egg whites until stiff, then carefully fold in.

3 Cook over a low heat until the mixture has set. Sprinkle the top with the remaining sugar, then brown under the hot grill. Serve immediately, straight from the pan, with soured cream or natural yogurt.

Apple Crumble

Countrywide The beauty of crumbles is that they are very easy to make. This recipe uses apple but any type of fruit can be used.

Serves 4 • Preparation 15 minutes • Cooking time 45 minutes

125g (4oz) plain flour
50g (2oz) unsalted butter, cubed
50g (2oz) golden caster sugar
450g (1lb) apples, peeled, cored and sliced
custard or double cream to serve

Nutrition per serving
425 cals | 18g fat (7g sats) |
74g carbs | 0.3g salt

1 Preheat the oven to 180°C (160°C fan oven) mark 4. Put the flour into a bowl, add the butter and rub in with your fingertips until the mixture resembles fine breadcrumbs. Stir in half the sugar. Put to one side.
2 Arrange half the apples in a 1.1 litre (2 pint) pie dish and sprinkle with the rest of the sugar. Add the remaining apple slices to the dish. Spoon the crumble mixture over the fruit.
3 Bake for 45 minutes or until the fruit is soft. Serve hot with custard or a drizzle of double cream.

Old-English Trifle

Countrywide The recipe for trifle has altered little over the centuries – at one time syllabub topped the custard, and fruit has not always been included.

Serves 6 • Preparation 20 minutes, plus soaking and cooling • Cooking time 15 minutes

600ml (1 pint) milk
½ vanilla pod
2 medium eggs, plus 2 egg yolks
2 tbsp caster sugar, plus extra to sprinkle
8 trifle sponges
175g (6oz) raspberry or strawberry jam
125g (4oz) macaroons, lightly crushed
100ml (3½ fl oz) medium sherry
300ml (½ pint) double cream

To decorate
40g (1½ oz) flaked almonds, toasted
50g (2oz) glacé cherries

Nutrition per serving
532 cals | 24g fat (9g sats) |
66g carbs | 0.3g salt

1 Bring the milk to the boil with the vanilla pod. Remove from the heat, cover and leave to infuse for 20 minutes.
2 Beat together the eggs, egg yolks and sugar, then strain on to the milk. Cook gently without boiling, stirring, until the custard thickens slightly. Pour into a bowl, lightly sprinkle the surface with sugar, then cool.
3 Spread the trifle sponges with jam, cut up and put into a 2 litre (3½ pint) shallow serving dish with the macaroons. Spoon the sherry over and leave for 2 hours. Pour the cold custard over.
4 Lightly whip the cream. Top the custard with half the cream. Pipe the remaining cream on top and decorate with almonds and cherries.

Boodles Orange Fool

The Southeast Boodle's Club, in London, was founded in 1764 and this luscious fool has been a speciality on the menu there for many years.

Serves 6 • Preparation 15 minutes, plus chilling

4–6 trifle sponges, cut into 1cm (½in)
thick slices
grated zest and juice of 2 oranges
grated zest and juice of 1 lemon
25–50g (1–2oz) sugar
300ml (½ pint) double cream
grated orange zest or orange slices or
segments to decorate

Nutrition per serving
325 cals | 28g fat (17g sats) |
17g carbs | 0.1g salt

1 Use the sponge slices to line the bottom and halfway up the sides of a deep serving dish or bowl.

2 Mix the orange and lemon zests and juice with the sugar and stir until the sugar has completely dissolved.

3 In another bowl, whip the cream until it just starts to thicken, then slowly add the sweetened fruit juice, whipping the cream as you do so. Whip until the cream is light and thickened and all the juice is absorbed.

4 Pour the mixture over the sponge and chill for at least 2 hours, longer if possible, so that the juice can soak into the sponge and the cream thicken. Serve decorated with orange zest or segments or slices of fresh orange.

Chilled Blackberry Snow

The Southeast Finish assembling this just before it is needed and serve immediately or it will start to lose some volume.

Serves 6 • Preparation 30 minutes, plus freezing

450g (1lb) blackberries, fresh or frozen,
thawed
2 medium egg whites
50g (2oz) caster sugar
300ml (½ pint) double cream

Nutrition per serving
303 cals | 27g fat (17g sats) |
13g carbs | 0.1g salt

1 Rub the blackberries through a nylon sieve. Pour the purée into a rigid container and freeze for about 2 hours or until mushy.

2 Whisk the egg whites until stiff, then gradually add the sugar, whisking until the mixture stands in soft peaks. Whip the cream until it just holds its shape.

3 Remove the frozen blackberry purée from the freezer and mash to break down the large ice crystals, being careful not to break it down completely.

4 Fold the cream and egg whites together, then quickly fold in the semi-frozen blackberry purée to form a 'swirled' effect. Spoon into tall glasses and serve immediately.

Damask Cream

The West This is also known as Devonshire junket. Don't serve it until you are ready to eat, as once it is cut the shape will disintegrate.

Serves 4 • Preparation 5 minutes • Cooking time 10 minutes, plus setting

600ml (1 pint) single cream
3 tbsp caster sugar
2 tsp vegetarian rennet essence
a large pinch of freshly grated nutmeg
1 tbsp brandy
4 tbsp clotted or double cream
1 tsp rosewater
rose petals to decorate (optional)

Nutrition per serving
417 cals | 37g fat (23g sats) |
15g carbs | 0.1g salt

1 Put the single cream and 2 tbsp of the sugar into a pan. Heat gently until tepid, stirring to dissolve the sugar. (When the mixture is tepid it will register 36.9°C on a sugar thermometer, or not feel hot or cold if you put your finger in it.) Stir in the rennet, nutmeg and brandy, then pour into a serving dish.
2 Leave for 2–3 hours until set. Do not disturb the junket during this time or it will not set.
3 When the junket is set, mix the remaining sugar, the cream and rosewater together and spoon carefully over the top. Decorate with rose petals, if you like.

Eton Mess

The Southeast This is served at the annual prize-giving of Eton College, one of Britain's most famous public schools. It's a marvellous summer dessert.

Serves 6 • Preparation 10 minutes

200g (7oz) fromage frais, chilled
200g (7oz) low-fat Greek yogurt, chilled
1 tbsp golden caster sugar
2 tbsp strawberry liqueur
6 meringues, roughly crushed
350g (12oz) strawberries, hulled and halved

Nutrition per serving
198 cals | 5g fat (3g sats) |
33g carbs | 0.1g salt

1 Put the fromage frais and yogurt into a large bowl and stir to combine.
2 Add the sugar, strawberry liqueur, meringues and strawberries. Mix together gently and divide among six dishes.

TRY SOMETHING DIFFERENT

▼▼▼▼▼▼▼▼▼▼

Caribbean Crush
Replace the sugar and liqueur with dulce de leche toffee sauce and the strawberries with sliced bananas.

Cranberry Christmas Pudding

The Southeast Christmas puddings were first made hundreds of years ago, and originally included meat broth, but they gradually evolved into the pudding we know and love today. Since they can be made so far in advance of Christmas, it's one less job to have to worry about.

Serves 12 • Preparation 20 minutes, plus soaking • Cooking time 6 hours

200g (7oz) currants
200g (7oz) sultanas
200g (7oz) raisins
75g (3oz) dried cranberries or cherries
grated zest and juice of 1 orange
50ml (2fl oz) rum
50ml (2fl oz) brandy
1–2 tsp Angostura bitters
1 small apple
1 carrot
175g (6oz) fresh breadcrumbs
100g (3½ oz) plain flour, sifted
1 tsp mixed spice
175g (6oz) light vegetarian suet
100g (3½ oz) dark muscovado sugar
50g (2oz) blanched almonds, roughly chopped
2 medium eggs
butter to grease
Frosted Berries and Leaves (see Cook's Tips) and icing sugar to decorate
Brandy Butter (see Cook's Tips) to serve

Nutrition per serving
448 cals | 17g fat (7g sats) |
68g carbs | 0.3g salt

1 Put the dried fruit, orange zest and juice into a large bowl. Pour the rum, brandy and Angostura bitters over, cover and leave to soak in a cool place for at least 1 hour or overnight.

2 Grate the apple and carrot, then add to the bowl of soaked fruit with the breadcrumbs, flour, mixed spice, suet, sugar, almonds and eggs. Use a wooden spoon to mix everything together well. Now's the time to make a wish!

3 Grease a 1.8 litre (3¼ pint) pudding basin and line with a 60cm (24in) square piece of muslin. Spoon the mixture into the pudding basin and flatten the surface. Gather the muslin up and over the top, then twist and secure with string.

4 Put the basin on an upturned heatproof saucer or trivet in the bottom of a large pan. Pour in enough boiling water to come halfway up the side of the basin. Cover with a tight-fitting lid and simmer for 6 hours. Keep the water topped up. Remove the basin from the pan and leave to cool. When the pudding is cold, remove it from the basin, then wrap it in clingfilm and a double layer of foil. Store in a cool, dry place for up to six months.

5 To reheat, steam for 2½ hours; check the water level every 40 minutes and top up with boiling water if necessary. Leave the pudding in the pan, covered, to keep warm until needed. Decorate with the Frosted Berries and Leaves and dust with icing sugar. Serve with Brandy Butter.

COOK'S TIPS

Frosted Berries and Leaves
Lightly beat 1 medium egg white and spread 25g (1oz) caster sugar out on a tray, making sure there are no lumps. Brush a few fresh cranberries and bay leaves with the beaten egg white. Dip the berries and leaves into the sugar, shake off any excess, then leave to dry on a tray lined with greaseproof paper or baking parchment for about 1 hour.

Brandy Butter
Put 150g (5oz) unsalted butter, at room temperature, into a bowl and whisk to soften. Gradually whisk in 150g (5oz) sifted golden icing sugar, then pour in 3 tbsp brandy just before the final addition of sugar. Continue whisking until the mixture is pale and fluffy, then spoon into a serving dish. Cover and chill until needed. Remove from the fridge 30 minutes before serving.

Spotted Dick

Countrywide This lovely old-fashioned pudding has been around since the 19th century, when it was often served in gentlemen's clubs. It is traditionally made in a roll, and not formed in a pudding basin.

Serves 4 • Preparation 20 minutes • Cooking time 2 hours

125g (4oz) fresh breadcrumbs
75g (3oz) self-raising flour, plus extra to dust
75g (3oz) shredded suet
50g (2oz) caster sugar
175g (6oz) currants
finely grated zest of 1 lemon
5 tbsp milk
Fresh Vanilla Custard (see page 217) to serve

Nutrition per serving
502 cals | 18g fat (10g sats) | 84g carbs | 0.8g salt

---

1 Half-fill a preserving pan or large pan with water and put on to boil.
2 Put the breadcrumbs, flour, suet, sugar, currants and lemon zest into a bowl and stir well until thoroughly mixed.
3 Pour in the milk and stir until well blended. Using one hand, bring the ingredients together to form a soft, slightly sticky dough.
4 Turn the dough out on to a floured surface and knead gently until just smooth. Shape into a neat roll about 15cm (6in) in length.
5 Make a 5cm (2in) pleat across a clean teatowel or pudding cloth. (Or pleat together sheets of greased greaseproof paper and strong foil.)

Encase the roll in the cloth (or foil), pleating the open edges tightly together.
6 Tie the ends securely with string to form a cracker shape. Make a string handle across the top. Lower the suet roll into the pan of boiling water and boil for 2 hours.
7 Using the string handle, lift the Spotted Dick out of the water. Put on a wire rack standing over a plate and allow the excess moisture to drain off.
8 Snip the string and gently roll the pudding out of the cloth or foil on to a warmed serving plate. Serve sliced with custard.

Syrup Sponge Pudding

Countrywide A nostalgic pudding evoking memories of schooldays in times gone by. Filling and warming, it's just the thing for a cold winter's day. For a change, try making the jam or chocolate versions.

Serves 4 • Preparation 15 minutes • Cooking time 1½ hours

125g (4oz) butter, plus extra to grease
2 tbsp golden syrup
125g (4oz) caster sugar
2 medium eggs, beaten
a few drops of vanilla extract
175g (6oz) self-raising flour, sifted
a little milk to mix
Fresh Vanilla Custard (see Cook's Tip) to serve

Nutrition per serving
582 cals | 29g fat (17g sats) |
77g carbs | 1.1g salt

---

1 Half-fill a steamer or large pan with water and put it on to boil. Grease a 900ml (1½ pint) pudding basin and spoon the syrup into the bottom.
2 Cream together the butter and sugar until pale and fluffy. Add the beaten eggs and the vanilla, a little at a time, beating well after each addition.
3 Using a metal spoon, fold in half the sifted flour, then fold in the rest, with enough milk to give a dropping consistency.
4 Pour the mixture into the prepared basin, cover with greased greaseproof paper or foil and secure with string. Steam for 1½ hours. Serve with custard.

TRY SOMETHING DIFFERENT

Steamed Jam Sponge Pudding
Put 4 tbsp raspberry or blackberry jam into the base of the basin instead of the syrup.

Steamed Chocolate Sponge Pudding
Omit the golden syrup. Blend 4 tbsp cocoa powder with 2 tbsp hot water, then gradually beat into the creamed mixture before adding the eggs.

•COOK'S TIP•
Fresh Vanilla Custard
Pour 600ml
(1 pint) whole milk into a pan.
Slit 1 vanilla pod lengthways and scrape out the seeds, adding them to the milk with the pod, or add 1 tsp vanilla extract. Slowly bring to the boil. Turn off the heat immediately and set aside to infuse for 5 minutes. Put 6 large egg yolks, 2 tbsp golden caster sugar and 2 tbsp cornflour into a bowl and whisk together. Gradually whisk in the warm milk, leaving the vanilla pod behind if using. Rinse the pan and pour the mixture back in. Heat gently, whisking or stirring gently for 2–3 minutes until the custard thickens – it should just coat the back of a wooden spoon in a thin layer. Serve immediately or cover the surface closely with a round of wet greaseproof paper, then cover with clingfilm and chill until needed. Serves 8.

Sticky Toffee Puddings

Countrywide The origin of this recipe is open to debate, with many restaurants and chefs claiming to have invented it, but what is cetain is that it is a firm favourite throughout the country. It's also good served with cream, ice cream or custard.

Serves 4 • Preparation 20 minutes • Cooking time 25–30 minutes, plus resting

1 tbsp golden syrup
1 tbsp black treacle
150g (5oz) butter, softened
25g (1oz) pecan nuts or walnuts, finely ground
75g (3oz) self-raising flour
125g (4oz) caster sugar
2 large eggs, beaten
cream or custard to serve

Nutrition per serving
565 cals | 38g fat (21g sats) |
53g carbs | 0.9g salt

1 Preheat the oven to 180°C (160°C fan oven) mark 4. Put the syrup, treacle and 25g (1oz) of the butter into a bowl and beat until smooth. Divide the mixture among four 150ml (¼ pint) timbales or ramekins and set aside.
2 Put the nuts into a bowl, sift in the flour and mix together well.
3 Put the remaining butter and the sugar into a food processor and whiz briefly. (Alternatively, use a hand-held electric whisk.) Add the eggs and the flour mixture and whiz or mix again for 30 seconds. Spoon the mixture into the timbales or ramekins, to cover the syrup mixture. Bake for 25–30 minutes until risen and golden.
4 Remove the puddings from the oven and leave to rest for 5 minutes, then unmould on to warmed plates. Serve immediately with cream or custard.

Jam Roly-poly

Countrywide This suet pudding is rolled in a similar fashion to a Swiss roll and then steamed. Another school dinner favourite, it is traditionally served with custard, although it also tastes good with cream. It's a truly warming winter pudding.

Serves 4 • Preparation 25 minutes • Cooking time 1 hour

butter to grease
6 tbsp jam
a little milk
Fresh Vanilla Custard (see page 217)
to serve

For the suet crust pastry
175g (6oz) self-raising flour, plus extra
to dust
¼ tsp salt
100g (3½ oz) shredded suet

Nutrition per serving
449 cals | 22g fat (13g sats) |
62g carbs | 0.7g salt

1 Preheat the oven to 180°C (160°C fan oven) mark 4. Grease a piece of foil 23 × 33cm (9 × 13in).

2 To make the pastry, sift the flour and salt into a bowl, added the shredded suet and stir to mix. Using a round-bladed knife, mix in enough cold water to make a soft dough – you will need about 100ml (3½ fl oz). If the dough seems too dry, add a little extra liquid. Knead very lightly until smooth.

3 Roll out the suet crust pastry on a lightly floured surface to a rectangle about 23 × 28cm (9 × 11in). Spread the jam on the pastry, leaving 5mm (¼in) clear along each edge. Brush the edges with milk and roll up the pastry evenly, starting from one short side.

4 Put the roll on the greased foil and wrap the foil around it loosely, to allow for expansion, but seal the edges well. Put a rack in a roasting tin. Fill with 2.5cm (1in) boiling water, making sure it does not come higher than the rack. Put the foil-covered roll on the rack. Cover the whole tray tightly with foil to make sure no steam escapes. Steam for 1 hour. Remove from the foil and serve with custard.

CAKES

The Perfect Victoria Sponge

Countrywide Named after Queen Victoria, who is said to have eaten this with afternoon tea, the Victoria sponge is a classic favourite. Light and airy, it is the perfect tea-time treat and will appeal to both young and old.

Cuts into 10 slices • Preparation 20 minutes • Cooking time about 25 minutes, plus cooling

175g (6oz) unsalted butter at room temperature, plus extra to grease
175g (6oz) golden caster sugar
3 medium eggs
175g (6oz) self-raising flour, sifted
3–4 tbsp jam
a little icing sugar to dust

Nutrition per slice
445 cals | 21g fat (11g sats) |
30g carbs | 0.8g salt

1 Preheat the oven to 190°C (170°C fan oven) mark 5. Grease two 18cm (7in) sandwich tins and base-line with greaseproof paper.

2 Put the butter and caster sugar into a large bowl and, using a hand-held electric whisk, beat together until pale and fluffy. Add the eggs one at a time, beating well after each addition and adding a spoonful of flour to the mixture if it looks as if it's about to curdle. Using a large metal spoon, fold in the remaining flour.

3 Divide the mixture evenly between the prepared tins and level the surface with a palette knife. Bake in the centre of the oven for 20–25 minutes until the cakes are well risen and spring back when lightly pressed in the centre. Loosen the edges with a palette knife and leave in the tins for 5 minutes.

4 Turn out, remove the lining paper and leave to cool on a wire rack. Sandwich the two cakes together with jam and dust icing sugar over the top. Slice and serve. Store in an airtight container. It will keep for up to three days. If stored in the fridge it will keep for up to one week.

Madeira Cake

Countrywide This cake does not contain Madeira wine but was originally made to eat accompanied by a glass of fortified wine. It has a firm, even but light texture and is traditionally flavoured with lemon.

Cuts into 12 slices • Preparation 20 minutes • Cooking time 50 minutes, plus cooling

175g (6oz) butter, softened, plus extra
to grease
125g (4oz) plain flour
125g (4oz) self-raising flour
175g (6oz) golden caster sugar
1 tsp vanilla extract
3 large eggs, beaten
1–2 tbsp milk (optional)
2–3 thin slices lemon peel

Nutrition per slice
260 cals | 14g fat (8g sats) |
31g carbs | 0.4g salt

1 Preheat the oven to 180°C (160°C fan oven) mark 4. Grease and line a deep 18cm (7in) round cake tin. Sift the plain and self-raising flours together.

2 Cream the butter and sugar together in a bowl until pale and fluffy, then beat in the vanilla extract. Add the eggs, a little at a time, beating well after each addition.

3 Using a metal spoon, fold in the sifted flours, adding a little milk if necessary to give a dropping consistency.

4 Spoon the mixture into the prepared tin and level the surface. Bake for 20 minutes. Lay the lemon peel on the cake and bake for a further 30 minutes or until a skewer inserted into the centre comes out clean. Turn out on to a wire rack and leave to cool.

TRY SOMETHING DIFFERENT

Add the grated zest of 1 lemon at step 2. Add the juice of the lemon instead of the milk at step 3.

Porter Cake

Northern Ireland A rich, dark fruit cake that keeps very well. The original recipe used porter, a weaker variety of stout, which used to be a very popular working man's pint. However, as porter died out with the advent of bitter and is rarely produced, stout makes an admirable substitute.

Cuts into 10 slices • Preparation 10 minutes • Cooking time 1½ hours, plus cooling

125g (4oz) butter, softened, plus extra
to grease
225g (8oz) self-raising wholemeal flour
½ tsp baking powder
125g (4oz) soft light brown sugar
1 tsp ground mixed spice
finely grated zest of 1 lemon
150ml (½ pint) stout
2 medium eggs
350g (12oz) mixed dried fruit

Nutrition per slice
296 cals | 10g fat (6g sats) |
49g carbs | 0.3g salt

1 Preheat the oven to 170°C (150°C fan oven) mark 3. Grease and line a deep 18cm (7in) cake tin.
2 Put the butter, flour, baking powder, sugar, spice, lemon zest, stout and eggs into a bowl and beat for 2–3 minutes until well mixed. Stir in the dried fruit.
3 Pour into the prepared tin and bake for about 1½ hours or until risen and firm to the touch. Leave to cool in the tin.
4 When the cake is cold, wrap it in greaseproof paper and foil and leave to mature for a week before eating.

Westmorland Pepper Cake

The North If you've never tried adding pepper to a sweet dish before now you'll be pleasantly surprised by its effect. It adds unusual spiciness to what is otherwise a fairly standard fruit cake and is just one example of the huge variety of fruit cake recipes that come from this part of the world.

Cuts into 8 slices • Preparation 10 minutes • Cooking time 1 hour 5 minutes, plus cooling

75g (3oz) butter, plus extra to grease
75g (3oz) raisins
75g (3oz) currants
125g (4oz) caster sugar
225g (8oz) self-raising flour
a pinch of salt
½ tsp ground ginger
a large pinch of ground cloves
½ tsp finely ground black pepper
4 tbsp milk
1 medium egg, beaten

Nutrition per slice
276 cals | 9g fat (5g sats) |
48g carbs | 0.6g salt

1 Preheat the oven to 180°C (160°C fan oven) mark 4. Grease the base of a deep 18cm (7in) round cake tin and line the base with greaseproof paper.
2 Put the butter, fruit, sugar and 150ml (¼ pint) water into a pan and bring to the boil. Simmer for 10 minutes, then leave to cool slightly. Put the flour, salt, spices and pepper into a large bowl and gently stir in the fruit mixture, milk and egg. Mix thoroughly together without beating.
3 Turn the mixture into the prepared tin and bake for about 50 minutes or until firm to the touch and golden brown. Turn out and leave to cool on a wire rack.

Dundee Cake

Scotland A traditional Scottish fruit cake that became popular at the end of the 19th century. It is often served at Christmas – when the Scots have been known to add a dram of whisky to the mixture.

Cuts into 16 slices • Preparation 20 minutes • Cooking time about 2 hours, plus cooling

225g (8oz) butter or margarine, softened, plus extra to grease
125g (4oz) currants
125g (4oz) raisins
50g (2oz) blanched almonds, chopped
125g (4oz) chopped mixed candied peel
300g (11oz) plain flour
225g (8oz) light muscovado sugar
finely grated zest of 1 lemon
4 large eggs, beaten
75g (3oz) split almonds, to finish

Nutrition per slice
350 cals | 18g fat (8g sats) |
45g carbs | 0.4g salt

1 Preheat the oven to 170°C (150°C fan oven) mark 3. Grease and line a deep 20.5cm (8in) round cake tin. Wrap a double thickness of brown paper around the outside and secure with string.

2 Combine the dried fruit, chopped nuts and peel in a bowl. Sift in a little flour and stir to coat the fruit.

3 Cream the butter and sugar together in a bowl until pale and fluffy, then beat in the lemon zest. Add the eggs a little at a time, beating well after each addition.

4 Sift in the remaining flour and fold in lightly, using a metal spoon, then fold in the fruit and nut mixture.

5 Turn the mixture into the prepared tin and, using the back of a metal spoon, make a slight hollow in the centre. Arrange the split almonds on top.

6 Bake on the centre shelf of the oven for 2 hours or until a skewer inserted into the centre comes out clean. Loosely cover the top of the cake with foil if it appears to be browning too quickly. Leave in the tin for 15 minutes, then turn out on to a wire rack and leave to cool completely. Wrap in greaseproof paper and foil and leave to mature for at least a week before eating.

Somerset Apple Cake

The West Both Somerset and Dorset lay claim to this deliciously moist cake, which is equally good served with cream and eaten warm as a pudding. It is best consumed within two days of being made.

Cuts into about 10 slices • Preparation 20 minutes • Cooking time 1½ hours, plus cooling

125g (4oz) butter, plus extra to grease
175g (6oz) dark soft brown sugar
2 medium eggs, beaten
225g (8oz) plain wholemeal flour
1 tsp ground mixed spice
1 tsp ground cinnamon
2 tsp baking powder
450g (1lb) cooking apples, peeled, cored and chopped
3–4 tbsp milk
1 tbsp clear honey
1 tbsp light demerara sugar

Nutrition per slice
248 cals | 10g fat (6g sats) |
38g carbs | 0.5g salt

1 Preheat the oven to 170°C (150°C fan oven) mark 3. Grease a deep 18cm (7in) round cake tin and line with greaseproof paper.

2 Cream the butter and soft brown sugar together until pale and fluffy. Add the eggs a little at a time, beating well after each addition. Add the flour, spices and baking powder and mix well. Fold in the apples and enough milk to give a soft dropping consistency.

3 Turn the mixture into the prepared tin and bake for 1½ hours or until well risen and firm to the touch. Turn out on to a wire rack to cool.

4 When the cake is cold, brush with the honey and sprinkle with the demerara sugar to decorate.

Sticky Ginger Ring

The Midlands/ The North Full of wonderful spicy flavours, this cake will fill the house with enticing aromas as it cooks. Ginger and cinnamon complement each other perfectly, while the black treacle gives the cake a rich colour.

Cuts into 8 slices • Preparation 15 minutes • Cooking time 1 hour, plus cooling and setting

100g (3½oz) unsalted butter, diced, plus extra to grease
100g (3½oz) light brown soft sugar
3 tbsp black treacle
100ml (3½fl oz) milk
2 tbsp brandy
1 large egg, beaten
150g (5oz) plain flour
2 tsp ground ginger
2 tsp ground cinnamon
1 tsp bicarbonate of soda
75g (3oz) ready-to-eat dried prunes, coarsely chopped

DECORATION
225g (8oz) golden icing sugar, sifted
2 pieces preserved stem ginger, drained of syrup (syrup reserved) and roughly chopped

Nutrition per slice
375 cals | 12g fat (7g sats) |
64g carbs | 0.3g salt

1 Preheat the oven to 150°C (130°C fan oven) mark 2. Generously grease a 21cm (8½in), 600ml (1 pint) round ring mould with butter.

.2 Put the butter, brown sugar and treacle into a pan and heat gently until melted, stirring all the time. Add the milk and brandy and leave to cool, then beat in the egg.

3 Sift the flour, spices and bicarbonate of soda into a large mixing bowl. Make a well in the centre, pour in the treacle mixture and stir until all the flour has been combined – it should be of a soft, dropping consistency. Stir in the chopped prunes. Pour the mixture into the prepared ring mould and level the surface.

4 Bake for 1 hour or until the cake is firm to the touch and a skewer inserted into the centre comes out clean. Cool in the tin for 10 minutes, then loosen the sides of the cake, turn out on to a wire rack and leave to cool completely.

5 To make the icing, mix the icing sugar with about 2 tbsp of the reserved ginger syrup to create a coating consistency. Drizzle over the cake and down the sides, then decorate with the stem ginger. Leave to set

FREEZING TIP

To freeze, complete the recipe to the end of step 4, then wrap the cake in clingfilm and foil. Freeze for up to one month. To use, thaw for 3 hours and complete the recipe.

Lemon Drizzle Loaf

Countrywide This modern classic is tangy, moist and refreshing and the perfect treat to have with a mid-afternoon cup of tea. It keeps well, and so can be made in advance for the family or for when friends are coming round.

Cuts into 8–10 slices • Preparation 20 minutes • Cooking time about 50 minutes, plus cooling

175g (6oz) unsalted butter, softened, plus extra to grease
175g (6oz) caster sugar
4 medium eggs, lightly beaten
3 lemons
125g (4oz) self-raising flour
50g (2oz) ground almonds
75g (3oz) sugar cubes

Nutrition per slice
424 cals | 25g fat (13g sats) |
46g carbs | 0.6g salt

1 Preheat the oven to 180°C (160°C fan oven) mark 4. Grease a 900g (2lb) loaf tin and line with baking parchment.

2 Using a hand-held electric whisk, beat together the butter and caster sugar in a large bowl until pale and fluffy, about 5 minutes. Gradually beat in the eggs, followed by the finely grated zest of 2 of the lemons and the juice of ½ a lemon.

3 Fold the flour and ground almonds into the butter mixture, then spoon into the prepared tin and bake for 40–50 minutes until a skewer inserted into the centre comes out clean. Cool in the tin for 10 minutes, then turn out on to a wire rack and leave to cool until warm.

4 Meanwhile, put the sugar cubes into a small bowl with the juice of 1½ lemons and the pared zest of 1 lemon (you will have 1 un-juiced lemon left over). Soak for 5 minutes, then use the back of a spoon to roughly crush the cubes. Spoon over the warm cake and leave to cool completely before serving in slices. Store in an airtight container. It will keep for up to four days.

.COOK'S TIP.
This recipe also works with gluten-free self-raising flour, for those on a coeliac diet.

Cappuccino and Walnut Cake

Countrywide Another modern classic, this moist iced cake is one for the coffee and nut lovers. It makes an attractive centrepiece for the tea-time table or a special occasion. The decoration of violets makes it extra special, but not to worry if you don't have them.

Cuts into 10 slices • Preparation 30 minutes • Cooking time about 45 minutes, plus cooling

65g (2½oz) unsalted butter, melted and cooled, plus extra to grease
100g (3½oz) plain flour
1 tsp baking powder
4 medium eggs
125g (4oz) caster sugar
1 tbsp chicory and coffee essence
75g (3oz) walnuts, toasted, cooled and finely chopped

To decorate
50g (2oz) walnuts
1 tbsp granulated sugar
¼ tsp ground cinnamon
fresh unsprayed violets (optional)

To ice
200g (7oz) good-quality white chocolate
4 tsp chicory and coffee essence
2 × 250g tubs mascarpone cheese

Nutrition per slice
449 cals | 30g fat (13g sats) |
36g carbs | 0.3g salt

---

1 Preheat the oven to 190°C (170°C fan oven) mark 5. Grease two 20.5 x 4cm deep (8 x 1½in deep) round cake tins and base-line each with a circle of greased greaseproof paper. Sift the flour and baking powder together twice.

2 Using an electric mixer, whisk the eggs and caster sugar in a large heatproof bowl set over a pan of barely simmering water for 3–4 minutes until light, thick and fluffy. Remove the bowl from the heat and continue whisking until the mixture has cooled and the whisk leaves a ribbon trail for 8 seconds when lifted out of the bowl.

3 Fold in the butter, coffee essence and chopped walnuts. Sift half the flour over the mixture, then fold in carefully but quickly with a metal spoon. Sift and fold in the rest, taking care not to knock out too much air. Pour into the prepared tins and tap them lightly on the worksurface. Bake for 20–25 minutes until the tops feel springy. Cool in the tins for 10 minutes, then turn out on to a wire rack and leave to cool completely.

4 To make the decoration, whiz the walnuts in a food processor or blender with the granulated sugar and cinnamon until finely chopped. Take care not to overprocess the nuts or they will become oily. Set aside.

5 To make the icing, break up the chocolate and put into a heatproof bowl set over a pan of gently simmering water, making sure the base of the bowl doesn't touch the water. Allow to melt slowly without stirring. In another bowl, add the coffee essence to the mascarpone and beat until smooth, then slowly beat in the melted chocolate.

6 Spread one-third of the icing on top of one cake, then sandwich with the other half. Smooth the remaining icing over the top and sides. Lift the cake on to a large piece of greaseproof paper and scatter the chopped nuts all around it. Then lift the greaseproof up to press nuts on to the sides. Transfer to a plate and decorate with the violets, if you like. Store in an airtight container in the fridge. It will keep for up to two days.

Carrot Cake

Countrywide Root vegetables were often used to lend sweetness to 18th-century cakes and puddings. Beetroots, parsnips and carrots were all common ingredients, but of these, only carrot is still favoured today. It makes a very pleasant, moist cake without any hint of carrot in the taste.

Cuts into 12 slices • Preparation 15 minutes • Cooking time 40 minutes, plus cooling

250ml (9fl oz) sunflower oil, plus extra
to grease
225g (8oz) light muscovado sugar
3 large eggs
225g (8oz) self-raising flour
a large pinch of salt
½ tsp each ground mixed spice,
grated nutmeg and ground cinnamon
250g (9oz) carrots, peeled and coarsely
grated

For the frosting
50g (2oz) butter, preferably unsalted,
at room temperature
225g pack cream cheese
25g (1oz) golden icing sugar
½ tsp vanilla extract
8 pecan halves, roughly chopped

Nutrition per slice
383 cals | 32g fat (10g sats) |
24g carbs | 0.3g salt

1 Preheat the oven to 180°C (160°C fan oven) mark 4. Grease two 18cm (7in) sandwich tins and base-line with greaseproof paper.
2 Using a hand-held electric whisk, whisk the oil and muscovado sugar together to combine, then whisk in the eggs, one at a time.
3 Sift the flour, salt and spices together over the mixture, then gently fold in, using a large metal spoon. Tip the carrots into the bowl and fold in.
4 Divide the cake mixture between the prepared tins and bake for 30–40 minutes until golden and a skewer inserted into the centre comes out clean. Remove from the oven and

leave in the tins for 10 minutes, then turn out on to a wire rack and leave to cool completely.
5 To make the frosting, beat the butter and cream cheese together in a bowl until light and fluffy. Sift in the icing sugar, add the vanilla extract and beat well until smooth. Spread one-third of the frosting over one cake and sandwich together with the other cake. Spread the remaining frosting on top and sprinkle with the pecan halves. Store in an airtight container. Eat within two days. Alternatively, the cake will keep for up to one week in an airtight container if it is stored before the frosting is applied.

Mince Pies

Countrywide Originally containing a sweet and savoury filling, the mince pie dates back hundreds of years, but by the Victorian era the addition of meat had fallen from fashion (although suet is still used). Today the mince pie is an essential part of the Christmas table.

Makes 24 • Preparation 15 minutes, plus chilling • Cooking time 12–15 minutes, plus cooling

225g (8oz) plain flour, plus extra to dust
125g (4oz) unsalted butter, chilled
and diced
100g (3½ oz) cream cheese
1 medium egg yolk
finely grated zest of 1 orange
400g jar mincemeat (see Try Something
Different and page 269)
1 medium egg, beaten
icing sugar to dust

Nutrition per pie
150 cals | 8g fat (4g sats) |
17g carbs | 0.2g salt

1 Put the flour into a food processor. Add the butter, cream cheese, egg yolk and orange zest and whiz until the mixture just comes together. Tip the mixture into a large bowl and bring the dough together with your hands. Shape into a ball, wrap in clingfilm and put in the freezer for 5 minutes.

2 Preheat the oven to 220°C (200°C fan oven) mark 7. Cut off about one-third of the pastry dough and set aside. Roll out the remainder on a lightly floured surface to 5mm (¼in) thick. Using a 6.5cm (2½in) cutter, stamp out circles to make 24 rounds, re-rolling the dough as necessary. Use the pastry circles to line two 12-cup patty tins. Roll out the reserved pastry and use a star cutter to stamp out the stars.

3 Put 1 tsp mincemeat into each pastry case, then top with pastry stars. Brush the tops with beaten egg, then bake for 12–15 minutes until golden. Remove from the tins and leave to cool on a wire rack. Serve warm or cold, dusted with icing sugar. Store in an airtight container for up to four days.

TRY SOMETHING DIFFERENT

▼▼▼▼▼▼▼▼▼

Improve the flavour of a jar of bought mincemeat by adding 2 tbsp brandy, the grated zest of 1 lemon and 25g (1oz) pecan nuts, chopped. Or, instead of the nuts, try a piece of preserved stem ginger in syrup, chopped.

Eccles Cakes

The North First sold in Eccles, near Manchester, in the late 18th century, Eccles cakes are now famous throughout the world. Crumbly puff pastry encloses a filling of buttery dried fruit, making them very moreish.

Makes 8 • Preparation 10 minutes, plus resting • Cooking time 15 minutes, plus cooling

215g pack puff pastry, thawed if frozen
plain flour to dust
25g (1oz) butter, softened
25g (1oz) soft dark brown sugar
25g (1oz) fine chopped mixed peel
50g (2oz) currants
caster sugar to sprinkle

Nutrition per cake
158 cals | 9g fat (2g sats) |
19g carbs | 0.3g salt

1 Roll out the pastry on a lightly floured surface and cut into 9cm (3½in) rounds.
2 For the filling, mix the butter, brown sugar, mixed peel and currants in a bowl.
3 Put 1 tsp of the fruit and butter mixture in the centre of each pastry round. Draw up the edges of each pastry round to enclose the filling and then reshape. Turn each round over and roll lightly until the currants just show through. Prick the top of each with a fork. Leave to rest for about 10 minutes in a cool place. Preheat the oven to 230°C (210°C fan oven) mark 8.
4 Put the pastry rounds on a damp baking sheet and bake for about 15 minutes or until golden. Transfer to a wire rack and leave to cool for 30 minutes. Sprinkle with caster sugar while still warm.

.COOK'S TIP.

Use a food processor to whiz the flour and butter together, if you prefer.

Rock Buns

Countrywide Quick and simple to make, these fruity buns are a great tea-time treat.

Makes 12 • Preparation 5 minutes • Cooking time 20 minutes, plus cooling

125g (4oz) butter or margarine, plus extra to grease
225g (8oz) plain flour
a pinch of salt
2 tsp baking powder
75g (3oz) demerara sugar
75g (3oz) mixed dried fruit
zest of ½ lemon
1 medium egg
milk

Nutrition per bun
192 cals | 9g fat (6g sats) |
26g carbs | 0.5g salt

1 Preheat the oven to 200°C (180°C fan oven) mark 6. Lightly grease two baking sheets.
2 Sift together the flour, salt and baking powder. Rub in the butter until the mixture resembles fine breadcrumbs. Add the sugar, fruit and lemon zest and mix together thoroughly.
3 Using a fork, mix to a moist but stiff dough with the beaten egg and a little milk.
4 Using two forks, shape into 12 rocky heaps on the baking sheets. Bake for 20 minutes or until golden brown. Transfer to a wire rack and leave to cool. Rock buns are best eaten on the day they are made.

Jam Tarts

Countrywide Perfect for the Mad Hatter's tea party, these tarts are sure to please the Queen of Hearts.

Makes 18 • Preparation 10 minutes, plus chilling • Cooking time 12–15 minutes

250g pack shortcrust pastry, thawed if frozen
a little plain flour to dust
seedless or no-bits raspberry jam

Nutrition per tart
70 cals | 3g fat (1g sats) |
12g carbs | 0.1g salt

•COOK'S TIP•

Use jams in several different flavours to give a colourful array of tarts.

1 Roll out the pastry to a thickness of 5mm (¼in) on a lightly floured surface. Using a 10 × 10cm (4 × 4in) heart-shaped cutter, cut out 18 hearts. Put on a non-stick baking sheet and leave to chill for 30 minutes. Preheat the oven to 200°C (180°C fan oven) mark 6.
2 Put a smaller heart-shaped cutter on top of each heart to use as a mould and spread jam inside. Bake the tarts for 12–15 minutes until golden. Leave to cool for 10 minutes. Store in an airtight container. They will keep for up to three days.

Fig Sly Cakes

Countrywide Sly cakes, or 'cheats', as they were sometimes called, got their name because of their deceptive appearance. On the outside they look plain and uninteresting. But concealed inside is a rich filling of figs, currants, nuts and raisins.

Makes 12 • Preparation 10 minutes, plus chilling • Cooking time 50 minutes, plus cooling

275g (10oz) plain flour
a pinch of salt
125g (4oz) butter, diced
75g (3oz) lard, diced
50g (2oz) caster sugar
225g (8oz) dried figs, chopped
75g (3oz) walnut pieces, chopped
50g (2oz) currants
50g (2oz) raisins
milk to glaze

Nutrition per cake
317 cals | 18g fat (7g sats) |
37g carbs | 0.3g salt

1 To make the pastry, put the flour and salt into a bowl, then rub in the butter and lard until the mixture resembles fine breadcrumbs. Stir in the sugar and enough water to bind the mixture together. Chill while preparing the filling.

2 Put the figs, walnuts, currants and raisins into a pan with 150ml (¼ pint) water and cook, uncovered, stirring continuously, until the water has evaporated and the fruit mixture is soft and thick. Leave to cool. Preheat the oven to 190°C (170°C fan oven) mark 5.

3 Divide the dough into two, then roll out one half to fit a shallow 18 x 28cm (7 x 11in) tin. Spread the fruit mixture over the dough, then roll out the remaining dough and use to cover the filling. Seal the edges well and mark into 12 squares. Brush the top with a little milk to glaze.

4 Bake for about 40 minutes or until golden brown. Leave to cool, then cut into the marked squares.

BISCUITS

Shrewsbury Biscuits

The Midlands Light, lemony biscuits, which need to be stored in an airtight container to keep their crispness. In other traditional recipes for Shrewsbury Biscuits, caraway seeds or currants were added to the basic mixture, to make pleasant variations.

Makes about 24 • Preparation 10 minutes • Cooking time 10 minutes

125g (4oz) butter, plus extra to grease
150g (5oz) caster sugar
2 medium egg yolks
225g (8oz) plain flour, plus extra to dust
finely grated zest of 1 lemon

Nutrition per biscuit
100 cals | 5g fat (3g sats) |
14g carbs | 0.1g salt

---

1 Preheat the oven to 180°C (160°C fan oven) mark 4. Lightly grease two or three baking sheets.
2 Cream the butter and sugar together until pale and fluffy. Add the egg yolks and beat in well. Stir in the flour and lemon zest and mix to a fairly firm dough.
3 Knead lightly on a lightly floured surface, then roll out until about 5mm (¼ in) thick. Using a fluted cutter, cut out 6.5cm (2½ in) rounds and put on the prepared baking sheets.
4 Bake for 9–10 minutes until lightly browned and firm to the touch. Transfer to wire racks to cool. Store in an airtight container for up to one week.

TRY SOMETHING DIFFERENT

Spice Biscuits
Omit the lemon zest and add 1 tsp mixed spice and 1 tsp ground cinnamon, sifted with the flour.

Fruit Squares
Make up the mixture and divide in half. Roll out both portions into rectangles and sprinkle 125g (4oz) chopped dried fruit over one piece. Cover with the other piece and roll out the mixture 5mm (¼ in) thick. Cut into squares.

Tonbridge Biscuits

The Southeast These originate from the small town in Kent. The caraway seeds sprinkled on top give them a distinctive flavour.

Makes about 24 • Preparation 10 minutes • Cooking time 10 minutes

75g (3oz) butter, diced, plus extra to grease
225g (8oz) plain flour, plus extra to dust
75g (3oz) caster sugar
1 medium egg, beaten
1 egg white, beaten, to glaze
caraway seeds to sprinkle

Nutrition per biscuit
71 cals | 3g fat (2g sats) |
11g carbs | 0.1g salt

1 Preheat the oven to 180°C (160°C fan oven) mark 4. Lightly grease two or three baking sheets.
2 Rub the butter into the flour until the mixture resembles fine breadcrumbs, then stir in the sugar. Add the egg and mix to a stiff paste.
3 Roll out on a lightly floured surface until about 5mm (¼in) thick, then prick the top with a fork. Using a 5cm (2in) plain cutter, cut into rounds. Brush with egg white and sprinkle on a few caraway seeds.
4 Put on to the prepared baking sheets and bake for about 10 minutes or until light brown. Transfer to wire racks to cool. Store in an airtight container for up to one week.

Scottish Oatcakes

Scotland The Scottish climate is well suited to growing oats, which don't mind the cold or rain. These griddle cakes are very simple but delicious.

Makes about 12 • Preparation 10 minutes • Cooking time 10 minutes

225g (8oz) fine or medium oatmeal, plus extra to dust
a pinch of salt
a pinch of bicarbonate of soda
15g (½ oz) lard
butter to serve

Nutrition per biscuit
46 cals | 2g fat (1g sats) |
6g carbs | 1.9g salt

1 Put the oatmeal, salt and bicarbonate of soda into a bowl.
2 Gently heat the lard and 150ml (¼ pint) water until the lard is melted, then quickly pour enough of it on to the dry ingredients to make a firm dough.
3 Roll out the dough on a surface sprinkled with oatmeal until about 3mm (⅛in) thick. Using a plain 7.5cm (3in) round cutter, cut out 12 rounds, re-rolling as necessary.
Or, cut into triangles, if preferred.
4 Cook the oatcakes on a hot griddle, on one side only for about 5–8 minutes, until they curl and are firm. (Alternatively, place on a greased baking sheet and bake at 180°C (160°C fan oven) mark 4 for 15–20 minutes until crisp.) Eat spread with butter.

Brandy Snaps

The North These brittle, sweet baked biscuits are moulded around the handle of a spoon while still warm from the oven, thus providing a cavity that can then be filled with whipped cream. Brandy snaps can be kept, unfilled, in an airtight container for up to a week.

Makes about 12 • Preparation 10 minutes • Cooking time 12 minutes, plus cooling

50g (2oz) butter, plus extra to grease
50g (2oz) caster sugar
2 tbsp golden syrup
50g (2oz) plain flour
½ tsp ground ginger
1 tsp brandy
finely grated zest of ½ lemon
150ml (¼ pint) double cream

Nutrition per biscuit
132 cals | 10g fat (6g sats) |
10g carbs | 0.1g salt

1 Preheat the oven to 180°C (160°C fan oven) mark 4. Line two or three large baking sheets with baking parchment.

2 Gently heat the butter, sugar and syrup until the butter has melted and the sugar has dissolved. Remove from the heat.

3 Sift the flour and ginger together, then stir into the melted mixture with the brandy and lemon zest.

4 Drop teaspoons of the mixture on to the prepared baking sheets, leaving 10cm (4in) between each one. Bake for 7 minutes or until cooked.

5 Using a palette knife, quickly remove from the baking sheets and roll each one around the buttered handle of a wooden spoon. Leave on the handles until set, then gently twist to remove. Cool on a wire rack.

6 If the biscuits set before they have been shaped, return them to the oven for a few minutes to soften. Store in an airtight container until required.

7 Just before serving, whip the cream until it just holds its shape. Spoon into a piping bag fitted with a star nozzle and pipe cream into the brandy snaps. Serve immediately.

Devon Flats

The West These delicious creamy biscuits are very easy to make and are not as rich as their list of ingredients might indicate.

Makes about 24 • Preparation 10 minutes • Cooking time 8–10 minutes, plus cooling

butter to grease
225g (8oz) self-raising flour, plus extra to dust
a pinch of salt
125g (4oz) caster sugar
125ml (4fl oz) clotted or double cream
1 medium egg, beaten
about 1 tbsp milk

Nutrition per biscuit
75 cals | 3g fat (2g sats) |
12g carbs | 0.1g salt

1 Preheat the oven to 220°C (200°C fan oven) mark 7. Lightly grease two or three baking sheets.
2 Mix the flour, salt and sugar together. Stir in the cream, egg and enough milk to make a stiff dough. If the dough feels at all sticky, cover it and chill to firm up.
3 Roll out the dough on a lightly floured surface until about 8mm (⅓in) thick. Using a 7.5cm (3in) cutter, cut out rounds.
4 Transfer to the prepared baking sheets and bake for 8–10 minutes until a light golden brown. Carefully transfer to wire racks and leave to cool. Store in an airtight container for up to two days.

Maidstone Biscuits

The Southeast These crisp and light biscuits include almonds and scented rosewater, an unusual flavouring that was popular with the Tudors.

Makes about 18 • Preparation 5 minutes • Cooking time 12–15 minutes, plus cooling

150g (5oz) plain flour, plus extra to dust
125g (4oz) butter
125g (4oz) caster sugar
1 tsp rosewater
50g (2oz) blanched almonds, chopped

Nutrition per biscuit
109 cals | 6g fat (3g sats) |
13g carbs | 0.1g salt

1 Preheat the oven to 180°C (160°C fan oven) mark 4. Lightly dust a baking sheet.
2 Cream the butter and sugar together until pale and fluffy. Fold in the flour, rosewater and almonds and mix to a stiff dough.
3 Place in small heaps on the prepared baking sheet, then bake for 12–15 minutes until golden brown. Cool on a wire rack. Store in an airtight container for up to a week.

Almond Macaroons

Countrywide Originally, macaroons were enjoyed mainly by the well-off, beause almonds were an expensive ingredient.

Makes 22 • Preparation 10 minutes • Cooking time 12–15 minutes, plus cooling

2 medium egg whites
125g (4oz) caster sugar
125g (4oz) ground almonds
¼ tsp almond extract
22 blanched almonds

Nutrition per macaroon
86 cals | 6g fat (1g sats) |
7g carbs | 0g salt

1 Preheat the oven to 180°C (160°C fan oven) mark 4. Line two baking sheets with baking parchment.
2 Whisk the egg whites in a clean, grease-free bowl until stiff peaks form. Gradually whisk in the sugar a little at a time, until thick and glossy. Gently stir in the ground almonds and almond extract.
3 Spoon teaspoonfuls of the mixture on to the prepared baking sheets, spacing them slightly apart. Press an almond into the centre of each one and bake in the oven for 12–15 minutes until just golden and firm to the touch.
4 Leave on the baking sheets for 10 minutes, then transfer to wire racks and leave to cool completely. On cooling, these biscuits have a soft, chewy centre; they harden up after a few days. Store in airtight containers for up to one week.

Ginger Biscuits

The Midlands These crunchy biscuits are ideal with a cup of tea at any time. Easy to make, they keep well so you can always have some to hand.

Makes 24 • Preparation 15 minutes • Cooking time about 12 minutes, plus cooling

50g (2oz) butter, plus extra to grease
125g (4oz) golden syrup
50g (2oz) dark muscovado sugar
finely grated zest of 1 orange
2 tbsp orange juice
175g (6oz) self-raising flour
1 tsp ground ginger

Nutrition per biscuit
55 cals | 2g fat (1g sats) |
10g carbs | 0.1g salt

1 Preheat the oven to 180°C (160°C fan oven) mark 4. Lightly grease two large baking sheets.
2 Put the butter, golden syrup, sugar, orange zest and juice into a heavy-based pan and heat very gently until melted and evenly blended.
3 Leave the mixture to cool slightly, then sift in the flour with the ginger. Mix thoroughly until smooth. Put small spoonfuls of the mixture on to the prepared baking sheets, spacing them well apart to allow room for spreading.
4 Bake for 12 minutes or until the biscuits are golden brown. Leave on the baking sheets for 1 minute, then carefully transfer to a wire rack and leave to cool. Store in an airtight container for up to five days.

Shortbread

Scotland Said to have been a favourite of Mary, Queen of Scots, shortbread is now popular throughout Great Britain. However, no Hogmanay (New Year) in Scotland would be complete without a gift of shortbread.

Makes 18 • Preparation 20 minutes, plus chilling • Cooking time 15–20 minutes, plus cooling

225g (8oz) butter, at room temperature
125g (4oz) golden caster sugar
225g (8oz) plain flour
125g (4oz) rice flour
a pinch of salt
golden or coloured granulated sugar
to coat
caster sugar to sprinkle

Nutrition per biscuit
190 cals | 10g fat (7g sats) |
23g carbs | 0.3g salt

1 Cream the butter and sugar together in a bowl until pale and fluffy. Sift the flours and salt together on to the creamed mixture and stir in, using a wooden spoon, until the mixture resembles breadcrumbs.

2 Gather the dough together with your hand and turn on to a clean surface. Knead very lightly until it forms a ball, then lightly roll into a sausage, about 5cm (2in) thick. Wrap in clingfilm and chill until firm.

3 Preheat the oven to 190°C (170°C fan oven) mark 5. Line two baking sheets with greaseproof paper. Remove the clingfilm and slice the dough into discs, 1cm (½in) thick. Pour some granulated sugar on to a plate and roll the edge of each disc in the sugar. Put the shortbread, cut side up, on the prepared baking sheets.

4 Bake the shortbread for 15–20 minutes, depending on thickness, until very pale golden. On removing from the oven, sprinkle with caster sugar. Leave on the baking sheets for 10 minutes, then transfer to a wire rack and leave to cool. Store in an airtight container for up to two weeks.

Traditional Flapjacks

Countrywide These moist, chewy squares are quick and easy to make, and the ingredients are inexpensive. Made in a tin and then cut up while still warm, they keep well and are just the thing to nibble on when hunger strikes.

Makes 12 squares • Preparation 10 minutes • Cooking time 25 minutes, plus cooling

200g (7oz) butter, plus extra to grease
150g (5oz) demerara sugar
4 tbsp golden syrup
1 tsp ground cinnamon
finely grated zest of ½–1 orange
400g (14oz) jumbo oats
100g (3½ oz) raisins or sultanas

Nutrition per square
354 cals | 17g fat (9g sats) |
50g carbs | 0.4g salt

1 Preheat the oven to 190°C (170°C fan oven) mark 5. Grease a 20.5cm (8in) square baking tin and line with baking parchment.
2 Melt the butter in a large pan and add the sugar, syrup, cinnamon and orange zest. Heat gently until the sugar dissolves.
3 Remove the pan from the heat and stir in the oats and raisins or sultanas. Press the mixture into the prepared tin and bake for 17–20 minutes until lightly golden. Cool before cutting into squares. Store the flapjacks in an airtight container for up to three days.

Christmas Biscuits

Countrywide Often designed to be hung on the Christmas tree, these biscuits, or cookies, can be cut into shapes such as holly or stars, and then iced and decorated. The children will enjoy adding their own designs in icing and silver balls.

Makes about 22 • Preparation 25 minutes, plus chilling • Cooking time 15 minutes, plus cooling

75g (3oz) unsalted butter, softened
100g (3½oz) caster sugar
1 medium egg
½ tsp vanilla extract
250g (9oz) plain flour, plus extra to dust
½ tsp baking powder
a selection of coloured ready-to-roll fondant icings, royal icing, food colourings and edible decorations

Nutrition per biscuit
94 cals | 3g fat (2g sats) |
17g carbs | 0.1g salt

1 Using a wooden spoon, cream the butter and sugar together in a large bowl until smooth. Beat in the egg and vanilla extract. Sift the flour and baking powder into the bowl and stir until combined. Tip out on to a lightly floured surface and knead gently to make a soft dough. Shape into a disc and wrap in clingfilm, then chill for 1 hour until firm.

2 Preheat the oven to 180°C (160°C fan oven) mark 4. Roll out the dough on a lightly floured surface until 5mm (¼in) thick. Using Christmas cookie cutters, stamp out shapes, re-rolling the trimmings if necessary. If the cookies are to be hung as decorations, use a skewer to make a 5mm (¼in) hole in each one. Put on two non-stick baking trays and bake for 10–15 minutes until pale golden and risen. Leave to cool on the sheets for 3 minutes to harden, then transfer to a wire rack to cool completely.

3 When the cookies are completely cool, decorate with different coloured fondant icings or royal icing and edible decorations. Store in an airtight container for up to two weeks.

BREADS & TEABREADS

Oatmeal Soda Bread

Northern Ireland An Irish country bread, this requires no rising or proving. The aroma wafting from the oven as the bread cooks will make you impatient for it to be done. Enjoy it with good butter and jam, or with cheese.

Cuts into about 10 slices • Preparation 10 minutes • Cooking time 25 minutes, plus cooling

25g (1oz) butter, plus extra to grease
275g (10oz) plain wholemeal flour
175g (6oz) coarse oatmeal
2 tsp cream of tartar
1 tsp salt
about 300ml (½ pint) milk and water, mixed

Nutrition per slice
183 cals | 4g fat (2g sats) |
31g carbs | 0.6g salt

1 Preheat the oven to 220°C (200°C fan oven) mark 7. Grease and base-line a 900g (2lb) loaf tin.
2 Mix together all the dry ingredients in a bowl. Rub in the butter, then add the milk and water to bind to a soft dough. Spoon into the prepared tin.
3 Bake in the oven for 25 minutes or until golden brown and well risen. Turn out on to a wire rack and leave to cool slightly. The bread is best eaten on the day it is made.

Marbled Chocolate Teabread

Countrywide The Victorians were very fond of marbled cakes. This recipe is so called because the feathery swirls of chocolate that are revealed when it is sliced make a pattern similar to that of Italian marble.

Cuts into about 10 slices • Preparation 15 minutes • Cooking time 1¼–1½ hours, plus cooling

225g (8oz) butter, plus extra for greasing
225g (8oz) caster sugar
4 medium eggs, beaten
225g (8oz) self-raising flour
finely grated zest of 1 large orange
1 tbsp orange juice
a few drops orange flower water (optional)
75g (3oz) plain chocolate
1 tbsp cocoa powder, sifted

Nutrition per slice
406 cals | 24g fat (14g sats) |
46g carbs | 0.1g salt

---

1 Preheat the oven to 180°C (160°C fan oven) mark 4. Grease a 900ml (2 pint) loaf tin and line the base and sides with greaseproof paper.

2 Cream the butter and sugar together until pale and fluffy, then gradually beat in the eggs, beating well after each addition. Fold in the flour.

3 Transfer half the mixture to another bowl and beat in the orange zest, juice and orange flower water, if using.

4 Break the chocolate into pieces, put into a small bowl and place over a pan of simmering water, making sure the base of the bowl doesn't touch the water. Stir until the chocolate melts. Stir into the remaining cake mixture with the cocoa powder.

5 Put alternate spoonfuls of the two mixtures into the prepared tin. Use a knife to swirl through the mixture to make a marbled effect, then level the surface.

6 Bake in the oven for 1¼–1½ hours until well risen and firm to the touch. Turn out on to a wire rack to cool. Serve cut in slices.

Cheese and Walnut Loaf

The West This tasty teabread combines two West Country specialities that are now readily available throughout the country: walnuts, which were originally grown in the Vale of Pewsey in Wiltshire, and Cheddar cheese (use a mature version for a stronger taste).

Makes 1 large loaf • Preparation 25 minutes, plus rising • Cooking time 45 minutes, plus cooling

oil to grease
15g (½oz) fresh yeast or 1½ tsp dried and a pinch of sugar
450g (1lb) strong wholemeal flour, plus extra to dust
1 tsp salt
½ tsp paprika
1½ tsp mustard powder
175g (6oz) Cheddar cheese, grated
125g (4oz) walnut pieces, finely chopped
3 tbsp chopped fresh mixed herbs or 1 tsp dried herbs

Nutrition per slice
176 cals | 9g fat (3g sats) |
18g carbs | 0.5g salt

1 Grease a 900g (2lb) loaf tin. Blend the fresh yeast with 300ml (½ pint) warm water. If using dried yeast, sprinkle it into 300ml (½ pint) warm water with the sugar and leave in a warm place for 15 minutes or until frothy.

2 Put the flour, salt, paprika, mustard powder, 125g (4oz) of the cheese, the walnuts and herbs into a large bowl and mix together. Make a well in the centre, then pour in the yeast liquid. Mix together to make a smooth dough that leaves the sides of the bowl clean.

3 Turn the dough out on to a lightly floured surface and knead well for about 10 minutes or until smooth and elastic. Put into a clean bowl, cover with a clean teatowel and leave in a warm place for about 1 hour or until doubled in size.

4 Turn the dough out on to a floured surface and knead lightly. Shape the dough to fit the prepared tin. Cover and leave in a warm place for 30 minutes or until the dough rises almost to the top of the tin. Preheat the oven to 190°C (170°C fan oven) mark 5.

5 Sprinkle the dough with the remaining cheese and bake for 45 minutes or until well risen and the loaf sounds hollow when tapped underneath. Turn out on to a wire rack to cool.

Barm Brack

Northern Ireland Similar breads, using a fruity yeast dough, are made in other parts of Britain. Scotland has its Selkirk bannock and Wales has bara brith, which means speckled bread, a reference to the fruit in the mixture. In Ireland, barm brack was traditionally eaten at Hallowe'en.

Makes 1 large loaf • Preparation 25 minutes, plus rising • Cooking time about 45 minutes, plus cooling

15g (½ oz) fresh yeast or 1½ tsp dried
and a pinch of sugar
25g (1oz) butter, plus extra to grease
450g (1lb) strong white flour, plus
extra to dust
4 tbsp caster sugar
½ tsp ground ginger
freshly grated nutmeg
175g (6oz) sultanas
175g (6oz) currants
50g (2oz) chopped candied peel

Nutrition per slice
252 cals | 2g fat (1g sats) |
56g carbs | 0.1g salt

1 Blend the fresh yeast with 300ml (½ pint) warm water. If using dried yeast, sprinkle it into 300ml (½ pint) warm water with the pinch of sugar and leave in a warm place for 15 minutes or until frothy.

2 Rub the butter into the flour, then stir in half the sugar, the ginger and nutmeg to taste. Stir in the fruit and peel and mix well together. Make a well in the centre and stir in the yeast liquid.

3 Beat well together until the dough leaves the sides of the bowl clean. Turn out on to a lightly floured surface and knead well for about 10 minutes, until smooth and elastic. Put into a clean bowl, cover with a clean teatowel and leave in a warm place for about 1 hour, until doubled in size. Lightly grease a baking sheet.

4 Turn the dough out on to a floured surface and knead lightly. Shape the dough into a large round or oval and place on the prepared baking sheet. Cover and leave in a warm place for about 30 minutes or until doubled in size. Preheat the oven to 230°C (210°C fan oven) mark 8.

5 Bake for 15 minutes, then reduce the oven temperature to 200°C (180°C fan oven) mark 6 and bake for a further 20–30 minutes until the bread sounds hollow when tapped underneath.

6 Dissolve the remaining sugar in 1 tbsp hot water and brush over the loaf to glaze. Return to the oven for 2–3 minutes, then transfer to a wire rack to cool.

Lardy Cake

The West Warm or cold, this cake is sweet, filling and delicious. Lardy cake originates from Wiltshire, and in the West Country local bakers still make it to their own recipes, cramming in as much lard, sugar and fruit as they or their customers choose.

Makes about 12 slices • Preparation 25 minutes, plus rising • Cooking time 30 minutes

75g (3oz) butter, diced, plus extra to grease

15g (½oz) fresh yeast or 1½ tsp dried and a pinch of sugar

450g (1lb) strong white flour, plus extra to dust

1 tsp salt

75g (3oz) lard, diced

175g (6oz) mixed sultanas and currants

50g (2oz) chopped mixed peel

50g (2oz) sugar

butter to serve (optional)

Nutrition per slice
296 cals | 12g fat (6g sats) |
45g carbs | 0.6g salt

---

1 Grease a 20.5 x 25.5cm (8 x 10in) roasting tin. Blend the fresh yeast with 300ml (½ pint) warm water. If using dried yeast, sprinkle it into 300ml (½ pint) warm water with the sugar and leave for 15 minutes or until frothy.

2 Put the flour and salt into a bowl and rub in 15g (½oz) of the lard. Make a well in the centre and pour in the yeast liquid. Beat together to make a dough that leaves the sides of the bowl clean, adding more water if necessary.

3 Turn out on to a lightly floured surface and knead well for about 10 minutes or until smooth and elastic. Put in a clean bowl, cover with a clean teatowel and leave in a warm place for about 1 hour or until doubled in size.

4 Turn the dough out on to a floured surface and roll out to a rectangle about 5mm (¼in) thick. Dot one-third of the remaining lard and the butter over the surface of the dough, then sprinkle with one-third of the fruit,

peel and sugar. Fold the dough in three, folding the bottom third up and the top third down. Give a quarter-turn, then repeat the process twice more.

5 Roll the dough out to fit the prepared tin. Put in the tin, cover and leave in a warm place for about 30 minutes or until puffy. Preheat the oven to 220°C (200°C fan oven) mark 7.

6 Score the top of the dough in a criss-cross pattern with a knife, then bake for 30 minutes or until well risen and golden brown. Turn out and serve immediately or leave to cool on a wire rack. Serve plain or with butter.

Sweet Cherry Bread

The Southeast Cherries first came to England with the Romans, and several varieties of sweet cherry are grown in Kent. With its topping of honey and icing, this bread is sure to be a welcome addition to afternoon tea, or a snack for the lunchbox.

Cuts into 8 slices • Preparation 40 minutes, plus rising • Cooking time 40 minutes, plus cooling

oil to grease
350g (12oz) strong white bread flour, plus extra to dust
½ tsp salt
2 tsp ground mixed spice
1 tsp ground cinnamon
25g (1oz) caster sugar
1 tbsp fast-action dried yeast
75g (3oz) unsalted butter, diced
200ml (7fl oz) warm milk
125g (4oz) white almond paste, roughly chopped
125g (4oz) glacé cherries
3 tbsp honey, warmed
75g (3oz) icing sugar, sifted

Nutrition per slice
310 cals | 4g fat (trace sats) | 66g carbs | 0.4g salt

1 Grease a 20.5cm (8in) round deep cake tin and base-line with greaseproof paper.
2 Sift the flour, salt, spices and caster sugar into a bowl. Add the yeast, then rub in the butter. Add the milk to make a dough (if the dough is too dry, add a little more milk). Turn out on to a lightly floured surface and knead for 10 minutes. Put the dough into a lightly oiled bowl, cover with oiled clingfilm and leave in a warm place for 2 hours or until doubled in size.
3 Turn out the dough on to a lightly floured surface and knead lightly. Shape into an oval, 60cm (24in) long. Scatter the almond paste and cherries over the surface and roll up the dough lengthways, then form it into a tight coil. Put in the cake tin, cover and leave in a warm place for 30 minutes or until doubled in size. Preheat the oven to 180°C (160°C fan oven) mark 4.

4 Bake for 40 minutes or until golden; it should sound hollow when tapped underneath. Turn out on to a wire rack and leave to cool completely. When cool, brush with honey. Mix the icing sugar with a few drops of water and drizzle over the bread. Store in an airtight container. It will keep for up to two days in an airtight container.

Plain Scones

Scotland Originally made with oats, and shaped like triangles, scones nowadays are baked with flour and come in various shapes. By varying the liquid and flour used, and adding extra ingredients such as dried fruit, lots of variations can be made.

Makes 8 • Preparation 15 minutes • Cooking time 10 minutes, plus cooling

40g (1½oz) butter, diced, plus extra
to grease
225g (8oz) self-raising flour, plus extra
to dust
a pinch of salt
1 tsp baking powder
about 150ml (¼ pint) milk
beaten egg or milk to glaze
whipped cream, or butter and jam,
to serve

Nutrition per scone
140 cals | 5g fat (3g sats) |
22g carbs | 0.7g salt

1 Preheat the oven to 220°C (200°C fan oven) mark 7. Grease a baking sheet. Sift the flour, salt and baking powder together into a bowl. Rub in the butter until the mixture resembles fine breadcrumbs. Using a knife to stir it in, add enough milk to give a fairly soft dough.

2 Gently roll or pat out the dough on a lightly floured surface to a 2cm (¾in) thickness (see Cook's Tip) and then, using a 6.5cm (2½in) plain cutter, cut out rounds.

3 Put on the baking sheet and brush the tops with beaten egg or milk. Bake for about 10 minutes or until golden brown and well risen. Transfer to a wire rack and leave to cool. Serve warm, split and filled with cream, or butter and jam.

•COOK'S TIP•

To ensure a good rise, avoid heavy handling and make sure the rolled-out dough is at least 2cm (¾in) thick

TRY SOMETHING DIFFERENT

Wholemeal Scones
Replace half the white flour with wholemeal flour.

Fruit Scones
Add 50g (2oz) currants, sultanas, raisins or chopped dates (or a mixture) to the dry ingredients.

Buttermilk Scones
Increase the flour to 300g (11oz) and the butter to 50g (2oz). Replace the milk with a 284ml carton buttermilk and add 25g (1oz) golden caster sugar. Bake for 12–15 minutes, then cool a little. Beat 250g (9oz) mascarpone in a bowl to soften. Add the seeds from 1 vanilla pod and beat well to combine. Serve the warm scones split and sandwiched together with the vanilla mascarpone and blueberry jam.

Cheese and Herb Scones

Scotland The Scots are famous for the variety of their scones. These are a savoury version and have a little hit of mustard in the mix.

Makes 8 • Preparation 15 minutes • Cooking time 10 minutes, plus cooling

40g (1½ oz) butter, diced, plus extra to grease
225g (8oz) self-raising flour, plus extra to dust
a pinch of salt
1 tsp baking powder
1 tsp mustard powder
2 tbsp finely chopped herbs
50g (2oz) finely grated Cheddar cheese, plus extra for sprinkling
about 150ml (¼ pint) milk
beaten egg or milk to glaze
butter to serve (optional)

Nutrition per scone
140 cals | 5g fat (3g sats) |
22g carbs | 0.7g salt

1 Preheat the oven to 220°C (200°C fan oven) mark 7. Grease a baking sheet. Sift the flour, salt, baking powder and mustard powder together into a bowl. Rub in the butter until the mixture resembles fine breadcrumbs. Add in the grated cheese and herbs, then, using a knife, stir in enough milk to give a fairly soft dough.

2 Gently roll or pat out the dough on a lightly floured surface to a 2cm (¾in) thickness. Using a 6cm (2½in) plain cutter, cut out rounds.

3 Put on the prepared baking sheet and brush the tops with beaten egg or milk, then sprinkle with a little cheese. Bake for about 10 minutes or until golden brown and well risen. Transfer to a wire rack and leave to cool. Serve warm, split and buttered, if you like.

Potato Scones

The North and Scotland These scones need to be made from floury potatoes, such as Pentland Squire or Maris Piper, which will mash well without lumps.

Makes about 8 • Preparation 10 minutes • Cooking time 40 minutes

450g (1lb) floury potatoes, peeled
1 tsp salt
25g (1oz) butter, plus extra to grease
about 125g (4oz) plain flour, plus extra to dust
butter to serve

Nutrition per scone
72 cals | 2g fat (1g sats) |
13g carbs | 0.5g salt

1 Cook the potatoes in lightly salted boiling water for about 20 minutes or until tender. Drain and mash until smooth. Add the salt and butter while the potatoes are still hot, then work in enough flour to make a stiff dough.

2 Turn out on to a floured surface, knead lightly and roll out until 1cm (½in) thick. Cut into 6.5cm (2½in) rounds.

3 Cook on a greased griddle or heavy-based frying pan for 4–5 minutes on each side until golden brown. Serve hot with butter.

.COOK'S TIP.
You can use leftover cold cooked potatoes, but for the best and lightest flavour boil them freshly.

Drop Scones (Scotch Pancakes)

Scotland These classic Scottish scones, looking more like a pancake, are traditionally cooked on a griddle, or girdle, and are good to eat at any time. They are best eaten when fresh and warm, with your choice of jam or honey.

Makes 15 • Preparation 10 minutes • Cooking time 12–18 minutes

125g (4oz) self-raising flour
2 tbsp caster sugar
1 medium egg, beaten
150ml (¼ pint) milk
vegetable oil to grease
butter, or whipped cream and jam,
to serve

Nutrition per scone
50 cals | 1g fat (0.2g sats) |
9g carbs | 0.1g salt

1 Mix the flour and sugar together in a bowl. Make a well in the centre and mix in the egg, with enough of the milk to make a batter the consistency of thick cream – working as quickly and lightly as possible.
2 Cook the mixture in batches: drop spoonfuls on to an oiled hot griddle or heavy-based frying pan. Keep the griddle at a steady heat and when bubbles rise to the surface of the scones and burst, after 2–3 minutes, turn them over with a palette knife.
3 Cook for a further 2–3 minutes until golden brown on the other side.
4 Put the cooked drop scones on a clean teatowel and cover with another teatowel to keep them moist. Serve warm, with butter, or cream and jam.

Muffins

The Southeast The correct way to toast muffins is not to split them and toast the two halves separately, as this makes them tough. Instead, cut them open, then close together again and toast slowly until warm right through, then open and butter each half.

Makes about 12 • Preparation 20 minutes, plus rising • Cooking time 15 minutes per batch

15g (½oz) fresh yeast or 1½ tsp dried yeast
300ml (½ pint) warm milk
450g (1lb) strong white flour, plus extra to dust
1 tsp salt
1 tsp plain flour
1 tsp semolina

Nutrition per muffin
142 cals | 1g fat (trace sats) |
30g carbs | 0.5g salt

1 Dissolve the yeast in the milk. If using dried yeast, sprinkle over the milk and leave in a warm place for 15 minutes or until frothy.
2 Sift the strong white flour and salt together, then make a well in the centre. Pour the yeast liquid into the well, draw in the flour and mix to a smooth dough.
3 Knead the dough on a lightly floured surface for about 10 minutes or until smooth and elastic. Put in a clean bowl, cover with a teatowel and leave in a warm place for about 1 hour or until doubled in size.
4 Using a lightly floured rolling pin, roll out the dough on a lightly floured surface to about 0.5–1cm (¼–½in) thick. Leave to rest, covered with a teatowel, for 5 minutes. Using a 7.5cm (3in) plain cutter, cut into rounds.
5 Put the muffins on a well-floured baking sheet. Mix together the plain flour and the semolina and use to dust the tops. Cover with a teatowel and leave in a warm place until doubled in size.
6 Grease a griddle or heavy frying pan and heat over a medium heat until a cube of bread turns brown in 20 seconds.
7 Cook the muffins on the griddle or frying pan for about 7 minutes each side or until golden brown.

Hot Cross Buns

Countrywide **A much-loved recipe, hot cross buns were traditionally eaten for breakfast on Good Friday and are still sold widely at Easter time. They were first made in the 18th century, when they were extra rich and spicy, and marked with a cross as a reminder of the festival.**

Makes 15 buns • Preparation 30 minutes, plus rising • Cooking time 15–18 minutes, plus cooling

100ml (3½ fl oz) warm milk, plus extra
to glaze
15g (½oz) fresh yeast or 7g sachet
(2 tsp) dried yeast
50g (2oz) golden caster sugar, plus
extra to glaze
350g (12oz) strong plain white flour,
sifted, plus extra to dust
a pinch of salt
vegetable oil to grease
a pinch of ground cinnamon
a pinch of freshly grated nutmeg
25g (1oz) chopped mixed candied peel
125g (4oz) mixed raisins, sultanas and
currants
25g (1oz) butter, melted and cooled
until tepid
1 medium egg, beaten

Nutrition per bun
140 cals | 2g fat (1g sats) |
28g carbs | 0.2g salt

1 Mix the warm milk with an equal quantity of warm water. Put the yeast into a small bowl with 1 tbsp of the warm liquid and 1 tsp of the sugar and set aside for 5 minutes.

2 Put 225g (8oz) of the flour and the salt into a large bowl, make a well in the centre and pour in the yeast mixture. Cover with a clean teatowel and leave in a warm place for 20 minutes or until frothy. Lightly oil a bowl and a large baking sheet.

3 Mix the remaining flour and sugar together with the spices, peel and dried fruit. Add to the yeast mixture with the melted butter and egg. Mix thoroughly to form a soft dough, adding a little more liquid if needed. Put the dough into the prepared bowl, cover and leave to rise in a warm place for 1–1½ hours until doubled in size.

4 Knock back the dough and knead lightly on a lightly floured surface for 1–2 minutes. Divide the dough into 15 equal-sized pieces and shape into buns. Put well apart on the prepared baking sheet. Make a deep cross on the top of each one with a sharp knife, then cover with a teatowel and leave in a warm place for 30 minutes or until doubled in size. Preheat the oven to 220°C (200°C fan oven) mark 7.

5 Brush the buns with milk and sprinkle with sugar, then bake for 15–18 minutes until they sound hollow when tapped underneath. Transfer to a wire rack and leave to cool. Serve warm.

TRY SOMETHING DIFFERENT

▼▼▼▼▼▼▼▼▼▼

Rather than mark crosses on the buns, brush with beaten egg to glaze, then top each with a pastry cross and glaze again. Bake as above.

Crumpets

The Midlands A traditional English comfort food, crumpets are perfect, hot and buttery, with afternoon tea. Popular in their present form since Victorian times, they were frequently toasted on the end of a toasting fork in front of the fire.

Makes about 24 • Preparation 20 minutes, plus rising • Cooking time about 35 minutes

350g (12oz) strong plain white flour
½ tsp salt
½ tsp bicarbonate of soda
1½ tsp easy-blend dried yeast
250ml (9fl oz) warm milk
a little vegetable oil
butter to serve

Nutrition per crumpet
60 cals | 1g fat (trace sats) |
12g carbs | 0.2g salt

1 Sift the flour, salt and bicarbonate of soda into a large bowl and stir in the yeast. Make a well in the centre, then pour in 300ml (½ pint) warm water and the milk. Mix to a thick batter.

2 Using a wooden spoon, beat the batter vigorously for about 5 minutes. Cover and leave in a warm place for about 1 hour or until sponge-like in texture. Beat the batter for a further 2 minutes, then transfer to a jug.

3 Put a large non-stick frying pan over a high heat and brush a little oil over the surface. Oil the insides of four crumpet rings or 7.5cm (3in) plain metal cutters. Put the rings, blunt edge down, on to the hot pan surface and leave for about 2 minutes until very hot.

4 Pour a little batter into each ring to a depth of 1cm (½in). Cook the crumpets for 5–7 minutes until the surface is set and appears honeycombed with holes.

5 Carefully remove each metal ring. Flip the crumpets over and cook the other side for 1 minute only. Transfer to a wire rack. Repeat to use all of the batter.

6 To serve, toast the crumpets on both sides and serve with butter.

Welsh Cakes

Wales Similar to scones, these are a popular Welsh snack, still eaten today as a tea-time treat. Not requiring an oven to cook them, they were easily made. However, unlike scones, they are not split and filled, although they are sometimes buttered.

Makes about 16 • Preparation 10 minutes • Cooking time 6 minutes per batch, plus cooling

50g (2oz) butter or margarine, plus extra to grease
225g (8oz) plain flour, plus extra to dust
1 tsp baking powder
a pinch of salt
50g (2oz) lard
75g (3oz) caster sugar
50g (2oz) currants
1 medium egg, beaten
about 2 tbsp milk

Nutrition per cake
123 cals | 6g fat (3g sats) |
18g carbs | 0.2g salt

1 Grease a griddle or heavy frying pan. Sift together the flour, baking powder and salt. Rub in the fats until the mixture resembles fine breadcrumbs, then add the sugar and currants.
2 Make a well in the centre, then add the egg and enough milk to make a stiff paste similar to shortcrust pastry.
3 Roll out on a lightly floured surface until 5mm (¼in) thick. Using a 7.5cm (3in) cutter, cut into rounds.
4 Cook the cakes slowly on the medium-hot griddle for 3 minutes on each side or until golden brown. Cool on a wire rack. Eat on the day they are made.

TRY SOMETHING DIFFERENT

Griddle Scones
Use self-raising flour instead of plain, with 1 tsp baking powder, a pinch of salt and ½ tsp freshly grated nutmeg. Omit the lard. Use 50g (2oz) golden caster sugar. Omit the currants. You may need 3–4 tbsp milk. Roll out to 1cm (½in) thick and cut into triangles. Cook for 5 minutes on each side. Serve warm, split and buttered.

PRESERVES

Rhubarb and Ginger Jam

Countrywide Forced, early rhubarb makes its appearance at the beginning of the year and by the late spring it is sprouting in gardens and the main crop is coming into the shops. Preserved ginger, which comes mostly from China, gives a good bite and extra flavour to the jam.

Makes about 1.4kg (3lb) • Preparation 10 minutes, plus steeping • Cooking time 20 minutes

1.1kg (2½lb) trimmed rhubarb, chopped
1.1kg (2½lb) sugar
juice of 2 lemons
25g (1oz) fresh root ginger, peeled
125g (4oz) preserved or crystallised ginger, chopped

Nutrition per tablespoon
50 calories | 0g fat (0g sats) | 13g carbs | 0.1g salt

1 Put the rhubarb into a large bowl in alternate layers with the sugar and lemon juice, then cover and leave overnight.

2 Next day, bruise the root ginger slightly with a weight or rolling pin and tie it in a piece of muslin. Put the rhubarb mixture into a preserving pan with the muslin bag, bring to the boil and boil rapidly for 15 minutes.

3 Remove the muslin bag, add the ginger and boil for a further 5 minutes or until the rhubarb is clear. Test for a set (see Cook's Tips) and, when setting point is reached, take the pan off the heat and skim the surface with a slotted spoon. Pot, seal and label (see Cook's Tips).

.COOK'S TIPS.

To test for a set, chill a saucer in the freezer. When the preserve is nearly ready, take the pan off the heat and spoon a blob of preserve on to a saucer and chill for a few minutes. When the preserve has cooled, push the surface with your finger; it is set if it wrinkles and doesn't break to reveal liquid.

To pot the preserve, wash jars or bottles in very hot soapy water, rinse thoroughly, then put upturned on a baking sheet in the oven at 140°C (120°C fan oven) mark 1 for 10–15 minutes until completely dry. Stand the jars upside down on a clean teatowel until the preserve is ready. Don't pot strawberry and other whole fruit jams Immediately or all the fruit will rise to the top; leave them in the pan for 15–20 minutes before potting. Spoon the preserve into the warm jars, filling them right to the top. Wipe the outside of the jars with a damp cloth while they are still warm and immediately put wax discs, wax side down, on the surface of the preserve, making sure they lie flat. Either cover immediately with a dampened round of cellophane and secure with a rubber band or string, or leave until quite cold before doing this. Label, then store in a cool, dark, dry place. Most preserves keep well for about a year, after which their flavour starts to deteriorate.

Strawberry Conserve

Countrywide Conserves are made from whole fruits, suspended in a thick, sweet syrup, and they do not set firmly. Use them as fillings for summer tarts or spread them on scones with cream.

Makes about 1.4kg (3lb) • Preparation 15 minutes, plus steeping • Cooking time 20 minutes, plus cooling

1.4kg (3lb) strawberries, hulled
1.4kg (3lb) sugar

Nutrition per serving
52 cals | 0g fat (0g sats) |
14g carbs | 0.1g salt

1 Put the strawberries in a large bowl in layers with the sugar. Cover and leave for 24 hours.
2 Put into a large pan and bring to the boil, stirring until the sugar dissolves. Boil rapidly for 5 minutes.
3 Return the mixture to the bowl, cover and leave in a cool place for a further two days.
4 Return to the pan again and boil rapidly for 10 minutes. Leave to cool for 15 minutes, then pot, seal and label as for jam (see Cook's Tips, page 262).

•COOK'S TIP•

Raspberries and loganberries can be conserved in the same way. For a quick dessert, serve with custard or milk puddings.

Bramble and Apple Jam

Countrywide Wild blackberries, or brambles, have always been in plentiful supply in British hedgerows, and have been gathered and used in many different ways for centuries. Commercially grown blackberries are often in the shops or on pick-your-own fruit farms.

Makes about 4.5kg (10lb) • Preparation 10 minutes • Cooking time 30 minutes

1.8kg (4lb) blackberries
700g (1½ lb) peeled, cored and sliced cooking apples
2.7kg (6lb) sugar
a knob of butter

Nutrition per serving
55 cals | 0.1g fat (0.1g sats) |
14 carbs | 0.1g salt

1 Put the blackberries into a large pan with 150ml (¼ pint) water and simmer gently until soft.
2 Meanwhile, put the apples into a separate preserving pan with 150ml (¼ pint) water and simmer gently until soft. Pulp with a wooden spoon or potato masher.
3 Add the blackberries and sugar to the apple pulp, stirring until the sugar has dissolved, then add a knob of butter.
4 Bring to the boil and boil rapidly, stirring frequently, for about 10 minutes. Test for a set (see Cook's Tips, page 262) and, when setting point is reached, take the pan off the heat and skim the surface with a slotted spoon. Pot, seal and label (see Cook's Tips, page 262).

Plum Jam

Countrywide British plums are at their best in late summer and this is just the time to get jam-making. Try the unusual variations too.

Makes about 4.5kg (10lb) • **Preparation 15 minutes, plus standing** • **Cooking time 50 minutes**

2.7kg (6lb) plums
2.7kg (6lb) sugar
knob of butter

Nutrition per tablespoon
40 cals | trace fat (0g sats) |
10g carbs | trace salt

1 Put the plums and 900ml (1½ pints) water into a preserving pan. Bring to the boil, then simmer gently for 30 minutes or until well reduced and the fruit is very soft.
2 Remove the pan from the heat, add the sugar, stirring until dissolved, then add the knob of butter. Bring to the boil and boil rapidly for 10–15 minutes until setting point is reached (see Cook's Tips, page 262), stirring frequently.
3 Take the pan off the heat. Using a slotted spoon, remove the plum stones and skim off any scum from the surface of the jam, then leave to stand for about 15 minutes. Pot, seal and label (see Cook's Tips, page 262).

TRY SOMETHING DIFFERENT

▼▼▼▼▼▼▼▼▼

Greengage Jam
Use greengages instead of plums and reduce the water to 600ml (1 pint).

Damson Jam
Use 2.3kg (5lb) damsons instead of plums. After adding the sugar, boil for 10 minutes only.

•COOK'S TIP•

If dessert plums are used rather than a cooking variety, add the juice of 1 large lemon.

Raspberry Jam

Scotland and Countrywide Scotland produces two-thirds of British raspberries and this is a good jam to make when they are at their peak and less expensive. It's quick to make and delicious.

Makes about 2.6kg (5¾lb) • **Preparation 10 minutes, plus standing** • **Cooking time about 45 minutes**

1.8kg (4lb) raspberries
1.8kg (4lb) golden caster sugar
knob of butter

Nutrition per tablespoon
50 cals | trace fat (0g sats) |
12g carbs | trace salt

1 Put the raspberries into a preserving pan and simmer very gently in their own juice for 15–20 minutes, stirring carefully from time to time, until soft.
2 Remove the pan from the heat and add the sugar, stirring until dissolved, then add the butter and boil rapidly for 20 minutes or until setting point is reached (see Cook's Tips, page 262).
3 Take the pan off the heat, remove any scum with a slotted spoon, then leave to stand for 15 minutes. Pot, seal and label (see Cook's Tips, page 262).

Gooseberry Jam

The Midlands Late June is the time to look for the hard, green, early gooseberries this recipe calls for. The jam can also be made later in the season, with riper, sweeter fruit. It will then have a light set and an attractive pale pink colour.

Makes about 4.5kg (10lb) • **Preparation 15 minutes** • **Cooking time 50 minutes**

2.7kg (6lb) gooseberries (slightly under-ripe), topped and tailed
2.7kg (6lb) sugar
a knob of butter

Nutrition per serving
55 cals | 0.1g fat (0.1g sats) |
14g carbs | 0.1g salt

1 Put the gooseberries into a preserving pan with 1.1 litres (2 pints) water. Simmer gently for about 30 minutes or until the fruit is really soft and reduced, mashing it to a pulp with a wooden spoon and stirring from time to time to prevent sticking.

2 Remove from the heat, add the sugar to the fruit pulp and stir until dissolved, then add a knob of butter.

3 Bring to the boil and boil rapidly for about 10 minutes. Test for a set (see Cook's Tips, page 262) and, when setting point is reached, take the pan off the heat and skim the surface with a slotted spoon. Pot, seal and label (see Cook's Tips, page 262).

TRY SOMETHING DIFFERENT

▼▼▼▼▼▼▼▼▼

Elderflower Gooseberry Jam
A delicious and unusual flavour can be given to gooseberry jam by adding 6–8 elderflower heads to each 1kg (2¼lb) fruit. Cut off the stems close to the flowers and tie the flowers in a piece of muslin. Add the muslin bag to the jam when it comes to the boil, removing it before the jam is potted.

Oxford Marmalade

The Southeast The tradition of making marmalade at home goes back at least 200 years, even though in those times oranges were something of a luxury, as they were expensive to import. Oxford marmalade is characteristically dark and chunky, with a slightly bitter flavour.

Makes about 4kg (9lb) • **Preparation 15 minutes, plus steeping** • **Cooking time 45 minutes, plus standing**

1.4kg (3lb) Seville oranges
2.7kg (6lb) sugar

Nutrition per serving
37 cals | 0g fat (0g sats) |
10g carbs | 0.1g salt

1 Peel the oranges and cut the peel into strips and the fruit into small pieces, reserving the pips. Put the pips into a small bowl. Put the strips of peel and chopped flesh into a large bowl.

2 Bring 3.4 litres (6 pints) water to the boil and pour 600ml (1 pint) over the pips and the remainder over the

orange peel and flesh. Cover both bowls and leave for several hours or overnight.

3 The next day, the pips will be covered with a soft transparent jelly which must be washed off them into the orange peel and flesh. To do this, lift the pips out of the water with a slotted spoon and put them into a nylon sieve. Pour the water the pips were soaking in over the pips into the large bowl. Repeat the process, using water from the large bowl. Discard the pips.

4 Boil the peel, flesh and water until the peel is very soft – the longer this mixture boils the darker the marmalade will be.

5 When the peel is quite soft, remove the pan from the heat and add the sugar, stirring until it has dissolved.

6 Boil very gently until the marmalade is as dark as you like it, then boil rapidly for about 15 minutes. Test for a set (see Cook's Tips, page 262) and, when setting point is reached, take the pan off the heat and skim the surface with a slotted spoon.

7 Leave to stand for 15 minutes, then stir to distribute the peel. Pot, seal and label (see Cook's Tips, page 262).

Currant and Port Jelly

The Southeast This is a good way to use up a glut of red or blackcurrants, and it has a richer flavour and deeper colour than usual. The port is added at the last moment, so none of the flavour is lost through boiling. The yield depends on the fruit's ripeness, and dripping time.

Preparation 10 minutes, plus straining • Cooking time 1 hour

1.4kg (3lb) red or blackcurrants
sugar
3 tbsp port

Nutrition per serving
45 cals | 0g fat (0g sats) |
12g carbs | 0.1g salt

1 There is no need to remove the currants from their stalks. Put the currants into a preserving pan with 600ml (1 pint) water and simmer gently for about 30 minutes or until the fruit is really soft and pulpy. Stir from time to time to prevent sticking.

2 Spoon the fruit pulp into a jelly bag or cloth attached to the legs of an upturned stool and leave to strain into a large bowl for at least 12 hours. Do not squeeze.

3 Discard the pulp remaining in the jelly bag. Measure the extract and return it to the pan with 450g (1lb) sugar for each 600ml (1 pint) extract.

4 Heat gently, stirring, until the sugar has dissolved, then boil rapidly for about 15 minutes. Test for a set (see Cook's Tips, page 262) and, when setting point is reached, remove the pan from the heat.

5 Stir in the port, then skim the surface with a slotted spoon. Pot, seal and label (see Cook's Tips, page 262).

Green Tomato Chutney

Countrywide The answer to the problem of what to do with tomatoes that refuse to ripen is to make this lightly spiced, smooth chutney, which goes well with cheese and all cold meats.

Makes about 1.4kg (3lb) • Preparation 15 minutes • Cooking time 2¼ hours

450g (1lb) cooking apples, peeled, cored and finely chopped
225g (8oz) onions, finely chopped
1.4kg (3lb) green tomatoes, thinly sliced
225g (8oz) sultanas
225g (8oz) demerara sugar
2 tsp salt
450ml (¾ pint) malt vinegar
4 small pieces of dried root ginger tied in a piece of muslin
½ tsp cayenne pepper
1 tsp mustard powder

Nutrition per serving
18 cals | 0g fat (0g sats) | 4g carbs |
0.1g salt

1 Put all the ingredients into a preserving pan. Bring to the boil, then simmer gently for about 2 hours, stirring occasionally, until the ingredients are tender, reduced to a thick consistency and no excess liquid remains.

2 Remove the ginger, spoon the chutney into preheated jars and cover at once with airtight, vinegar-proof tops (see Cook's Tips, page 262).

Apple and Mint Jelly

Countrywide A delicious herb jelly, made in the traditional way, to go with roast lamb. The yield will depend on the ripeness of the fruit and the time allowed for dripping.

Preparation 10 minutes, plus straining • Cooking time 1¼ hours

2.3kg (5lb) cooking apples, such as
Bramleys
a few large fresh mint sprigs
1.1 litres (2 pints) distilled white
vinegar
sugar
6–8 tbsp freshly chopped mint
a few drops of green food colouring

Nutrition per serving
46 cals | 0g fat (0g sats) |
12g carbs | 0.1g salt

1 Remove any bruised or damaged portions from the apples and roughly chop them into thick chunks without peeling or coring. Put them into a preserving pan with 1.1 litres (2 pints) water and the mint sprigs. Bring to the boil, then simmer gently for about 45 minutes or until soft and pulpy.

Stir from time to time to prevent sticking. Add the vinegar and boil for a further 5 minutes.

2 Spoon the apple pulp into a jelly bag or cloth attached to the legs of an upturned stool and leave to strain into a large bowl for at least 12 hours. Do not squeeze.

3 Discard the pulp remaining in the jelly bag. Measure the extract and return it to the preserving pan with 450g (1lb) sugar for each 600ml (1 pint) extract.

4 Heat gently, stirring, until the sugar has dissolved, then boil rapidly for about 10 minutes. Test for a set (see Cook's Tips, page 262) and, when setting point is reached, take the pan off the heat and skim the surface with a slotted spoon.

5 Stir in the chopped mint and add a few drops of green food colouring. Allow to cool slightly, then stir well to

distribute the mint. Pot, seal with vinegar-proof tops and label (see Cook's Tips, page 262).

TRY SOMETHING DIFFERENT

▼▼▼▼▼▼▼

Herb Jellies
Other fresh herbs, such as rosemary, parsley, sage and thyme, can be used equally as well as mint. Serve these herb jellies with roast meats – rosemary jelly with lamb; parsley jelly with gammon; sage jelly with pork; thyme jelly with poultry.

Bread and Butter Pickle

Countrywide This pickle is good with dishes such as sandwiches or bread and butter – hence its name. The yield will depend on how tightly the vegetables are packed and the jars' capacity.

Preparation 15 minutes, plus steeping • Cooking time 10 minutes, plus maturing

3 large ridged or smooth-skinned
cucumbers, thinly sliced
4 large onions, sliced
3 tbsp salt
450ml (¾ pint) distilled white vinegar
150g (5oz) sugar
1 tsp celery seeds
1 tsp black mustard seeds

Nutrition per serving
12 cals | 0g fat (0g sats) |
3g carbs | 0.5g salt

1 Layer the cucumber and onion slices in a large bowl, sprinkling each layer with salt. Leave for 1 hour, then drain and rinse well.

2 Put the vinegar, sugar and celery and mustard seeds into a pan and heat gently, stirring, until the sugar has dissolved. Bring to the boil and boil for 3 minutes.

3 Pack the vegetable slices into preheated jars (see Cook's Tips, page 262) and add enough hot vinegar mixture to cover. Cover immediately with airtight, vinegar-proof tops and label.

4 This pickle must be stored in a dark place or the cucumber will lose its colour. Store for two months to mature before eating.

Beetroot Relish

The North There are two types of beetroot: long and globe-shaped. Use either for this spicy pickle, which makes an excellent accompaniment to cold meats. This is a good recipe for using up the large, tougher maincrop beetroots, available all year.

Makes about 700g (1½lb) • Preparation 15 minutes • Cooking time 40 minutes, plus maturing

900g (2lb) cooked beetroot, skinned and diced
450g (1lb) white cabbage, finely shredded
75g (3oz) fresh horseradish, grated
1 tbsp mustard powder
600ml (1 pint) malt vinegar
225g (8oz) sugar
a pinch of cayenne pepper
salt and ground black pepper

Nutrition per serving
18 cals | 0g fat (0g sats) |
4g carbs | 0.1g salt

1 Combine all the ingredients in a large pan. Bring slowly to the boil, then simmer for 30 minutes, stirring occasionally.
2 Spoon into preheated jars (see Cook's Tips, page 262) and cover at once with airtight, vinegar-proof tops.
3 Label, then store in a cool, dry, dark place and leave to mature for two–three months before eating.

Fruit Vinegars

Countrywide Flavoured vinegars can be used wherever you would use ordinary vinegar, and add a subtle flavour all of their own. The fruit vinegars make very successful salad dressings.

Preparation 15 minutes, plus standing • Cooking time 15 minutes

raspberries, blackberries or blackcurrants
red or white wine vinegar
sugar

Nutrition per tablespoon
20 cals | 0g fat (0g sats) |
5g carbs | 0.1g salt

1 Put the fruit into a bowl and break it up slightly with the back of a wooden spoon. For each 450g (1lb) fruit, pour in 600ml (1 pint) red or white wine vinegar. Cover with a cloth and leave to stand for three to four days, stirring occasionally.
2 Strain through muslin and add 450g (1lb) sugar to each 600ml (1 pint). Boil for 10 minutes, then cool and strain again. Pour into bottles (see Cook's Tips, page 262), seal with airtight and vinegar-proof tops and label. Add a few whole pieces of fruit to each bottle, if you like. Use when making salad dressings.

Herb Vinegars

Countrywide You can use one favourite herb by itself, or a mixture of several. Use pretty bottles, label and seal, and give as presents.

sprigs of fresh herbs, such as
rosemary, tarragon, mint, thyme,
marjoram, basil, dill, sage, parsley
red or white wine vinegar

Nutrition per tablespoon
3 cals | 0g fat (0g sats) |
0.1 carbs | 0.1g salt

1 Fill bottles with sprigs of fresh herbs. Use either a mixture of herbs or one variety. Fill with red or white wine vinegar.
2 Seal with vinegar-proof tops, then label and leave in a cool, dry place for about 6 weeks. Use when making salad dressings.

Mincemeat

Countrywide The use of beef suet is reminiscent of the days when meat was always included in the recipe – hence its name. It was originally made to preserve meat through the winter.

Makes about 2.5kg (5½lb) • Preparation 20 minutes, plus standing and maturing

1.6kg (3½lb) dried mixed fruit
225g (8oz) cooking apples, peeled, cored and grated
125g (4oz) blanched almonds, chopped
450g (1lb) soft dark brown sugar
175g (6oz) shredded beef suet
1 tsp freshly grated nutmeg
1 tsp ground cinnamon
grated zest and juice of 1 lemon
grated zest and juice of 1 orange
300ml (½ pint) brandy or sherry

Nutrition per serving
78 cals | 2g fat (1g sats) |
14g carbs | 0.1g salt

1 Put all the ingredients into a large bowl, then mix together thoroughly.
2 Cover the mincemeat and leave to stand for two days. Stir well, put into jars and cover. Allow at least two weeks to mature before using.

•COOK'S TIP•

For mincemeat that will keep well, use a firm, hard type of apple, such as Wellington; a juicy apple, such as Bramley's Seedling, may make the mixture too moist.

FROM THE SHOP TO THE KITCHEN

BUYING FRESH FOOD

Knowing what to look for and how to select wisely are important factors when buying foods. The following notes will help you in your choice.

CHOOSING MEAT

When choosing meat, it helps to bear in mind the cooking method that you intend using. If you want something to cook quickly by a dry heat method such as grilling or roasting, it must be a lean, tender cut from a prime-quality animal and will inevitably be more expensive. Slower cooking with added moisture is suitable for one of the tougher, probably fattier cuts, which will be cheaper. If in doubt, ask your butcher for advice. Many pre-packaged meat cuts carry labels suggesting suitable methods of cooking, and these should be considered. The nutritional quality of the cheaper cuts is the same as that of the dearer cuts and the flavour of both is just as good if cooked properly.

Generally speaking, choose meat which has no undue amount of fat surrounding it; what fat there is should be firm and free from dark marks or discoloration. The colour of fat may vary for a number of reasons, none of which will affect the taste. Lean meat should be finely grained, firm and slightly elastic; a fine marbling, or flecks of fat in the meat, will help to keep the meat moist during cooking and often gives a better flavour. Coarse-grained meat is usually an indication that the meat is suitable only for stewing or braising. Do not worry about the colour of meat. The redness of meat will vary after cutting and exposure to air, but this need not affect your choice.

Whether you choose fresh or frozen meat is a matter mainly of personal preference, but frozen meat that has been thawed should not be refrozen unless cooked first.

CHOOSING POULTRY AND GAME

If buying *fresh poultry*, choose a bird that looks plump and well rounded. The skin should be free from blemishes and bruising. In a young chicken the tip of the breast bone will be soft and flexible; if it is hard and rigid the bird is probably too old to roast satisfactorily although it will be suitable for steaming or boiling.

Modern poultry production methods ensure a moist, tender-fleshed bird. Prompt freezing also guarantees freshness, so you can expect high quality from any of the well-known brands of frozen poultry. Traditionally reared farmyard birds are inclined to have more flavour.

Larger birds generally give the best value, as the proportion of meat to bone is higher and the extra meat, particularly chicken and turkey, left over from the first meal is excellent cold or made up in another dish. Remember that packaged poultry, frozen or fresh, is sold by oven-ready weight, but a fresh bird bought from a traditional poulterer or butcher will probably be sold at 'plucked' weight' – plucked but not drawn. The butcher will draw it for you, but

after weighing and pricing. You will need to allow for this in estimating the size of bird you require.

Game birds are best eaten young. The plumage is a guide as all young birds have soft even feathers. With pheasants and partridge, the long wing feathers are V-shaped in a young bird, as distinct from the rounded ones of an older bird. Smooth, pliable legs, short spurs and a firm, plump breast are other points to look for. Most game birds need to be hung so check this with your butcher or poulterer. He will probably pluck and draw it for you if you ask. If game is not hung, the flesh will be tough and tasteless. Look out for game in supermarkets too, where the game is ready for the oven.

CHOOSING FISH AND SEAFOOD

Really fresh *whole fish* has clear, bulging eyes and bright red gills. Avoid any with sunken, cloudy eyes and faded pink or grey gills. The body of the fish should be firm and springy to the touch, with shining skin and bright, close-fitting scales. *Fish fillets* and *steaks* should look freshly cut, the flesh moist and firm-textured, showing no signs of dryness or discoloration. The bones should be firmly embedded in the flesh; if they are loose and coming away from the flesh this indicates that the fish has been cut for some time and is past its best.

When buying *frozen fish*, make sure that it is solidly frozen, clear in colour and free of ice crystals. Any smell should be mild and clean, exactly as for fresh fish. Breadcrumbs or batter coatings on frozen fish portions should be crisp and dry looking. Avoid frozen fish that has a brownish tinge or that is in any way damaged.

Shellfish should be very fresh as they are more perishable than other fish. They should have a clean sea smell and clear fresh colour; avoid any that are dull looking. Prawns and shrimps should have tails curled well under them. Look for tightly closed shells where applicable.

While it is unwise to freeze your own shellfish – since the temperature required for satisfactory preservation of shellfish is lower than that normally obtainable in any domestic freezer – commercially *frozen shellfish* are useful when the type you require is out of season. You can also freeze very fresh shellfish in made-up dishes such as soups, fish pies and quiches.

CHOOSING DAIRY PRODUCE

When buying fresh *milk*, *cream* and *yogurt*, look at their date stamps, then keep them cool, clean and covered to ensure they stay fresh.

Cheese can be bought from specialist cheese shops and supermarkets. *Freshly cut cheese* should look fresh, with no dried or greasy areas on the surface. It is important that the cut surface of cheese is always covered and that a mild-flavoured cheese is not kept alongside a strong cheese. If buying *pre-packed cheese*, check that it does not look sweaty or excessively runny and that it is within the life of its date stamp. If buying a *ripened soft cheese*, such as Lymesworld, well before the expiry of the date stamp, you may prefer to keep it to allow it to ripen to your liking.

When buying pre-packed *eggs* in shops you can get some idea of how old they are by checking the week number given on the box. Week 1 falls at the end of December or beginning of January.

CHOOSING FRESH FRUIT AND VEGETABLES
When buying fruit and vegetables always choose them carefully and make sure that they are fresh. Fruits should be bought with unblemished skins. Root vegetables, such as potatoes, carrots and swedes, should be bought firm and unwrinkled. Buy little and often to ensure freshness.

STORING FOOD
Storage of perishable foods such as meat, fish, dairy products, soft fruit and vegetables is of vital importance to keep them as fresh as possible. The best place to keep them is in the refrigerator or, failing this, a cool larder. Perishable foods intended for long-term storage can be kept in a freezer.

All foods that are stored in the refrigerator should be covered or well wrapped to prevent the flavours drifting from one to another and to prevent the food from drying out. Store *cheese* in the bottom of the refrigerator, so it does not get too cold, but it's best to remove it from the refrigerator half an hour before serving to allow it to come up to room temperature and regain its flavour. *Milk*, *cream* and *yogurt* will keep for several days, but check date stamps when buying them. The same applies to cartons of fresh fruit juice. UHT milk will keep well even without a refrigerator but is best stored in a cool place.

Put *meat* in the refrigerator as soon as possible after buying. Remove any paper wrappings, rewrap the meat loosely in polythene or foil, leaving an end open for ventilation, and place the package on a plate in case it drips. If the meat is prepackaged in polythene or cling film, just loosen the wrapping to allow air to circulate. When buying meat in vacuum packs or controlled atmospheric packaging, follow the manufacturer's instructions.

Most fresh meat can be stored in the refrigerator for up to three or four days; minced meat and offal are more perishable and should be used within 24 hours. Cooked meat should be cooled quickly, wrapped in foil or polythene and, if possible, put into the refrigerator within 1½–2 hours of cooking. Store for up to four days. Frozen meat should be left in its wrappings and stored in the freezer or frozen food compartment of the refrigerator.

To store fresh *poultry*, remove the giblets from inside the bird as soon as you get it home. Remove any tight packaging, cover the bird loosely with a polythene bag that will allow the air to circulate and store in the refrigerator for 1–2 days. The giblets should preferably be cooked straight away, as they deteriorate more quickly than the rest of the bird, but in any case they should be stored separately.

Stuffings can be prepared in advance, but store them separately too and stuff the bird just before cooking.

Fresh fish, from the fishmonger, should be loosely wrapped and stored in the refrigerator. Cook it within 24 hours of purchase. Store *frozen fish* in the freezer or frozen food compartment in its original wrapping.

Eggs are best kept in a rack in a cool place. If you have to store them in a refrigerator, keep them well away from the ice compartment (there is often a special egg storage rack) and away from foods like cheese, fish or onions whose smells may transfer to the eggs.

Store eggs pointed end down and use them at room temperature; eggs that are too cold will crack when boiled and are also difficult to whisk. Fresh eggs can be stored for 2–3 weeks in the refrigerator or 1–2 weeks in a cool place.

Salad ingredients should be kept at the bottom of the refrigerator, loosely wrapped in polythene bags. Unwashed, most will keep for a week. Mushrooms are best kept in a paper bag and then wrapped in a polythene bag. Once washed, dry salad ingredients well before returning to the refrigerator in a polythene bag.

Green leafy vegetables are also best stored at the bottom of the refrigerator. Trim away any damaged parts and wrap the vegetables in paper before refrigerating. *Root vegetables* like onions, potatoes and carrots should be stored in a cool, airy place such as a vegetable rack so that air can circulate around them. If you buy potatoes ready washed in polythene bags it is best to transfer them to a paper bag so that they do not become soft and spongy. *Fruits* such as apples and pears are best kept in a fruit bowl.

COMMERCIAL FREEZING OF BRITISH FRUIT AND VEGETABLES
All fruit and vegetables, from the moment they are picked, begin to lose their nutritional value and flavour.

Freezing is a convenient way of preserving fresh fruit and vegetables and if blanched and frozen with minimal delay, they remain as close to their natural state as possible.

Commercial quick-freezing produces small ice crystals, which means there is little deterioration of the flavour, colour and nutritive value of fruit and vegetables. Frozen produce can thus often be fresher than the fresh fruit and vegetables in the shops.

PICK YOUR OWN
Fruit and vegetable picking can be an enjoyable day out and it's satisfying to come home laden with fresh produce. There is a wide variety of produce available, including soft fruits, green and root vegetables. Don't, however, get so carried away that you have to spend hours freezing, or making jam which you didn't plan to do because you have picked too much to consume. Check with the supplier concerning the suitability of their produce for freezing.

Try to choose a part of the field that hasn't already been well-picked – usually the further away from the entrance the better. The best fruit and vegetables tend to grow at the edge of the plant so tread carefully as you walk along the rows.

Select fresh, firm produce and when picking soft fruits don't pile them up so much in your basket that you squash the fruit below. The best way to pick fruits such as strawberries is to pinch the stem and snap it off above the fruit; don't pull the fruit from the plant.

When you get the fruit or vegetables home, use them quickly to avoid them going to waste. If you intend to freeze them, lay them singly on trays and put in the coldest part of the freezer. When solid, pack in polythene bags or rigid containers.

FROM FREEZER TO MICROWAVE

Home freezing is an ideal way of preserving food since you can have a store of produce readily available and you can buy food to preserve at the height of the season when they are cheap.

A freezer and microwave cooker can be ideal companions. The microwave will thaw food in a fraction of the time normally required for complete thawing, which allows you the convenience of being able to select food from the freezer at short notice.

Most foods can be frozen and microwaved without impairing the quality. The thawing process is very fast and because there is a risk that some parts of the food will start to cook while others are still frozen always use the DEFROST or LOW settings.

Pack food in containers suitable for using in both freezer and microwave, never microwave in foil containers and remove metal tags. Open all cartons and remove lids and slit or pierce polythene bags.

To help foods thaw evenly, stir when possible, moving frozen parts to the outside of the dish, separate chunks of food and turn large items over.

Some foods, such as joints of meat, also need to be given a standing time after thawing to ensure that they are completely thawed.

WHEN FRUIT ARE IN SEASON

THIS IS TO SHOW WHEN BRITISH-GROWN FRUIT IS AVAILABLE

		January	February	March	April	May	June	July	August	September	October	November	December
Apples	Cooking	•	•	•	•	•	•			•	•	•	•
	dessert	•	•	•							•	•	•
Blackberries										•	•		
Black/redcurrants							•	•	•				
Crab Apples										•	•		
Cherries							•	•	•				
Chestnuts											•	•	•
Damsons									•	•	•		
Elderberries										•	•		
Gooseberries							•	•	•				
Greengages								•	•				
Loganberries								•	•				
Medlars											•	•	
Mulberries								•	•				
Pears		•	•	•					•	•	•	•	•
Plums							•	•	•	•	•		
Quinces											•	•	
Raspberries							•	•	•				
Rhubarb			•	•	•	•							
Strawberries							•	•	•	•	•	•	

WHEN VEGETABLES ARE IN SEASON

THIS IS TO SHOW WHEN BRITISH-GROWN VEGETABLES ARE AVAILABLE

Vegetable	Variety	January	February	March	April	May	June	July	August	September	October	November	December
Artichokes	Globe						●	●	●	●			
	Jerusalem	●	●	●	●						●	●	●
Asparagus						●	●						
Beans	Broad						●	●					
	Runner							●	●	●	●		
	Kidney						●	●	●	●			
Beetroot		●	●	●	●	●	●	●	●	●	●	●	●
Broccoli	Calabrese						●	●	●				
	Sprouting			●	●	●							
Brussels	Top	●									●	●	●
	Sprouts	●	●	●	●						●	●	●
Cabbage	January King	●	●	●	●						●	●	●
	Drum Head								●	●			●
	Spring Green	●	●	●								●	●
	Red	●	●										●
Carrot		●	●	●	●	●	●	●	●	●	●	●	●
Cauliflower		●	●	●	●	●	●	●	●	●	●	●	●
Celeriac		●	●	●						●	●	●	●
Celery				●	●	●	●	●	●	●	●	●	●
Chicory		●	●						●	●	●	●	●
Chinese Leaves						●	●	●	●	●	●	●	●
Courgettes								●	●	●	●		
Cucumbers			●	●	●	●	●	●	●				
Endive					●	●	●	●					
Kale		●	●	●	●							●	●
Leeks		●	●	●	●				●	●	●	●	●
Lettuce		●	●	●			●	●	●	●	●	●	●
Marrows							●	●	●	●	●		
Mint					●	●	●	●	●	●			
Mushrooms		●	●	●	●	●	●	●	●	●	●	●	●
Mustard and Cress		●	●	●	●	●	●	●	●	●	●	●	●
Onions										●	●	●	
Parsley					●	●	●	●	●	●	●		
Parsnips		●	●	●	●					●	●	●	●
Peppers					●	●	●	●	●	●			
Peas						●	●	●	●	●	●		
Potatoes	New						●	●	●				
	Maincrop	●	●	●	●	●				●	●	●	●
Pumpkin									●	●	●		
Radishes				●	●	●	●	●	●	●	●		
Seakale		●	●	●									●
Shallots		●								●	●	●	
Spinach (best Mar/Apr)			●	●	●	●	●	●	●	●			
Spring Onions					●	●	●	●	●				
Swedes		●	●	●	●	●				●	●	●	●
Sweetcorn									●	●	●		
Tomatoes					●	●	●	●	●	●			
Turnips		●	●	●				●	●	●	●	●	●
Watercress		●	●	●	●	●	●	●	●	●	●	●	●

INDEX

REGIONAL INDEX

RECIPE INDEX

NOTES

Both metric and imperial measures are given for the recipes. Follow either set of measures, not a mixture of both, as they are not interchangeable.

All spoon measures are level. 1 tsp = 5ml spoon; 1 tbsp = 15ml spoon.

Ovens and grills must be preheated to the specified temperature.

Use sea salt and freshly ground black pepper unless otherwise suggested.

Fresh herbs should be used unless dried herbs are specified in a recipe.

Medium eggs should be used except where otherwise specified. Free-range eggs are recommended.

Note that some recipes contain raw or lightly cooked eggs. The young, elderly, pregnant women and anyone with an immune-deficiency disease should avoid these because of the slight risk of salmonella.

ACKNOWLEDGEMENTS & PICTURE CREDITS

Richard Ehrlich has written about food and drink for every major national newspaper in the UK. He is the author of eight cookbooks and has served on the Committee of the Guild of Food Writers, of which he is currently Chairman, for a total of eight years.

Richard McComb is the food critic for the Birmingham Post. He writes widely on food and drink in the Midlands and covers national and international food-based travel.

Tracey Barker was born into a Cambridgeshire farming family but is now based in Suffolk. She has been writing professionally about food since 1995, and is currently compiling an online compendium which celebrates excellence in food and drink produced across the East of England.

Roger Protz, one of the world's leading authorities on beer, is the author of 20 books including the *World Guide to Beer, The Taste of Beer* and the best-selling *300 Beers to Try Before You Die.* He has edited 20 editions of the annual *Good Beer Guide* and is the co-proprietor of www.beer-pages.com.

Emma Sturgess is a food writer and award-winning restaurant critic who has written for numerous publications including the *Guardian, Restaurant,* and *Metro.* She trained in food and wine at Ballymaloe Cookery School and lives near Manchester.

Andrea Leeman has lived in the West Country for over 20 years and specialises in recipe development, local and seasonal produce, and smaller producers. She is the author of *A Taste of Somerset, A Taste of Devon* and *A Taste of Gloucestershire.*

Sue Lawrence is a cookery writer, novelist and specialist in the food and cooking of her native Scotland. Her books include *Scots Cooking, A Cook's Tour of Scotland,* and *Eating In.*

Juliet Harbutt, one of the world's leading experts on cheese, runs the annual British Cheese Awards. Her books include *World Cheese Book* and *Cheese Classified: A Cheese Lover's Companion.* She received a Food Hero Award in the 2008 Good Housekeeping Food Awards.

Colin Pressdee is an award-winning food writer and consultant. His books include *Food Wales, Food Wales: A Second Helping, Food Wales Eating Out Guide,* and *London Oyster Guide.*

Illustrations: Nicole Heidaripour
Photographers: Neil Barclay (pages 62 and 67); Steve Baxter (page 245); Nicki Dowey (pages 60, 64T, 65B, 69, 74, 76, 80T, 81, 82, 83, 84, 85, 86, 93, 96, 100, 101, 108, 109, 113, 121, 127, 134, 140T, 145, 147, 154, 157, 163, 164, 174, 182, 184B, 188T, 190, 192, 195, 196, 197,199, 204B, 212B, 214, 218, 224, 225, 227, 228, 232, 236, 241, 242T, 246, 249, 250, 251, 252, 253 and 255T); Fiona Kennedy (pages 58, 72, 75, 78, 88, 95, 97, 98, 104, 105, 115T, 116, 117, 118, 122, 126, 128, 130, 131, 132, 133, 136, 137, 141, 144, 152, 158, 166, 167, 180, 183, 184T, 188B, 194, 200, 201T, 202, 209, 210, 212T, 213T, 234B, 235, 238, 239, 240, 255B and 257); Gareth Morgans (page 159); Myles New (pages 87 and 277); Craig Robertson (pages 63, 64B, 65T, 79, 90, 91, 94, 99, 111, 112, 115B, 120, 125, 151, 153, 155, 162, 170, 179,187T, 198, 204T, 205T, 206, 207 and 217); Brett Stevens (page 129); Roger Stowell (page 150); Lucinda Symons (pages 66, 70, 73, 80B, 102, 106, 110, 114, 119, 138, 140B, 142, 143, 146, 148, 156, 160, 165, 169, 171, 172, 173, 175,176, 185, 186, 187B, 189, 191, 201B, 205B, 208, 211, 213B, 216, 219, 223, 226, 230, 231, 233, 234T, 242B, 243, 244, 248, 254, 256, 258, 260 and 261); Martin Thompson (page 222); Kate Whitaker (page 229).
Home Economists: Joanna Farrow, Emma Jane Frost, Teresa Goldfinch, Alice Hart, Lucy McKelvie, Kim Morphew, Aya Nishimura, Bridget Sargeson, Kate Trend and Mari Mererid Williams.
Stylists: Tamzin Ferdinando, Wei Tang, Helen Trent and Fanny Ward.